Speaking *for* Success

second edition

Jean H. Miculka

Associate Professor Emerita

Communication Department

The University of Texas at El Paso

THOMSON

✳

SOUTH-WESTERN

Australia · Brazil · Canada · Mexico · Singapore · Spain · United Kingdom · United States

THOMSON
———— * ————™
SOUTH-WESTERN

Speaking for Success, 2E

Jean H. Miculka

VP/Editorial Director
Jack W. Calhoun

VP/Editor-in-Chief
Karen Schmohe

Executive Editor
Eve Lewis

Developmental Editor
Karen Hein

Consulting Editor
Leslie Kauffman

Marketing Manager
Courtney Schulz

Content Project Manager
Colleen A. Farmer

Manufacturing Coordinator
Kevin Kluck

Marketing Coordinator
Angela Glassmeyer

Production House
Interactive Composition Corporation

Printer
Edwards Brothers

Art Director
Tippy McIntosh

Internal & Cover Designer
Lou Anne Thesing

Front Cover Photo Credit
Imagezoo

For more information about our products, contact us at:

Thomson Higher Education
5191 Natorp Boulevard
Mason, Ohio 45040
USA

Reviewers

Carla Bradley
Teacher/Dept. Chair, Business Department
Burlington High School
Burlington, WI

Lona Dittmar
Oral Communications Teacher, Debate & Forensics Coach
Marysville High School
Marysville, KS

Madge Gregg
Business Teacher
Hoover High School
Hoover, AL

Dennis G. Kaczor
Business/Marketing Teacher and Professional Speaker
Mosinee High School and TPOPT Productions
Mosinee, WI

Sherry Lowell-Lewis
Lecturer, Communication Department
University of Texas, El Paso
El Paso, TX

Susan Schonauer
Marketing Technology Instructor
Indian Hill Satellite via Great Oaks Institute of Technology
Cincinnati, OH

About the Author

Jean H. Miculka is an Associate Professor Emerita from the Speech Communication Department at the University of Texas, El Paso. Her long career began as a radio announcer, attending classes at NBC. She graduated with an M.A. from Northwestern University's School of Speech and taught at the elementary through high school levels for 14 years. Relocating to Texas, she set up a speech program at Frank Phillips Junior College, then moved on to the University of Texas at El Paso where she taught public speaking, oral interpretation, creative drama, and choral speaking for the next 24 years.

Professor Miculka has published a variety of books in the Speech/Communication field and has been a member of the National Communication Association and the Texas Speech Communication Association. She enjoys traveling and has visited all seven continents since her retirement.

Contents

UNIT 2: Communicating Person to Person

What's New in This Edition

In this second edition of *Speaking for Success*, the number of chapters has been reduced from 14 to 12, blending materials from some chapters into new combinations. Chapters have been renamed to show an updated focus on the speaking process. Increased coverage of topics such as paralanguage, debate, persuasive speaking, and critical thinking offers a more comprehensive look at the subject matter.

Because each teacher has his/her own way of approaching the exciting field of teaching public speaking, the units of *Speaking for Success* are arranged for adaptation to individual teaching styles. Although the units begin with principles of communication, move to interpersonal study, then to group work, and finally to audience situations, each chapter contains applications and projects in each of these areas. The basic premise is to get students speaking in every class session—with a partner, in a small group, or in front of the class. Formal instruction in presentational speaking comes in the last unit, but needed information can be tapped at any time during the course. Models are provided for each of the major speaking assignments in the early chapters.

Making Connections is a new end-of-chapter section that ties chapter material to other curriculum areas. Winning Edge assignments aid students who participate in competitive speech events.

Supplements

New to this edition is an *Annotated Instructor's Edition* that contains helpful teaching notes at point-of-use in the margins. The notes provide a guide for teachers, supplement the text, and offer suggested solutions for text assignments as well as enrichment activities. An *Instructor's Resource CD* also provides additional teacher support material, including lesson plans, quizzes, and PowerPoint® presentations to accompany each chapter. This text is also available as an *eBook on CD* (0-538-44397-9). eBooks are viewed on a computer with a free Adobe® Acrobat® Book Reader™ and look exactly like the printed version—including photos, graphics, and rich fonts.

Organization

UNIT ONE—COMMUNICATING ON ALL CHANNELS provides a broad introduction to the ongoing, ever-changing process of communication. Topics include the receipt and processing of information and the role of speaking, as well as paralanguage, listening, and nonverbal communication.

UNIT TWO—COMMUNICATING PERSON TO PERSON is based on the principles of interpersonal communication, beginning with stage fright, its causes, and ways to reduce it. Self-image, the role of mentors, methods of handling criticism, and ways of building self-confidence are discussed. Interpersonal workplace skills and types and techniques of interviews are also explained.

UNIT THREE—GROUP COMMUNICATION discusses speaking within and to groups and explores group dynamics, group decision making, and informative and persuasive speaking purposes. Parliamentary procedure, task- and process-oriented roles, and leadership styles are introduced, as well as group problem-solving models, critical thinking, and debate as formal argument.

UNIT FOUR—COMMUNICATING WITH AN AUDIENCE is devoted to the process of preparing and delivering a dynamic presentation. Topics include audience analysis, research techniques, organization and support of ideas, selection and use of visual aids, styles of delivery, and question-and-answer sessions.

Features in Every Chapter

Features designed to provide a variety of experiences are found in each of the 12 chapters.

- **Objectives**—listed at the beginning of each unit and chapter to point out skills to be learned in the text.

- **Key Terms and Concepts**—listed at the beginning of each chapter to call attention to highlighted material in the text.

- **Idea Box**—a student focus on chapter content, speech topics, immediate involvement, and future assignments.

- **Cartoons**—a humorous poke at concepts within the chapter.

- **Communication at Work**—case studies of business persons demonstrating the use of speaking skills in specific work situations.

- **Language Traps**—examples of everyday speaking errors and suggestions for correcting them

- **Quotations**—illustrations of the wise words of famous or knowledgeable people regarding speaking skills and success.

- **Personal Check-Up**—questions for students' evaluation of their understanding of chapter concepts.

- **Chapter Summary**—a brief recap of the major ideas in the chapter.

- **Chapter Review**—a brief quiz to check knowledge of chapter concepts.

- **Can You Define These Terms?**—an exercise in matching vocabulary terms with definitions from the chapter.

- **Applications**—two or three activities, exercises, or challenges at the end of each chapter that reinforce chapter concepts.
- **Making Connections**—assignments that apply text content to other subject areas.
- **Projects**—speaking assignments with sample outlines and critique sheets.
- **Winning Edge**—specific exercises designed to prepare students for DECA, FBLA, and BPA competitive events.

Understanding the Icons

The following graphic icons will help you easily identify different types of activities in the end-of-chapter assignments.

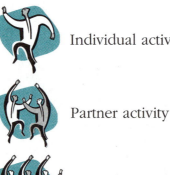 Individual activity

 Applies speaking skills to other academic areas

Partner activity

 Applies speaking skills to professional situations

Group activity

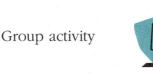 Indicates opportunity for speaking in front of a partner or group

Now We're Talking

In this age of technological training, people skills need honing too. We are surrounded by others, and our ability to connect with them lies within our speaking skills—whether we talk one-on-one, in an informal group, or in the spotlight in front of an audience. *Speaking for Success, 2e* is designed to lay a foundation for real-life situations and provide an opportunity for speaking skills to be practiced.

Filled with individual, partner, and group activities, chapters in *Speaking for Success, 2e* challenge students to participate in learning situations where they first interact and then evaluate the experience. These skills come slowly—but they evolve successfully when studied, discussed, and practiced.

ENGAGE STUDENT INTEREST

Paralanguage Flavors the Verbal Message

3

CHAPTER OBJECTIVES

After completing this chapter, you should be able to

- Identify the role of paralanguage in spoken messages.
- Explain the difference between content and intent in speaking.
- Apply practice tips for improving vocal qualities.
- Describe and apply empathetic listening techniques.
- Identify appropriate and effective communication styles for each circle of your communication network.
- Explain how language and paralanguage tools are adjusted to fit a variety of communication situations.

KEY TERMS AND CONCEPTS

mixed message	timbre	listening for intent
pitch	diction	empathy
rate	articulation errors	empathetic listening
volume/intensity	pronunciation errors	small talk

IDEA BOX

Make a list of people with whom you talk. The list should cross a wide spectrum of categories. (Suggested categories are listed below.) Consider how topics and language styles vary from person to person.

Family	Coworkers
Friends	Teammates
Neighbors	Customers
Teachers	Acquaintances
Employers	Strangers
Classmates	

Chapter Objectives are clearly stated learning goals.

Key Terms and Concepts are vocabulary words/ideas that will be defined within the chapter.

Idea Box gets students thinking about speech topics and offers immediate involvement in chapter contents.

Quotations provide motivational words from authors and leaders regarding speaking skills and success.

"*People think the goal is to be relaxed in front of an audience. Absolutely not. You must be at discipline, but be at ease. You want to convey the message, 'I'm glad to be here.'*"

—Dorothy Sarnoff

In an audience situation, listeners' attention focuses on the speaker's voice as eardrums respond to variety in the vibrations beating against them. In other words, speaking in public should sound somewhat conversational, or at least the pitch should change frequently. Problems with pitch may occur in public speaking when the words to be spoken are written out in front of the speaker. When the speaker reads, the pitch tends to flatten out, rather than rise and fall conversationally. The voice becomes *monotone*. Sound pats the listening eardrums gently, lulling the listener to sleep, rather than beating against the eardrums for attention.

Tip: If you are asked to read aloud or to speak from a prepared manuscript, do all you can to make your voice sound conversational. Take little pauses. Change your pitch pattern. Sound as if you are talking to your audience, not just reading to them.

RATE The speed with which words are spoken determines the pace or **rate** of delivery. Just as with pitch, the more variety in the rate, the easier it is to listen. Speakers do not say one word or one sentence at a time. Rather, they speak in phrases—producing groups of word sounds punctuated by pauses of different lengths. Some phrases spill out rapidly, while others move more deliberately.

Tip: To achieve improvements in rate, practice giving your speech aloud. When you prepare a presentation, "talk" your speech out in the privacy of your room. Phrase ideas carefully, slowing to focus on important ideas, tossing off unimportant words, and using effective pauses of different lengths. Make it sound spontaneous. Practice, practice, practice. Suit your overall rate of speaking to the size of the group—slow down for larger audiences, but make your speech sound like conversation.

VOLUME OR INTENSITY The **volume/intensity** indicates the degree of loudness with which a message is spoken. A loud voice can indicate feelings of excitement, anger, or need for attention. A level that is too soft may give the impression that the speaker is hesitant, fearful, or unprepared. The intensity of a vocal sound reveals something about a speaker's feelings. In ordinary conversation, in an interview situation, or in public, it is important to adjust your volume level to your listeners. For a listening audience, it is annoying to have difficulty hearing the speaker. When a microphone is used, it should effectively project the speaker's voice at the proper auditory level. But, microphones are not always available. Your effective speaking voice should be as loud as the occasion and the listeners warrant.

Tip: To keep listeners' attention, change the volume of your voice occasionally. Some phrases or ideas might be delivered with greater force for emphasis, some with less. The variation of sound waves beating against the listeners' ears keeps attention. The secret is to watch individuals in your audience. You can tell if they can't hear you or are losing interest. Direct your voice to the person farthest away

Language trap

Don't say, "She seen the movie."
Say, "She saw the movie." or "She has seen the movie."

Listening

© 1999 Ted Goff

"And should there be a sudden loss of consciousness during this meeting, oxygen masks will drop from the ceiling."

There are many ways to listen.

- *Appreciatively* to your favorite music.
- *Comprehensively* to your doctor's instructions.
- *Critically* to evaluate the claims of a commercial.
- *Intently* to a single voice in a crowd.
- *With empathy* to encourage a good friend.

Your responses—facial expressions, muscular tension, eye contact, and so forth—clearly indicate your listening style and set the stage for interaction to continue (or perhaps discontinue). Real listening is difficult to fake.

- Can't hear—"That microphone isn't working."
- Don't hear—"I do wish she wouldn't mumble."
- Won't hear—"He never says anything important."
- Can't understand—"I don't speak French."
- Don't understand—"Why do I push this button?"
- Won't understand—"I never did like math."

Personal CHECK-UP

Identify four barriers to listening. Give examples.

Poor Listening Is Costly in Business

There are many reasons for improving your listening skills at work. Your job will require you to listen to supervisors, co-workers, customers, and perhaps to your own employees. In fact, 55 percent of your waking time is spent listening. Your attention shifts in and out. You focus and refocus. Think of the cost to a business of people who listen poorly.

- Accidents cause physical injury.
  "I didn't hear anyone say this is a hard-hat area."

- Production breakdowns result in losses.
  "I don't remember him saying to insert the bolt from the left side."

- Lost sales and dissatisfied customers hurt business.
  "Why did she get so angry? I didn't understand her complaint."

- Misunderstandings between employees slow production.
  "Why didn't you pay attention when I gave you that deadline?"

Chapter 2   Speech Is an Oral Language Code   *19*

"*Nobody ever listened himself out of a job.*"

—Calvin Coolidge

- Conflict between workers and management affects work environment.
  "I keep telling the boss that we'd save time if we combined the two steps into one. No one listens to those of us who do the job."

Improving Listening Skills

Listening is a complex process that includes *decoding* (converting sound into meaning), *comprehending* (understanding how the message relates to the topic), *decision making* (deciding how to respond), and *feedback* (reacting verbally, nonverbally, or not at all). Disciplined listening is actually hard work.

LISTENING FOR CONTENT   Consider what you bring to a communication situation—your experience of living, your attitudes, your beliefs, your ideas, and your value system. Clearly, you do not listen as if you were an empty glass waiting to be filled. You take in the message, but you use your skills to understand, to relate, to remember, and to retain.

When you are required to listen to a presentation in a business setting or in school, you are expected to listen for the *content,* or the information contained in the speech. A student in American history class, for example, would listen to a lecture by

- Assessing the speaker's purpose and credibility.
- Searching for the central idea of the speech.
- Noting the main points that develop the central idea.
- Paying attention to factual data, such as places, names, and dates.

COMMUNICATION AT WORK

The task of a social worker is to form a relationship with each client during the first meeting. Marta Kishun says everything happens in a "talking frame" in her private sessions, but that counseling includes more than speech communication. She establishes a rapport in the beginning with speech, but as the client talks, the social worker's job is to listen actively. A vital part of active listening is feedback. Marta uses physical indicators, such as maintaining eye contact, nodding, and facial expressions of concern, to show that she is listening. Marta needs to understand what particularly upsets or troubles a client, even if the client doesn't say so directly. She also asks questions to help her clients approach their experiences from new angles. Marta knows it's a giant step for people to come and ask for help. She uses all of her communication skills to put them at ease and to help them find a new perspective.

©Getty Images/PhotoDisc

20   Unit 1   Communicating on All Channels

ENHANCE STUDENT LEARNING

■ **Quality control**—You *verify* information, confirming that what you perceive is accurate and what you say is true, just as a company assures the quality of its goods and services.

All of this activity takes place through the perceptive process we call thinking. Indeed, *thinking* is the key to effective communication. It is because we are creatures who are able to reflect, contemplate, and decide that we make choices about the ways we speak and listen. These choices influence our life relationships and our business encounters with others.

Communication—The Process

Communicating is more complex than just speaking and listening. It is affected by a variety of elements that make each situation different, especially by our perception of the world around us. Consider how each of the following perception factors affects the way you speak.

How You See Yourself

The picture you have of yourself as a person makes a difference. For example, a shy individual who lacks confidence might talk very softly and refuse to make eye contact. An assertive, confident person might speak energetically and hold eye contact.

How Others See You

The picture others have of you affects how they approach you. If your image says "trustworthy," you might be asked for advice. If your image says "athletic," you might be invited to play on a team.

How You Feel at the Moment

Your current feelings of satisfaction, frustration, stress, or "the blues" can change your speaking manner. A normally open and friendly person might respond with "I don't want to talk about it now, OK?" if he or she were having a difficult day.

How You Think About Things

Life experiences shape your attitudes, beliefs, and values and affect the way you communicate. As you mature and gain more experience, you change. June and Glen are not the same now as they were when they were in fifth grade. When they were children, they spoke as children. As adults, their communication styles are based on a broader range of experiences.

Through your appearance and through ... send constant messages.

Personal Check-Up assists with review and comprehension of key concepts.

How You Behave

Your actions and behaviors affect your interaction with others. Think how the physical distance you choose when having a conversation makes the communication situation friendly or difficult. An appropriate distance may seem friendly and acceptable. A too-close distance may seem hostile, aggressive, or inappropriate, whereas keeping a too-far distance may make you seem standoffish or disinterested.

Speech—A Part of the Process

Throughout the ages, people have communicated with each other. From smoke signals to semaphore to sonar to the Internet, humans have designed symbolic codes to represent messages. Probably the most satisfying and useful of these devices is **speech**—putting words into sound waves.

Speech is a means of getting to know and understand people. It is a way of verbalizing what you think and believe so that others can appreciate you. Good speech will be necessary in your future job, but you also apply it in many ways today.

To Create Social Contact

In a social context, speech is used to greet friends, co-workers, and customers. It is used to exchange social conversation, converse about illnesses and accidents, chat about upcoming events, and maintain personal relationships. We also use speech to report important information such as deadlines, promotions, special occasions, and appointments.

Language trap

Don't say, "Juan and her gave the party." Say, "Juan and she gave the party."

Language Trap provides examples of common grammatical errors and suggestions for correcting them.

Friends use speech to create social contact.

REVIEW AND ASSESSMENT

CHAPTER SUMMARY

We are all communication channels because coded messages come from us and through us. We each perceive the world in a unique way and respond by encoding and decoding our reactions according to our perceptions. Oral language, paralanguage, and nonverbal codes are important means used to communicate with others and to maintain human relationships in both work and social life. Feedback is important because it lets us know how we are being received. We pay attention to feedback to understand others and ourselves.

CHAPTER REVIEW

1. In what ways do you send messages even when you are not speaking?
2. Communication is more than just speaking and listening. What factors make each situation different?
3. What are the ways in which we use speech in our daily lives?
4. How important is feedback to communication?
5. What does Joseph DeVito's quote "Communication is a package of signals" really mean to you?
6. Why do we say that communication is a process?

CAN YOU DEFINE THESE TERMS?

Match each description with the appropriate term. Write the correct letter in the blank preceding the sentence. Some terms will not be used.

Terms:

1. ___ The process by which an idea or message is transformed into oral language
2. ___ The source of a verbal or nonverbal message
3. ___ The verbal or nonverbal response the receiver gives back to the sender
4. ___ Putting words into sound waves
5. ___ Clues to meaning revealed by the tone of voice, volume, rate of speaking, pauses, and so forth
6. ___ Ideals or views held dear
7. ___ Firm convictions about something
8. ___ The process of making sense of the world through the use of your senses to observe and be aware of your surroundings
9. ___ The mental process of converting sound into meaning
10. ___ Symbolic ways of representing ideas or feelings
11. ___ A means of sending or receiving messages
12. ___ Made up of words carried by sound waves and gestures or movement carried by light waves

a. attitudes
b. beliefs
c. channel
d. codes
e. decoding
f. encoding
g. feedback
h. message
i. paralanguage
j. perception
k.
l.
m.
n.

Chapter Summary provides a brief recap of the major ideas in the chapter.

Chapter Review offers thought-provoking questions to test understanding of chapter concepts.

CHAPTER SUMMARY

Each time we speak, we use a powerful, symbolic language code. The code is fluid, changing and adapting over time, and we may attach personal meanings to the words. The dictionary provides denotative meanings, and we add connotations by calling up mental images and associations from our experiences. Communication problems result when we make assumptions that a speaker's point of reference is similar to our own. Speaking skills can be improved if we are aware of language levels. Reporting language focuses on verifiable facts. Inferential language is based on reasoning, although sometimes flawed, that adds personal opinions. Judgmental language includes the speaker's evaluation. Developing good listening skills is an important part of speech training. Listening barriers are more often psychological than physical, and poor listening causes problems in the workplace. Suggestions for improvement include listening for content and paraphrasing to determine accuracy.

CHAPTER REVIEW

1. Give an example of a word that has different referents depending on the context.
2. Explain the difference between connotative and denotative meanings.
3. Give one example of each of the three levels of language.
4. Why do businesses desire employees who possess good listening skills?
5. List three phrases you might use to begin a paraphrase of a message.
6. List ways you might paraphrase, "Ain't no way you're getting on this squad."

CAN YOU DEFINE THESE TERMS?

Match each description with the appropriate term. Write the correct letter in the blank preceding the sentence. Some terms will not be used.

Terms:

1. ___ The items to which words refer
2. ___ Feelings that people attach to words because of personal experiences
3. ___ Specific definitions generally agreed upon by educated speakers of a language
4. ___ Conclusions reached when we take for granted that others perceive things as we do
5. ___ Verifiable statements based on observation
6. ___ To repeat the message in your own words
7. ___ Statements that evaluate good/bad, right/wrong, ugly/pretty, and so forth
8. ___ When the brain focuses on the meaning of sounds
9. ___ Statements of opinion that draw conclusions by a reasoning process

a. assumptions
b. connotations
c. denotations
d. hearing
e. inferential language
f. judgmental language
g. listening
h. paraphrase
i. referents
j. reporting language

Can You Define These Terms? matches vocabulary terms with definitions from within the chapter.

APPLICATIONS

Sign on the Bottom Line

Meeting new people and knowing how to get another person's approval or signature are important workplace skills. During the next 20 minutes, try to find classmates who correspond to the descriptions listed below. Introduce yourself to them and try to convince them to sign your book next to the words that describe them. No one should sign your book more than once, and no one should sign next to a description that he or she doesn't truly match.

1. Works on weekends _____
2. Drives a truck _____
3. Loves biology _____
4. Has interviewed a celebrity _____
5. Is taller than 5'7" _____
6. Reads *People* magazine _____
7. Enjoys speaking before an audience _____
8. Is a salesperson _____
9. Has seen *Titanic* three times _____
10. Was born under the sign of Aquarius _____
11. Has an e-mail address _____
12. Believes it is time a woman was elected president _____
13. Plays a musical instrument _____
14. Is job hunting _____
15. Frequently attends hockey games _____
16. Owns a scaly pet _____
17. Has read at least one Shakespeare play _____
18. Has an October birthday _____
19. Is a vegetarian _____
20. Has visited Hawaii _____

What was the most difficult part of this exercise?

How many of your classmates can you now call by name?

What information did you use to match classmates to descriptions?

Applications provide activities and exercises that help reinforce chapter concepts.

MAKING CONNECTIONS

History

Until the development of the Internet, people used other methods of communicating with each other over distances. Choose an earlier form of communication (smoke signals, signal flags, telegraph, pony express, hobo signs, telephone, and so forth).

Research its creation, purpose, and development and how it changed business and/or society. Write a brief, one-page paper sharing your information. Jot down topic ideas here.

_____
_____
_____
_____

Technology

Using terms presented in this chapter that describe speech communication, describe aspects of the computer that have a similar function.

Write your comparisons below.

_____
_____
_____
_____
_____
_____

PROJECTS

Presenting Yourself—Small Group Speech

Read the following list and choose a topic you can comfortably discuss with a small group of classmates. In a group of four or five classmates, take turns introducing yourselves and talking about one of the areas. Each topic has the potential to tell something about you and interest your audience. Choose the topic that best expresses who you are or what interests you.

- What is the first ...
  What would you ...

- Of all the gifts you ...

- Order what you'd ...

- Tell how you fee...
  explain how you ...

- If you could be ...
  you choose to liv...

Making Connections activities demonstrate the link between core academic areas or career situations and essential speaking skills.

Projects provide opportunities for preparing presentations and speaking in front of an audience.

BPA Extemporaneous Speech

Extemporaneous speaking involves being able to pull together your thoughts on a subject and present a short speech on the spur of the moment. You must effectively demonstrate communication skills in arranging, organizing, and presenting information orally with limited preparation time.

You will draw two different business topics from a hat. You will have the option to select either topic. You will have ten minutes to develop the topic (key idea). You may jot down notes for reference on cards provided by the event proctor. No previously prepared notes or visual aids may be used for the presentation.

Possible topics will include:

- Government Incentives for the Manufacture of Hybrid Cars
- Flexible Work Weeks—More Leisure Time
- Tax Incentives for Small Businesses
- Bailing Out the Airline Industry
- Clamping Down on Corporate Scandal
- Natural Disasters Stimulate Business
- The Importance of International Business
- Professional Networking for Success

The length of the speech must be between one and three minutes. You will speak before a panel of judges and a timekeeper—no audience will be allowed at this event. The timekeeper will signal when one minute and thirty seconds of speaking time remain on the clock.

Performance Indicators Evaluated

- Illustrate an understanding of the topic.
- Organize thoughts into a meaningful presentation.
- Communicate a clear presentation backed by examples and facts.
- Develop a conclusion that is supported by the facts presented.
- Present the information with confidence.

For more detailed information, go to the BPA web site.

Think Critically

1. Why is it important to keep up to date on current domestic and international events?
2. List two strategies for remaining calm while preparing and presenting an extemporaneous speech.
3. Give an example of a business situation where you might be called upon to give an extemporaneous speech.
4. Why is it important to sort out your opinions when preparing a speech?

http://www.bpa.org/

Winning Edge features competitive-event scenarios for the DECA, FBLA, and BPA organizations.

Communicating on All Channels

Unit Objectives

After completing this unit, you should be able to

- Define channels and codes.
- Recognize how perception affects communication.
- Discuss the human communication process.
- Describe the role of communication in professional and social contexts.
- Identify ways in which oral language serves as a code.
- Name the basic elements in speech communication.
- Perform the listening skills that facilitate communication.
- Describe the role of paralanguage in spoken messages.
- Explain the importance of nonverbal channels of communication.
- Begin speech organization and delivery.

1 You Are a Coded Communication Channel

CHAPTER OBJECTIVES

After completing this chapter, you should be able to

- Explain how perception affects communication.
- Discuss the importance of effective communication skills in professional and social contexts.
- Identify elements of the speech communication process and their functions.
- Define the concept of feedback, and explain how it helps the flow of communication.

KEY TERMS AND CONCEPTS

channel	beliefs	sender	receiver
codes	values	encoding	decoding
paralanguage	perception	message	feedback
attitudes	speech		

IDEA BOX

If you asked your closest friends to describe you, what would they say? Make a list of the ten words or phrases that best describe you. Be honest.

Friendly?

Trustworthy?

Cool?

Ambitious?

Procrastinator?

Opinionated?

Shy?

Energetic?

Funny?

Smart?

Communication—Channels and Codes

Like a computer, you operate as a communication **channel**—a means of sending and receiving messages. Your *sensory equipment*—eyes, ears, nose, tongue, and skin—serve as channels for seeing, hearing, smelling, tasting, and touching. On these channels are codes that have a recognized meaning and make communication possible between people. **Codes** are symbolic ways of representing ideas or feelings. Similar to the binary code that permits your computer to send messages, spoken words and phrases serve as a *verbal code*. You learned these language symbols as a child by listening and repeating sounds that got an adult's attention. When you and a stranger know the same language, you can listen to each other and exchange messages.

The sound of the speaking voice is a second code that provides clues as to what the speaker means. By paying attention to **paralanguage** (tone, volume, rate of speaking, pauses, and so forth), an impression is added to the spoken words. Based on the tone of someone's voice, you might conclude that "she is angry with me" or "he is just joking around." Paralanguage helps you understand how the speaker *feels* about what is being said.

Most fascinating of all is the part that sight plays in human communication. Eyes are constantly noting messages through observation of *nonverbal codes,* such as eye contact, hand movements, or facial expressions. Verbal messages are usually spoken intentionally, but the accompanying paralanguage and nonverbal codes are often expressed unintentionally. Speakers may be unaware of the muscular tensions or other physical behaviors they are manifesting as they speak. You "read" people by listening to the way something is said, watching for eye contact, and verifying whether words and voice match the nonverbal clues. Other people read you the same way.

Language trap

Don't say, "The patient should lay on the table."
Say, "The patient should lie on the table."

COMMUNICATION AT WORK

Ed Wong is a sales representative for General Motors, Buick. Communicating with customers is perhaps the most critical part of his job. Ed must be friendly, open, and courteous and show that he is deeply interested in finding the right car for each individual. He adjusts his approach to the needs of each customer. He might emphasize safety features for customers with children, or he might stress style and color for a young, unmarried customer. Ed has to describe and explain the features of the cars to all of his prospective customers, regardless of how much they know or don't know about cars. After the initial contact, Ed sometimes negotiates or answers further questions on the phone. As always, he makes sure that he gives complete, accurate information and that both he and the customer understand just what needs to happen next.

©Getty Images/PhotoDisc

This book is designed to help you become aware of the dynamics of human communication. Your gained understanding will help you handle any fears you may have about speaking in business or social situations. A well-planned resume and successful interview may result in winning the job you want. Understanding how to give instructions, how to listen, how to evaluate critically, and how to organize and deliver a presentation will help you succeed in any job you choose. So, take action now. Read, learn, practice the suggested activities, and apply what you know. Your goal is to be a successful oral communicator, and the goal is within your reach!

Perception—Basis for Communication

How did you become such a unique, complex bundle of feelings, attitudes, beliefs, and values? Why are you both different from and like other people? From just living on this planet day to day, you have gathered

- **Attitudes**—the way you think or feel about an object, person, event, and so forth.

- **Beliefs**—firm convictions about something.

- **Values**—ideals or views held dear.

Like a sponge, you absorb impressions from every event happening in the world around you. Through your five senses—seeing, hearing, smelling, tasting, and touching—you pick up data from a million sensations. You sort and store these impressions to create your personal view of the world. No other human being is exactly like you. No one sees things exactly as you do.

The process of making sense of the world through the use of your senses to observe and be aware of your surroundings is known as **perception**. It can be compared to five operations in a company. You accept and handle stimuli from the outside world in the following businesslike ways.

- **Receiving**—Your five senses respond by taking in information, just as a business receives its many deliveries of goods and supplies.

- **Purchasing**—You can't give equal attention to everything, so you respond to the most interesting or demanding, just as a business selectively purchases the best supplies and services it needs.

- **Warehousing**—Your busy brain makes sense of all this input by sifting it, comparing it to what you already know, arranging it, and storing it in your memory bank like a business stores products in its warehouses.

- **Administrating**—You make supervisory decisions about what the incoming data means and how you will respond to it, similar to a company's administrators making business decisions and relaying information.

- **Quality control**—You *verify* information, confirming that what you perceive is accurate and what you say is true, just as a company assures the quality of its goods and services.

All of this activity takes place through the perceptive process we call thinking. Indeed, *thinking* is the key to effective communication. It is because we are creatures who are able to reflect, contemplate, and decide that we make choices about the ways we speak and listen. These choices influence our life relationships and our business encounters with others.

Personal CHECK-UP

Of the five perception factors listed, which most greatly influences your speaking?

Communication—The Process

Communicating is more complex than just speaking and listening. It is affected by a variety of elements that make each situation different, especially by our perception of the world around us. Consider how each of the following perception factors affects the way you speak.

How You See Yourself

The picture you have of yourself as a person makes a difference. For example, a shy individual who lacks confidence might talk very softly and refuse to make eye contact. An assertive, confident person might speak energetically and hold eye contact.

How Others See You

The picture others have of you affects how they approach you. If your image says "trustworthy," you might be asked for advice. If your image says "athletic," you might be invited to play on a team.

How You Feel at the Moment

Your current feelings of satisfaction, frustration, stress, or "the blues" can change your speaking manner. A normally open and friendly person might respond with "I don't want to talk about it now, OK?" if he or she were having a difficult day.

How You Think About Things

Life experiences shape your attitudes, beliefs, and values and affect the way you communicate. As you mature and gain more experience, you change. June and Glen are not the same now as they were when they were in fifth grade. When they were children, they spoke as children. As adults, their communication styles are based on a broader range of experiences.

Through your appearance and through words, you send constant messages.

©Getty Images/PhotoDisc

How You Behave

Your actions and behaviors affect your interaction with others. Think how the physical distance you choose when having a conversation makes the communication situation friendly or difficult. An appropriate distance may seem friendly and acceptable. A too-close distance may seem hostile, aggressive, or inappropriate, whereas keeping a too-far distance may make you seem standoffish or disinterested.

Language trap

Don't say, "Juan and her gave the party." Say, "Juan and she gave the party."

Speech—A Part of the Process

Throughout the ages, people have communicated with each other. From smoke signals to semaphore to sonar to the Internet, humans have designed symbolic codes to represent messages. Probably the most satisfying and useful of these devices is **speech**—putting words into sound waves.

Speech is a means of getting to know and understand people. It is a way of verbalizing what you think and believe so that others can appreciate you. Good speech will be necessary in your future job, but you also apply it in many ways today.

To Create Social Contact

In a social context, speech is used to greet friends, co-workers, and customers. It is used to exchange social conversation, converse about illnesses and accidents, chat about upcoming events, and maintain personal relationships. We also use speech to report important information such as deadlines, promotions, special occasions, and appointments.

Friends use speech to create social contact.

© 2005 Ted Goff

"This baby is going to make all human contact obsolete!"

Communication Technology

In our world of technology, information flows faster and easier to a great many people. Contact on a personal level may happen less and less frequently. When used effectively, technology can enhance communication. But it can cause barriers if used ineffectively. When you use the various forms of communication technology, use them appropriately. Don't simply send messages. Pay careful attention to feedback you receive. Listen for it, look for it, respond to it, and confirm your understanding.

To Exchange Information

Speech is critical in gathering and exchanging information. With speech, we can ask for further explanation, outline an idea or process, clear up a difficult point, illustrate a concept by giving an example, and answer or ask questions. We can also expand ideas by presenting research sources, lecturing on a new topic, participating in a dialogue, itemizing facts, or relating our experiences.

To Influence the Behavior of Others

We can use speech to stimulate appropriate attitudes, present new and different viewpoints, convince others to take action, or encourage an open exchange of ideas. We can counsel or give advice, share personal convictions, praise the work of others, reason with logic, cite evidence, and describe personal experiences.

To Solve Business or Personal Problems

In the workplace and in our personal lives, we use speech to identify and define problems. We then use our speech to isolate causes, consider alternative courses of action, and propose possible solutions to these problems.

Speech—The Basic Elements

If human speech is so important, how does it work? The following terms are used to describe a model of speech communication. Figure 1-1 illustrates the speech communication model in action as it relates to perception.

- **Sender**—the source of a verbal message (words) or nonverbal message (actions, gestures, tone).

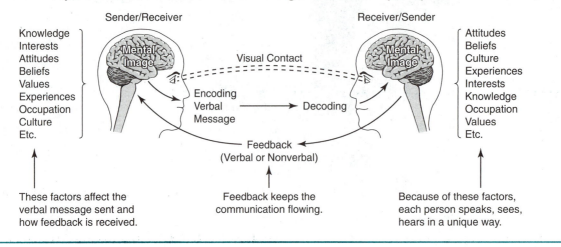

Sender/Receiver   Receiver/Sender

Knowledge
Interests
Attitudes
Beliefs
Values
Experiences
Occupation
Culture
Etc.

Mental Image

Visual Contact

Encoding
Verbal
Message

Decoding

Feedback
(Verbal or Nonverbal)

Attitudes
Beliefs
Culture
Experiences
Interests
Knowledge
Occupation
Values
Etc.

These factors affect the verbal message sent and how feedback is received.

Feedback keeps the communication flowing.

Because of these factors, each person speaks, sees, hears in a unique way.

- **Encoding**—the process by which an idea or message is transformed into oral language.

- **Message**—made up of words carried by sound waves and gestures or movement carried by light waves.

- **Receiver**—the person who hears or sees the message sent.

- **Decoding**—the mental process of converting sound into meaning.

- **Feedback**—the verbal or nonverbal response the receiver gives back to the sender.

Every person has mental images based on a variety of personal experiences. Even with common events, our responses may be different. Say the word "cat" and you get positive responses from feline-lovers who coo about those precious, furry kitties. You may get no reaction from others or twisted-up noses and disgusted voices saying, "I hate cats."

Although each person brings different attitudes, beliefs, and values to an interaction, we can still talk to each other and understand one another, provided we recognize that each person has the right to perceive the world differently. Of course, we should be using the same language. To be understood, we learn to trigger similar mental images for each other via spoken words. Someone says, "We'll meet on Tuesday." The receivers of that message should understand which Tuesday the speaker had in mind. The date could be specified for clarity.

Keep in mind that an *interaction* is not necessarily an alternating process in which two people take turns speaking and listening to each other. It is much more than that! We humans are capable of far greater skills. We can send and receive multiple messages all at the same time. Unlike Internet e-mail where one person writes to a receiver who waits for the message and then answers, in face-to-face communication a person can speak (encode an oral message) while watching the

Personal
CHECK-UP

Name two participants in a speech communication process and explain the variety of tasks they must do to keep communication flowing.

receiver's feedback (decoding the nonverbal message). In other words, if the speaker, Lori, is talking to David, she checks David's response to her verbal message as she speaks. A questioning look, a shrug of the shoulders, or a frown can be noted immediately, and this feedback sends a nonverbal message to the speaker.

Feedback—Aid to Communication Flow

Feedback frequently occurs while a message is being sent. This is valuable to the speaker because it allows the speaker to make adjustments in the message while it is being spoken. For example, if Anita sees a glazed look in the eyes of her friend, it may cause her to realize that she's repeating a story she's already told. Now Anita can explain why she's telling it again, shift to another topic, or just stop.

Because speakers who are energetically involved in a communication transaction are watching, listening, and speaking all at once, transmissions of sending and receiving can be almost simultaneous. Both individuals serve as senders and receivers operating at the same time.

As author Joseph A. DeVito says, "Communication is a package of signals." You are now in the business of learning how these verbal and nonverbal codes work. Messages, as signals, flow through the channels of voice, body language, space, time, appearance, and words. In presenting yourself to others, it is wise to be aware of how others see you and how you look at the world in which we live. No one but you can make changes in the way you communicate. You are the only one who can apply the principles of this book to your life and career.

©Getty Images/PhotoDisc

In presenting yourself to others, it is wise to be aware of how others see you and how you look at the world in which you live.

CHAPTER SUMMARY

We are all communication channels because coded messages come from us and through us. We each perceive the world in a unique way and respond by encoding and decoding our reactions according to our perceptions. Oral language, paralanguage, and nonverbal codes are important means used to communicate with others and to maintain human relationships in both work and social life. Feedback is important because it lets us know how we are being received. We pay attention to feedback to understand others and ourselves.

CHAPTER REVIEW

1. In what ways do you send messages even when you are not speaking?
2. Communication is more than just speaking and listening. What factors make each situation different?
3. What are the ways in which we use speech in our daily lives?
4. How important is feedback to communication?
5. What does Joseph DeVito's quote "Communication is a package of signals" really mean to you?
6. Why do we say that communication is a process?

CAN YOU DEFINE THESE TERMS?

Match each description with the appropriate term. Write the correct letter in the blank preceding the sentence. Some terms will not be used.

Terms:

1. ____ The process by which an idea or message is transformed into oral language
2. ____ The source of a verbal or nonverbal message
3. ____ The verbal or nonverbal response the receiver gives back to the sender
4. ____ Putting words into sound waves
5. ____ Clues to meaning revealed by the tone of voice, volume, rate of speaking, pauses, and so forth
6. ____ Ideals or views held dear
7. ____ Firm convictions about something
8. ____ The process of making sense of the world through the use of your senses to observe and be aware of your surroundings
9. ____ The mental process of converting sound into meaning
10. ____ Symbolic ways of representing ideas or feelings
11. ____ A means of sending or receiving messages
12. ____ Made up of words carried by sound waves and gestures or movement carried by light waves

a. attitudes
b. beliefs
c. channel
d. codes
e. decoding
f. encoding
g. feedback
h. message
i. paralanguage
j. perception
k. receiver
l. sender
m. speech
n. values

APPLICATIONS

Sign on the Bottom Line

Meeting new people and knowing how to get another person's approval or signature are important workplace skills. During the next 20 minutes, try to find classmates who correspond to the descriptions listed below. Introduce yourself to them and try to convince them to sign your book next to the words that describe them. No one should sign your book more than once, and no one should sign next to a description that he or she doesn't truly match.

1. Works on weekends _____

2. Drives a truck _____

3. Loves biology _____

4. Has interviewed a celebrity_____

5. Is taller than 5′7″ _____

6. Reads *People* magazine _____

7. Enjoys speaking before an audience_____

8. Is a salesperson _____

9. Has seen *Titanic* three times_____

10. Was born under the sign of Aquarius_____

11. Has an e-mail address _____

12. Believes it is time a woman was elected president _____

13. Plays a musical instrument_____

14. Is job hunting_____

15. Frequently attends hockey games _____

16. Owns a scaly pet _____

17. Has read at least one Shakespeare play _____

18. Has an October birthday_____

19. Is a vegetarian _____

20. Has visited Hawaii _____

What was the most difficult part of this exercise?

How many of your classmates can you now call by name?

What information did you use to match classmates to descriptions?

MAKING CONNECTIONS

History

Until the development of the Internet, people used other methods of communicating with each other over distances. Choose an earlier form of communication (smoke signals, signal flags, telegraph, pony express, hobo signs, telephone, and so forth).

Research its creation, purpose, and development and how it changed business and/ or society. Write a brief, one-page paper sharing your information. Jot down topic ideas here.

_____

_____

_____

Technology

Using terms presented in this chapter that describe speech communication, describe aspects of the computer that have a similar function.

Write your comparisons below.

_____

_____

_____

_____

_____

PROJECTS

Presenting Yourself—Small Group Speech

Read the following list and choose a topic you can comfortably discuss with a small group of classmates. In a group of four or five classmates, take turns introducing yourselves and talking about one of the topics. Explain why that particular subject interests you.

- What is the first thing you would buy if you won $600,000 in a lottery? What would you do next?

- Of all the gifts you have received, which one meant the most to you? Why?

- Order what you'd like to eat for your last meal on earth. Make us enjoy it.

- Tell how you feel about your name. If you have a nickname, state it and explain how you got it.

- If you could be transferred to another city or another state, where would you choose to live? Why?

Standing Up Front—Individual Speech

Select two or three items from the list of descriptions you wrote for the Idea Box at the beginning of the chapter. Identify the ones you would like your classmates to know about you.

Get up in front of the class and introduce yourself. Begin with your name. Spell it, if necessary, and write it on the board or an overhead transparency. Repeat your name. Ask the group to repeat it as well. If you prefer a nickname, tell why.

Explain the two or three items you selected from your Idea Box description list. State why you think those words describe you. Give examples. Close with a planned ending, such as "Don't forget to call me Dude," or "I always answer to the name Maricarmen," or "Think of me as talkative, trustworthy Tom."

FBLA Public Speaking I

This event gives participants the opportunity to demonstrate leadership through effective speaking skills. The topic for your speech is Ethanol—Alternative for a Fuel Crisis. Ethanol is made from corn. Assume your state ranks second in corn production. You will be presenting your speech to members of Congress (the judges). The main purpose of your speech is to request federal financial support for additional ethanol production plants in your state, which in turn will decrease the fuel crunch. Your speech should be four minutes in length. You may use note cards, but no visual aids may be used.

Performance Indicators Evaluated

- Clearly state the purpose of ethanol for fuel production.
- Convince the audience to invest government funds for ethanol production.
- Explain the importance of developing alternatives to fossil fuels.
- Demonstrate a logical sequence of ideas to support ethanol production.

You will be evaluated for your

- Knowledge of the topic.
- Organized presentation of the topic.
- Confidence, quality of voice, and eye contact.
- Relationship of the topic to business strategy.

For more detailed information, go to the FBLA web site.

Think Critically

1. Why is fuel an important current topic?
2. What major advantages should you emphasize for the increased production of ethanol?
3. How is your proposal beneficial to your state?
4. How is your proposal beneficial to the nation?

http://www.fbla-pbl.org/

2 Speech Is an Oral Language Code

CHAPTER OBJECTIVES

After completing this chapter, you should be able to

- Explain how language is constantly changing.
- Describe denotative and connotative meanings.
- Define and give examples of reporting, inferential, and judgmental language.
- Identify listening barriers and how they negatively affect business.
- Apply the technique of paraphrasing to confirm understanding of a message.

KEY TERMS AND CONCEPTS

referents	reporting language	listening
denotations	inferential language	paraphrase
connotations	judgmental language	
assumptions	hearing	

IDEA BOX

Tune your ear to correct expressions that meet standard English usage. Try not to be trapped in the colloquial language that you often hear. Standard English is the choice of professional people in all fields. Only you can change your speaking habits. Practice saying the corrected versions if they sound unfamiliar to you.

Ain't = Am not
All the farther = As far as
Between you and I = Between you and me
Could care less = Could not care less
Data is = Data are
Graduate college = Graduate from college

The Power of Words

Spoken words are awesome tools. They flow together to provide verbal messages that resound with information.

> *"The smartphone, T-Mobile Sidekick II, has PDA functions for e-mail and IM fans who can also surf the Web, take snapshots, and make phone calls for $249.99 after a $50 mail-in rebate."*

Words deliver messages that snap listeners into action.

> *"Forward! March!"*

Words may also send a wave of delight through listeners.

> *"The weather report indicates that blizzard conditions are imminent, so classes will be canceled for the rest of the day."*

Language is indeed an astonishing invention—a product of creative human brains. Springing out of a human need, a *verbal code* was devised by people to symbolize and shape meaning. As a tool for thinking, *symbols* such as words help make sense of the experience of living. We observe, associate, reflect, contemplate, and talk to ourselves. As a means of interacting with others, we exclaim, joke, ask, describe, explain, and chat almost as easily as we breathe. Speech is so important that it is almost a sixth sense!

Language Symbols

Words often mirror our thinking processes. They symbolize the ideas in our heads. A word can't *be* a thing—it can only *stand for* something. It is a symbol, although we sometimes act as if it really exists. Ideas are encoded into words and transmitted as sound waves into the air. You hear, listen, and decode to clearly understand the message. Of course, it helps if the sender and receiver are sharing the same verbal code.

Coded Meanings

How do words get their meanings? We tend to think of a word as fixed and forever frozen on a page so we can count on its pronunciation and meaning. Not so! Spoken language is constantly changing as people use it. Different meanings are added, and new uses discovered. Consider how the advent of personal computer

> **"Words are not reality. They're only expressions of what people see...(hear and touch)"**
>
> —Elizabeth George

FIGURE 2-1   Real objects are represented by language symbols

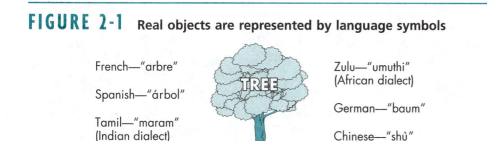

French—"arbre"

Spanish—"árbol"

Tamil—"maram" (Indian dialect)

TREE

Zulu—"umuthi" (African dialect)

German—"baum"

Chinese—"shù"

Language trap

Don't say, "Where's the fax machine at?" Say, "Where is the fax machine?"

systems has added new meaning to the word "mouse." Computer definitions have been added to many familiar words that were already in use—scroll, menu, file, disk, floppy, port, chip, desktop, windows, browsing, surfing, server, net, web, and so forth. Used outside of a computer context, the same words have totally different meanings. Inside the world of computers, these terms have specific **referents**— the items (devices, programs, or functions) to which the words refer.

DENOTATIVE MEANINGS A dictionary lists words and explains the ways in which people have used those words in the past. Specific definitions generally agreed upon by educated speakers of a language are known as **denotations**. For example, if it is accepted that "up" stands for a particular direction, it is so coded. But, "up" has also been used as an expression for feeling good. The beauty of language is that there is no direct, one-to-one relationship of a word to a specific, real item. The symbols are adapted to express our feelings, our beliefs, our ideas, and figments of our imaginations.

CONNOTATIVE MEANINGS **Connotations** are the feelings that people attach to words because of personal experiences. Many words trigger emotional meanings. For example, "exam," "work," "school," and "holiday" all have specific denotative meanings listed in the dictionary. But think of how you add your personal feelings to these words. You create connotations for yourself. The words call up your individual experiences. "Beach" is defined as "an expanse of sand along the edge of a body of water." Your mental image of a beach may trigger positive thoughts of warmth, relaxation, pleasant breezes, and sparkling,

© Getty Images/PhotoDisc

A listener must decide what the words mean and what the speaker means by those words.

emerald water. Someone else may think of a cold, fishy, wet place with itchy, hard-to-get-rid-of sand. It is the same referent, but a different perception. We cannot make **assumptions**, or take for granted, that others perceive things the same way we do. We sometimes jump to a conclusion of a speaker's intended meaning before we realize the speaker's point of reference. It is no wonder we sometimes have communication problems.

Language Levels

One of the most delightful aspects of language is its ability to operate on a number of levels. From precise details of a science experiment, to the lengthy explanation of a government document, to the lyrics of a love song or the creation of a poem, language fills many needs. One of the first steps in your own improvement in speaking is to become aware of the level of language you are using. Then you can make gentle corrections.

Reporting language consists of statements based on observation. The words are concrete and specific, saying only what can be seen, touched, heard, measured, and so forth. This information can be confirmed by the listener as well as the person speaking. Consider the statement, "The cash receipts for today are $1,588.68." Because money can be counted to verify the truth of the statement, this is considered reporting language. People usually accept such statements because they can check them for accuracy. In conversation, you can often avoid friction by using reporting language.

Inferential language uses statements that draw conclusions by a reasoning process that may or may not be faulty. Inferences include more than reporting. They blend assumptions, knowledge, experiences, and attitudes into statements that infer or set up opinions about a subject. Because they reflect the mindset of the speaker, inferences often tell a listener more about the person talking than about the topic. If you monitor your own speech, you'll find inferences to be common and convenient. To improve, you might adjust your comments to be closer to reporting language or add phrases like "In my opinion . . ." to your statement. Consider the statement, "We weren't very busy at the restaurant today." The receiver of the statement may not know what constitutes "busy" in the speaker's mind. How many people must one serve to be busy? How much money must be taken in? The speaker might instead say, "In my opinion, we weren't very busy today" or "We didn't have as many customers as usual today."

Judgmental language contains statements that evaluate good/bad, right/wrong, ugly/pretty, and so forth. "This sandwich tastes like road kill" is an example. Judgments about what we like or dislike are so frequent that we don't always recognize them when we speak. They slip easily off our tongues. To avoid sounding too critical, add the phrase "to me" or "I believe" or "as I see it" when you state your outlook. Not everyone will agree with your evaluation, but if you qualify the statement as your viewpoint, you will not offend or provoke an argument.

Personal CHECK-UP

Identify a time when a misunderstanding occurred because you and someone else had different connotations for a word. Think of food, cars, or movies.

The Listener's Role

Hearing and listening are different. When the ear responds to vibrations caused by sound waves and transmits nerve impulses to the brain, we are **hearing**. When the brain focuses on the meaning of the sounds being heard, we are **listening**. Rock music, cell phone messages, barking dogs, a teacher's voice, a friend's whisper—of all the noises surrounding us, we choose the ones to which we will pay attention. We focus on what most interests us, and we let other noises fade into the background.

There are techniques that speakers may use to get our attention. For example, louder sounds strike the membrane harder, creating greater vibrations on the eardrum. Softer sounds require us to focus carefully in order to understand. Speakers pay attention to their voice levels if they want to be heard, and they vary them to hold our interest. The role of a listener in communication is vital. As you learn to speak for success, you must also learn to receive messages successfully. Listening is an action we often take for granted, but practice is necessary in order to become a good listener.

Listening Barriers

Some obstacles that interfere with listening may be physical. It is possible that something might be wrong with the hearing mechanism or the technology used to facilitate transmission. More often than not, however, barriers are psychological—resulting from resistant attitudes, irritated feelings, or lack of awareness. The following barriers may cause breakdowns in communication.

> *"Sound knocks on your eardrums and you hear it; listening is what you do with what you hear."*
>
> **—Source Unknown**

FIGURE 2-2   The process of hearing

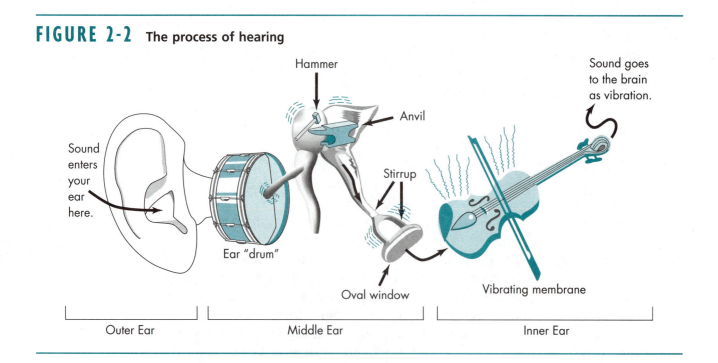

Hammer

Sound goes to the brain as vibration.

Anvil

Sound enters your ear here.

Stirrup

Ear "drum"

Oval window

Vibrating membrane

Outer Ear | Middle Ear | Inner Ear

© 1999 Ted Goff

"And should there be a sudden loss of consciousness during this meeting, oxygen masks will drop from the ceiling."

Listening

There are many ways to listen.

- *Appreciatively* to your favorite music.
- *Comprehensively* to your doctor's instructions.
- *Critically* to evaluate the claims of a commercial.
- *Intently* to a single voice in a crowd.
- *With empathy* to encourage a good friend.

Your responses—facial expressions, muscular tension, eye contact, and so forth—clearly indicate your listening style and set the stage for interaction to continue (or perhaps discontinue). Real listening is difficult to fake.

- Can't hear—"That microphone isn't working."
- Don't hear—"I do wish she wouldn't mumble."
- Won't hear—"He never says anything important."
- Can't understand—"I don't speak French."
- Don't understand—"Why do I push this button?"
- Won't understand—"I never did like math."

Poor Listening Is Costly in Business

There are many reasons for improving your listening skills at work. Your job will require you to listen to supervisors, co-workers, customers, and perhaps to your own employees. In fact, 55 percent of your waking time is spent listening. Your attention shifts in and out. You focus and refocus. Think of the cost to a business of people who listen poorly.

- Accidents cause physical injury.
  "I didn't hear anyone say this is a hard-hat area."

- Production breakdowns result in losses.
  "I don't remember him saying to insert the bolt from the left side."

- Lost sales and dissatisfied customers hurt business.
  "Why did she get so angry? I didn't understand her complaint."

- Misunderstandings between employees slow production.
  "Why didn't you pay attention when I gave you that deadline?"

Personal CHECK-UP

Identify four barriers to listening. Give examples.

- Conflict between workers and management affects work environment.

"I keep telling the boss that we'd save time if we combined the two steps into one. No one listens to those of us who do the job."

Improving Listening Skills

Listening is a complex process that includes *decoding* (converting sound into meaning), *comprehending* (understanding how the message relates to the topic), *decision making* (deciding how to respond), and *feedback* (reacting verbally, nonverbally, or not at all). Disciplined listening is actually hard work.

LISTENING FOR CONTENT Consider what you bring to a communication situation—your experience of living, your attitudes, your beliefs, your ideas, and your value system. Clearly, you do not listen as if you were an empty glass waiting to be filled. You take in the message, but you use your skills to understand, to relate, to remember, and to retain.

When you are required to listen to a presentation in a business setting or in school, you are expected to listen for the *content,* or the information contained in the speech. A student in American history class, for example, would listen to a lecture by

- Assessing the speaker's purpose and credibility.
- Searching for the central idea of the speech.
- Noting the main points that develop the central idea.
- Paying attention to factual data, such as places, names, and dates.

COMMUNICATION AT WORK

The task of a social worker is to form a relationship with each client during the first meeting. Marta Kishun says everything happens in a "talking frame" in her private sessions, but that counseling includes more than speech communication. She establishes a rapport in the beginning with speech, but as the client talks, the social worker's job is to listen actively. A vital part of active listening is feedback. Marta uses physical indicators, such as maintaining eye contact, nodding, and facial expressions of concern, to show that she is listening. Marta needs to understand what particularly upsets or troubles a client, even if the client doesn't say so directly. She also asks questions to help her clients approach their experiences from new angles. Marta knows it's a giant step for people to come and ask for help. She uses all of her communication skills to put them at ease and to help them find a new perspective.

©Getty Images/PhotoDisc

- Guessing the meaning of unfamiliar words from the context.
- Discovering similar ideas expressed in different words.

Language trap

Don't say, "I done the assignment."
Say, "I have done the assignment already."
or "I did the assignment."

Although there may be a short question-and-answer period after a speech, opportunity to clarify misunderstandings is often limited. To listen well, you must block out distractions and focus your attention. Of course, taking and comparing notes with classmates is a good idea.

PARAPHRASING In a one-to-one situation, or in a small group, it is possible to use feedback to determine the accuracy of your listening. A technique called *paraphrasing* is useful to clarify the content of a speech message. To **paraphrase** means to repeat in your own words the message you heard. Start with one of the following phrases.

- "If I understand correctly, you said . . ."
- "So, your idea is . . ."
- "Do I understand you to mean . . . ?"
- "In other words . . ."
- "Do I hear you saying . . . ?"

Practice these introductions to paraphrasing so that you can slide into them easily. You will be able to restate what you heard, and this response will give the speaker a chance to add further information, explain a point, or correct your misunderstanding. More effective communication results when you paraphrase messages to ensure understanding.

©Getty Images/PhotoDisc

Use feedback and paraphrasing to determine the accuracy of your listening.

CHAPTER SUMMARY

Each time we speak, we use a powerful, symbolic language code. The code is fluid, changing and adapting over time, and we may attach personal meanings to the words. The dictionary provides denotative meanings, and we add connotations by calling up mental images and associations from our experiences. Communication problems result when we make assumptions that a speaker's point of reference is similar to our own. Speaking skills can be improved if we are aware of language levels. Reporting language focuses on verifiable facts. Inferential language is based on reasoning, although sometimes flawed, that adds personal opinions. Judgmental language includes the speaker's evaluation. Developing good listening skills is an important part of speech training. Listening barriers are more often psychological than physical, and poor listening causes problems in the workplace. Suggestions for improvement include listening for content and paraphrasing to determine accuracy.

CHAPTER REVIEW

1. Give an example of a word that has different referents depending on the context.
2. Explain the difference between connotative and denotative meanings.
3. Give one example of each of the three levels of language.
4. Why do businesses desire employees who possess good listening skills?
5. List three phrases you might use to begin a paraphrase of a message.
6. List ways you might paraphrase, "Ain't no way you're getting on this squad."

CAN YOU DEFINE THESE TERMS?

Match each description with the appropriate term. Write the correct letter in the blank preceding the sentence. Some terms will not be used.

Terms:

a. assumptions
b. connotations
c. denotations
d. hearing
e. inferential language
f. judgmental language
g. listening
h. paraphrase
i. referents
j. reporting language

1. ___ The items to which words refer
2. ___ Feelings that people attach to words because of personal experiences
3. ___ Specific definitions generally agreed upon by educated speakers of a language
4. ___ Conclusions reached when we take for granted that others perceive things as we do
5. ___ Verifiable statements based on observation
6. ___ To repeat the message in your own words
7. ___ Statements that evaluate good/bad, right/wrong, ugly/pretty, and so forth
8. ___ When the brain focuses on the meaning of sounds
9. ___ Statements of opinion that draw conclusions by a reasoning process

APPLICATIONS

Language Levels

Identify each statement as reporting (R), inferential (I), or judgmental (J) language.

1. ___ We've got the best team in the city!
2. ___ "Epoch" is a noun standing for a particular period of history.
3. ___ See this yummy candy bar? It has dark chocolate with mint filling.
4. ___ These snakes won't hurt anybody because they're a garden variety.
5. ___ In my opinion, this ocean-side room is not worth the extra cost.
6. ___ Skateboards are dangerous; I broke my elbow riding one.

Uncritical Inference Test *developed by William V. Haney*

Read the following brief story. Assume that all of the information presented in it is definitely accurate and true. Read it carefully because it has ambiguous parts designed to lead you astray. There is no need to memorize it, though. You may refer back to it whenever you wish.

Then, read the statements following the story and indicate whether you consider each statement to be definitely true (T), definitely false (F), or possibly true or false (?). If any part of a statement is doubtful, circle the "?". Answer each statement in order, and do not go back to change any answer later or reread any statements after you have answered them. Doing so will distort your score.

To start, here is a sample story followed by statements with the correct answers circled.

SAMPLE STORY   You arrive home late one evening and see that the lights are on in your living room. There is only one car parked in front of your house. The words "Jerome R. Jones, M.D." are spelled in small gold letters across one of the car doors.

1. The car parked in front of your house has lettering on one of its doors.   (T) F ?
   (This is a "definitely true" statement because it is directly specified by the story.)

2. Someone in your family is sick.   T F (?)
   (This could be true, but could be false. Perhaps Dr. Jones is paying a social call at your home, perhaps he has gone to the house next door or across the street, or perhaps someone else is using his car.)

3. No car is parked in front of your house.   T (F) ?
   (This is a "definitely false" statement because the story directly contradicts it.)

4. The car parked in front of your house belongs to a man named Johnson.   T F (?)
   (This may seem false, but can you be sure? Perhaps the car has just been sold.)

This sample should warn you of some of the traps to look for when taking the test. Now, begin the actual test. Remember, mark each statement in order. Do not skip around or change your answers.

TEST STORY   A businessman had just turned off the lights in the store when a man appeared and demanded money. The owner opened a cash register. The contents of the cash register were scooped up, and the man sped away. A member of the police force was notified promptly.

1. A man appeared after the owner had turned off his store lights.   T   F   ?

2. The robber was a man.   T   F   ?

3. The man who appeared did not demand money.   T   F   ?

4. The man who opened the cash register was the owner.   T   F   ?

5. The storeowner scooped up the contents of the cash register and ran away.   T   F   ?

6. Someone opened a cash register.   T   F   ?

7. After the man who demanded money scooped up the contents of the cash register, he ran away.   T   F   ?

8. While the cash register contained money, the story does not say how much.   T   F   ?

9. The robber demanded money of the owner.   T   F   ?

10. A businessman had just turned off the lights when a man appeared in the store.   T   F   ?

11. It was broad daylight when the man appeared.   T   F   ?

12. The man who appeared opened the cash register.   T   F   ?

13. No one demanded money.   T   F   ?

14. The story concerns a series of events in which only three persons are mentioned—the owner of the store, a man who demanded money, and a member of the police force.   T   F   ?

15. The following events occurred: someone demanded money, a cash register was opened, its contents were scooped up, and a man dashed out of the store.   T   F   ?

Your instructor will read the correct answers. Score your correct answers. Discuss the following questions in small groups, and report your answers to the class.

1. When reading the statements, what mental images did you add to the words in the story?

2. What questions would you ask to clarify the messages in the story?

3. If you were a witness to this scene, how would you describe the incident to the police officer? Write the script for what you would say. (You may make up details that you would like to add.)

4. What conclusions can be drawn from this test about using language carefully?

MAKING CONNECTIONS

Speech Communication

Write a sentence that feeds back a paraphrase of each of the following messages to determine the content.

1. The vice president's cousin was promoted over people who have worked here longer.

   _____

   _____

   _____

2. The reporter said that CNN unofficially documented a report from unknown Pentagon informants who believe that unidentified objects may have been sighted.

   _____

   _____

   _____

3. I heard a drug manufacturer say at a meeting recently that more than 10 million sleeping pills are taken by Americans each night.

   _____

   _____

   _____

4. Retail gasoline prices hit another record high over the past weeks, mirroring a rapid increase in the cost of crude oil.

_____

_____

_____

5. The American Medical Association says long-term research shows that alcohol impairs the brain development of youths younger than 21.

_____

_____

_____

English

Use a dictionary to help with words in which you are unsure of the pronunciation or meaning. Write a sentence using each word below correctly. Be prepared to read your sentences aloud.

anxious/eager   avocation/vocation

assure/ensure/insure   pronounce/pronunciation

accept/except

_____

_____

_____

_____

_____

_____

_____

_____

_____

_____

_____

_____

_____

_____

PROJECTS

Businessperson's Calendar

Your instructor will read aloud some specific directions that will require you to fill out the diagram below. Listen carefully to the reading, and fill in the spaces. Your instructor will also ask some questions to be answered in the numbered spaces below.

_____

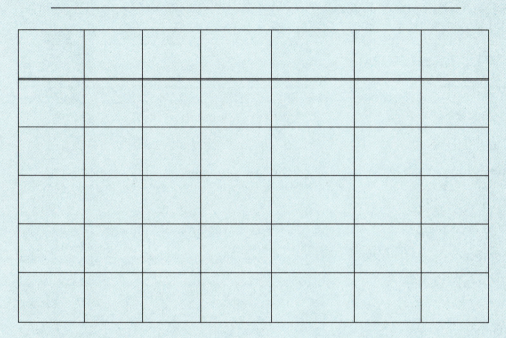

Answer the questions "true" or "false" according to the information provided. Write your answers below.

1. _____   6. _____

2. _____   7. _____

3. _____   8. _____

4. _____   9. _____

5. _____   10. _____

Score _____

Oral Report to a Group

An oral report is designed to provide an audience with information concerning a topic that they know little about. You are to report on an organization that you know very well. Think of a social club, team, business, high school club, sorority, community organization, or other organization. Prepare a brief (two- to four-minute) report to be presented to a group of your classmates. Select a key idea and develop it with two or three main points. Plan the introduction and conclusion. Prepare a rough, one-page outline that you may follow as you speak. It should include words and phrases to jog your memory.

SAMPLE OUTLINE FORM

Introduction

(Get attention)	A. Use a quip, a quote, or a humorous remark.
(Involve listeners)	B. Ask a question using the word "you."
(Establish your credibility)	C. Explain how you know this information.

Key Idea

(Write it on the board so everyone understands what you are going to talk about.)

Development of Key Idea

Main point I.

Main point II.

Main point III.

Conclusion

(Summarize)	A. Restate your key idea and main points.
(Focus)	B. State what you want your audience to remember and why.

CRITIQUE SHEET FOR ORAL REPORTS

Circle "Average," "Good," or "Excellent" for each of the following points.

1. Did the speaker seem well prepared?   Average   Good   Excellent

2. Was the information organized in an interesting manner and explained clearly?   Average   Good   Excellent

3. Did the introduction do the three things required of it?   Average   Good   Excellent

4. Was the key idea clearly stated?   Average   Good   Excellent

5. Did the conclusion summarize and focus?   Average   Good   Excellent

6. Was the report informative and well practiced?   Average   Good   Excellent

7. Was the speaker's voice loud enough?   Average   Good   Excellent

8. Did you learn new information?   Average   Good   Excellent

Comments:

_____

_____

_____

_____

_____

_____

_____

_____

BPA Extemporaneous Speech

Extemporaneous speaking involves being able to pull together your thoughts on a subject and present a short speech on the spur of the moment. You must effectively demonstrate communication skills in arranging, organizing, and presenting information orally with limited preparation time.

You will draw two different business topics from a hat. You will have the option to select either topic. You will have ten minutes to develop the topic (key idea). You may jot down notes for reference on cards provided by the event proctor. No previously prepared notes or visual aids may be used for the presentation.

Possible topics will include:

- Government Incentives for the Manufacture of Hybrid Cars
- Flexible Work Weeks—More Leisure Time
- Tax Incentives for Small Businesses
- Bailing Out the Airline Industry
- Clamping Down on Corporate Scandal
- Natural Disasters Stimulate Business
- The Importance of International Business
- Professional Networking for Success

The length of the speech must be between one and three minutes. You will speak before a panel of judges and a timekeeper—no audience will be allowed at this event. The timekeeper will signal when one minute and thirty seconds of speaking time remain on the clock.

Performance Indicators Evaluated

- Illustrate an understanding of the topic.
- Organize thoughts into a meaningful presentation.
- Communicate a clear presentation backed by examples and facts.
- Develop a conclusion that is supported by the facts presented.
- Present the information with confidence.

For more detailed information, go to the BPA web site.

Think Critically

1. Why is it important to keep up to date on current domestic and international events?
2. List two strategies for remaining calm while preparing and presenting an extemporaneous speech.
3. Give an example of a business situation where you might be called upon to give an extemporaneous speech.
4. Why is it important to sort out your opinions when preparing a speech?

http://www.bpa.org/

Paralanguage Flavors the Verbal Message

3

CHAPTER OBJECTIVES

After completing this chapter, you should be able to

- Identify the role of paralanguage in spoken messages.
- Explain the difference between content and intent in speaking.
- Apply practice tips for improving vocal qualities.
- Describe and apply empathetic listening techniques.
- Identify appropriate and effective communication styles for each circle of your communication network.
- Explain how language and paralanguage tools are adjusted to fit a variety of communication situations.

KEY TERMS AND CONCEPTS

mixed message	timbre	listening for intent
pitch	diction	empathy
rate	articulation errors	empathetic listening
volume/intensity	pronunciation errors	small talk

IDEA BOX

Make a list of people with whom you talk. The list should cross a wide spectrum of categories. (Suggested categories are listed below.) Consider how topics and language styles vary from person to person.

Family	Coworkers
Friends	Teammates
Neighbors	Customers
Teachers	Acquaintances
Employers	Strangers
Classmates	

Spoken Language—Words Plus Voice

There's more to speech than just words. Your voice adds the tone that makes words meaningful. Your voice is part of your image—its sound identifies you. Your speaking voice is an instrument that reflects your personality, health, feelings, moods, and attitudes. It adds positive messages, such as warmth, friendliness, and sincerity, or negative messages, reflecting the opposite.

It is important to know the speech communication tools of pitch, rate, volume, timbre, and diction. When your vocal tones are vibrant and clear, your words carry power and impact. Words and voice work together—we only separate them for study purposes.

Paralanguage Reveals the Speaker's Intent

Familiar words on a printed page conjure images in the reader's mind. Spoken words do more. The way the words are expressed provides a wealth of additional information to the listening ear. In fact, the tone of voice may be more meaningful than the words. When the words say one thing and the voice indicates another, we are hearing a **mixed message**, and we tend to give more credibility to the voice. "Of course, I'd love to go," cooed in a soft, sweet tone provides a different response than the same words snapped in a sharp, abrupt manner. Although speakers may choose words carefully, vocal cues often expose what the speaker really feels. We call the vocal sound *paralanguage*. The Greek word "para" (meaning "beside" or "beyond") attached to "language" creates a speech term representing the additional clues to meaning beyond the spoken words. Facial expressions and body movement provide additional paralanguage clues. Paying attention to paralanguage helps to determine a variety of speaker emotions, such as contempt, indifference, grief, anger, anxiety, sadness, or happiness.

Words (language) and vocal sounds (paralanguage) are delivered together. As listeners, we get meaning from both the words and the way they are spoken. We learned in the last chapter that words carry the *content* of a message, so it is important to understand the language—English, Spanish, and so forth. However, it is paralanguage that reveals a speaker's *intent* or feeling about what is being said. When we were first learning to talk, it was paralanguage that we understood before words. We were more aware of the *subtext* (meaning beneath the words) because of what was going on with the speaker, and we learned to associate the words. Now, we are even more sensitive to the way that voices sound as words are spoken. We put the language and sound together to figure out the true meaning of the message. Both speech communication tools—words plus vocal sounds—are dynamic codes adaptable to all levels of conversation.

Vocal Qualities Accompany Verbal Messages

When a close friend calls you on the phone, there is little need for that person to identify himself or herself. You recognize the voice immediately. Often your friend's mood is also evident. Voices have characteristics that provide vocal codes for communication. What are the characteristics of paralanguage? As we examine these, we'll add tips for improving your speaking voice.

"It's not what you said, it's the way that you said it."
—**Source Unknown**

PITCH   **Pitch** is the variation in relative vibration frequency—high to low—of the human voice that contributes to the total meaning of speech. Because they are easy to listen to, people often respond favorably to relaxed, controlled, well-pitched (neither too high nor too low) voices. However, pitch tends to rise whenever a speaker is under tension and muscles tighten. This higher pitch may indicate nervousness, anger, or other strong feelings.

Tip: If your pitch tends to go high when you speak to a group, you'll want to get good control of your breathing before you begin speaking. Consciously take a couple of deep breaths and breathe out slowly. Then imagine rolling a bowling ball down an alley. Think "low, smooth, controlled" and let your opening words be at a comfortable, relaxed pitch.

When you talk with your friends in ordinary conversation, your pitch is at its normal level, but as you speak, it rises and falls in spontaneous, interesting patterns. Listen to several people talking together and notice how their pitch varies. The variation adds interest.

Your vocal tones can reflect attitudes and feelings that add to the words you speak.

In an audience situation, listeners' attention focuses on the speaker's voice as eardrums respond to variety in the vibrations beating against them. In other words, speaking in public should sound somewhat conversational, or at least the pitch should change frequently. Problems with pitch may occur in public speaking when the words to be spoken are written out in front of the speaker. When the speaker reads, the pitch tends to flatten out, rather than rise and fall conversationally. The voice becomes *monotone*. Sound pats the listening eardrums gently, lulling the listener to sleep, rather than beating against the eardrums for attention.

Tip: If you are asked to read aloud or to speak from a prepared manuscript, do all you can to make your voice sound conversational. Take little pauses. Change your pitch pattern. Sound as if you are talking to your audience, not just reading to them.

RATE   The speed with which words are spoken determines the pace or **rate** of delivery. Just as with pitch, the more variety in the rate, the easier it is to listen. Speakers do not say one word or one sentence at a time. Rather, they speak in phrases—producing groups of word sounds punctuated by pauses of different lengths. Some phrases spill out rapidly, while others move more deliberately.

Tip: To achieve improvements in rate, practice giving your speech aloud. When you prepare a presentation, "talk" your speech out in the privacy of your room. Phrase ideas carefully, slowing to focus on important ideas, tossing off unimportant words, and using effective pauses of different lengths. Make it sound spontaneous. Practice, practice, practice. Suit your overall rate of speaking to the size of the group—slow down for larger audiences, but make your speech sound like conversation.

Language trap

Don't say, "She seen the movie."
Say, "She saw the movie." or "She has seen the movie."

VOLUME OR INTENSITY   The **volume/intensity** indicates the degree of loudness with which a message is spoken. A loud voice can indicate feelings of excitement, anger, or need for attention. A level that is too soft may give the impression that the speaker is hesitant, fearful, or unprepared. The intensity of a vocal sound reveals something about a speaker's feelings. In ordinary conversation, in an interview situation, or in public, it is important to adjust your volume level to your listeners. For a listening audience, it is annoying to have difficulty hearing the speaker. When a microphone is used, it should effectively project the speaker's voice at the proper auditory level. But, microphones are not always available. Your effective speaking voice should be as loud as the occasion and the listeners warrant.

Tip: To keep listeners' attention, change the volume of your voice occasionally. Some phrases or ideas might be delivered with greater force for emphasis, some with less. The variation of sound waves beating against the listeners' ears keeps attention. The secret is to watch individuals in your audience. You can tell if they can't hear you or are losing interest. Direct your voice to the person farthest away from you, shift the loudness, drop to a quieter tone, build to an intense volume, or pause before or after an important point. Such vocal techniques will keep your audience listening, and their cues of interest will build your confidence.

TIMBRE   The distinctive qualities and tone that make your voice uniquely yours are referred to as **timbre**. Variations in these qualities signal your mood, physical condition, or emotional response to events. In public speaking, a pleasing vocal quality results from the relaxed use of your resonators (throat, nose, and mouth) and a desire to communicate.

Tip: If you feel your jaw and tongue tighten before speaking, drop your head and try a relaxing yawn along with a whole body stretch. Do this out of sight of your audience, of course.

DICTION   The care and precision with which you use your tongue and jaw to create clear speech sounds is called **diction**. Consonant sounds supply crispness and punch to speech (think of "k," "p," and "t"). Vowel sounds (represented by "a, e, i, o, and u") add richness and melody. **Articulation errors** occur when you do not make sounds clearly and accurately. **Pronunciation errors** occur when you do not make the correct sounds or you place the accent on the wrong syllable. Have you noticed that you use a particular level of diction and word style with your closest friends? You use a different language level in an interview or when giving a public speech.

Tip: When in doubt, look up words to be sure of accepted pronunciations when preparing for a presentation. The following are common errors you'll want to avoid. Practice saying the words correctly.

- Adding vowel sounds—"ath-a-lete" for "athlete"
- Omitting vowel sounds—"natcherly" for "naturally" and "pome" for "poem"
- Substituting vowel sounds—"git" for "get" and "crick" for "creek"
- Adding consonant sounds—"sta-stis-tics" for "statistics"
- Omitting consonants—"gover-ment" for "govern-ment"
- Reversing consonants—"liberry" for "library," "hunderd" for "hundred," and "childern" for "children"
- Nasalizing nonnasal sounds—"kaow" for "cow" and "touwn" for "town"
- Substituting consonants—"Babtist" for "Baptist," "wide" for "white," "assessory" for "accessory," and "congradulations" for "congratulations"
- Slurring sounds—"doncha" for "don't you," "whajado" for "what did you do?," and "gunna" for "going to"

© 2005 Ted Goff

"Your job will be to look at things in a new way and translate them to the old way for me."

Listening in the Workplace

Listening may be one of the most important communication tools you bring to your job. It certainly is the one you will use the most. Your job will require you to listen precisely and to interpret paralanguage and its characteristics of pitch, rate, volume or intensity, timbre, and diction. Reading the meaning behind the words and translating the message for others is viewed as a key workplace skill—one that may take practice and time to perfect.

DYSFUNCTIONAL CLUES When a speaker is uncomfortable talking, there is a tendency to use sounds to fill up silences. A person who continually pauses may fill the "dead space" with vocalized sounds, such as "er," "um," and "ah," or filler words, such as "you know" and "like." These repeated distractions may destroy the communicator's effectiveness. Such dysfunctional communication announces the speaker's nervousness or perhaps lack of preparation.

Tip: Listen to your own speech in conversation. Do you use filler words or sounds? To avoid such problems in speaking before a group, practice giving the speech aloud several times to help overcome the tendency.

Listening for Intent

If paralanguage is important, how does active listening apply to it? While some people believe that meaning is transferred like a gift, where one person gives and another receives, this is not always true. Listening to an upset friend requires different skills than does listening to a lecture for information. If a speaker expresses strong feelings with a flow of loud, dynamic expressions, the listener is put in the position of deciding what the words mean and why the speaker chose to deliver them in that manner. **Listening for intent** involves zeroing in on the unspoken "why" in the spoken message. Why has the speaker said this? What is the speaker feeling? Why is the speaker telling you?

People close to you, such as partners, friends, and family members, have interpersonal relationships with you that rely on empathy. **Empathy** is the ability to perceive another's point of view and to sense what others are feeling. Often what they want from you is the kind of listening that is concerned with the *person* speaking rather than with the message being spoken. This quality of paying attention is known as **empathetic listening**. More than trying to make sense of content and words, it can be described as listening for the "why." It requires an intense, focused "listening with the third ear," or "listening at the second level," or "absorbing through the pores." However you describe it, this tuned-in reception gets beneath the words to the emotions. You listen to learn the often unexpressed intent of the speaker. You choose this listening technique when the speaker's unspoken message is more important than the words.

Feedback Techniques

Empathetic listening is more than silently paying attention with an occasional nod. It is an active willingness to be completely receptive. To do this, you focus on the emotional intent that gives rise to the message. Let your eyes read facial clues and your ears pick up the vocal code that indicates sensibilities beneath the words. Your feedback is different from the active listening response of paraphrasing discussed earlier. In active listening, you responded to words, but now the focus is on feelings. You might respond with

Why is it important to listen carefully and to use appropriate feedback techniques in response to another person?

- ■ "That makes you feel happy then?"
- ■ "You must be worried about them."
- ■ "You seem pretty upset about this mistake."
- ■ "You're really angry about that comment?"
- ■ "These results seem to disturb you."

Note that you respond by talking about feelings. Practice these and similar phrases until they feel easy on your tongue. They are ways of going below the surface and inviting expressions of deeper emotions. These statements make no judgments about the speaker's message, nor do they indicate your reaction. The speaker can continue to talk without stopping to worry about your response. Your personal relationships will thrive because of your ability to listen empathetically.

Your Communication Network

Visualize Figure 3-1, not as a target, but as a way of charting your network of communication relationships. Think of the people whose names popped up when you completed the Idea Box at the beginning of the chapter. Do you communicate with each person/group in exactly the same way? Probably not. Start at the center. Think of your closest relationships as those in the inner circle, and those you contact least as outside the circle. Appropriate and effective communication styles are important for maintaining and developing these different levels of relationships.

FIGURE 3-1   Network of communication relationships

- Center: Deep personal sharing area
- First Ring: Close friendships
- Second Ring: Business and school communication
- Third Ring: Casual encounters
- Outside the Circles: Strangers

Deep Personal Sharing

In the heart of the circle are the people closest to you—the ones with whom you feel free to share your private thoughts and feelings. There may be only one name. Consider the amount and quality of time you spend with, the feelings you are willing to express with, your eagerness to talk and listen to, and the ties you have in common with those in your inner circle.

This inner circle is essential to most people. You are lucky if you have people in your life who provide deep sharing time for you. With these individuals, you can feel safe in revealing your inner thoughts. It takes time to form this type of solid relationship that is based on mutual trust. With your center persons, you have confidence to say what you truly believe without risk of judgment. You do not hesitate to ask for feedback from these special individuals, and you typically receive support and caring responses in return. These relationships build your self-esteem.

©Getty Images/PhotoDisc

Empathetic listening is concerned with the person speaking rather than with the message being spoken.

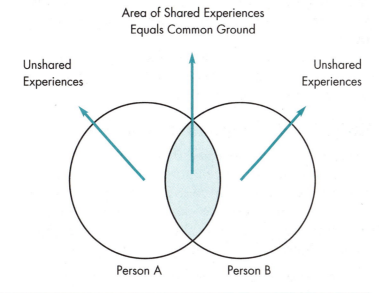

Close Friendships

In the first ring from the center are the names of your very good friends—people with whom you like to "hang out," see on an ongoing basis, or enjoy being around. This is a close circle of comrades. Here, the focus of your conversations includes common interests, daily events, hobbies, entertainment, jobs, family, and so forth. You laugh together, sympathize with one another, and look forward to seeing each other. The more common ground you share (Figure 3-2), the closer to the center of your communication network (Figure 3-1) another person is likely to be.

Business and School Communication

Not everyone whose name appears in the next ring is your buddy. This type of communication relationship is with people with whom you spend time in a particular setting—you work in the same office or have the same class. You talk about assignments and projects, people you both know, and shared goals, but you are not necessarily close friends. You probably do not share your deepest concerns, unless they currently involve work or school.

Casual Encounters

The outer ring is for those acquaintances with whom you may share a common activity or interest—you ride the same bus, eat in the same lunchroom, or are members of the same gym. You may not even know each other's full names. Conversations tend to be polite **small talk**—light or casual conversation about such topics as the weather, sports, or current events.

Personal CHECK-UP

Describe an experience when you felt that someone really listened to you and understood what you said. What clues indicated real listening?

Strangers

Outside the circle are folks with whom you speak because you recognize them from other encounters. You may not know their names, but you might pause for friendly greetings or at least acknowledge each other in passing.

Note that the personal level of sharing, the choice of topics, and the range and frequency of communication are less intimate as the circle widens. And indeed, the type and style of communication change too.

Choosing Appropriate Communication

By now you have realized that language and paralanguage are tools that can be adjusted to fit a variety of communication situations. The language you use with your close friends is probably different from the words you draw on to explain a math problem in class or to ask for help from your boss. You shift language style and the way you reveal your feelings to fit particular situations.

- **Informal situations**—casual conversation, slang, and relaxed comments.

- **Business situations**—clear reporting language, careful inferences, cautious judgments. Technical language or specialized terms used to describe products, types of tools, and processes may be used when professionals share the same vocabulary.

- **Formal situations**—careful use of standard English, limited as to topics and personal views.

COMMUNICATION AT WORK

As a professional landscaper, Donna Anders works closely with clients to learn what trees and shrubs they want planted and how much time they have to care for their yards. She frequently attends presentations with other landscape experts to gain new information about disease control and recently developed varieties of plants. In Donna's company, she meets weekly with her employees to solve problems regarding their suppliers of plants, trees, and other landscaping materials and to collaborate on plans for securing new clients. They also discuss ways to maintain high-quality service. Donna and her employees must listen for content as well as intent when talking with customers. It is important to watch customers' paralanguage to determine their true needs and any concern they may have about Donna's services. Donna and her employees must also be masters of small talk to maintain a friendly, customer-oriented atmosphere.

©Getty Images/PhotoDisc

CHAPTER SUMMARY

Words (language) combined with voice (paralanguage) reveal a speaker's true intent. With mixed messages, it is more often the tone of voice that receives the credibility. Vocal qualities include pitch, rate, volume, timbre, and diction. These vocal qualities can be improved for public speaking with proper practice. To an empathetic listener, words reveal content but paralanguage reveals the underlying emotions of the speaker. Listeners can use carefully worded feedback to acknowledge and support the speaker without offering personal reactions or passing judgment. Appropriate communication styles vary at each level of your communication network and are important for maintaining and developing the different levels of relationships. Language and paralanguage tools can be adjusted to fit a variety of communication situations.

CHAPTER REVIEW

1. If you were to describe a car to a friend, your boss, and a mechanic, how would your language change? Write a complete sentence for each situation.

2. Name a person whose speaking voice you like. Identify the characteristics that make it appealing.

3. Think of a person whose paralanguage and spoken words often send mixed messages. Which do you tend to believe? Give an example.

4. Your classmate has just blown up because of a bad grade and tells you all about it in an intense voice. Write two empathetic listening responses.

5. What is the difference between content and intent in a speaker's message?

CAN YOU DEFINE THESE TERMS?

Match each description with the appropriate term. Write the correct letter in the blank preceding the sentence. Some terms will not be used.

Terms:

1. ___ The degree of loudness

2. ___ When you do not make sounds clearly

3. ___ The ability to perceive another's point of view and to sense what others are feeling

4. ___ The speed with which words are spoken

5. ___ Concerned more with the person speaking rather than with the message being spoken

6. ___ The variation in relative vibration frequency— high to low—of the human voice

7. ___ The care and precision with which you use your tongue and jaw to create clear speech sounds

8. ___ The distinctive qualities and tone that make your voice uniquely yours

9. ___ Light or casual conversation about such topics as the weather, sports, or current events

a. articulation errors

b. diction

c. empathetic listening

d. empathy

e. listening for intent

f. mixed message

g. pitch

h. pronunciation errors

i. rate

j. small talk

k. timbre

l. volume/intensity

APPLICATIONS

Vocal Qualities Accompany Verbal Messages

Match each example of speech with the term of voice quality or type of language to which it corresponds. Write the correct letter in the blank preceding the example. Some examples may receive more than one term, and some terms will not be used.

1. ____ "She speaks so fast that I can't understand her at all."

2. ____ "You seem pretty upset about the way it happened."

3. ____ "Well, she said she was sorry, but she didn't sound like it."

4. ____ "His voice is low and soothing; I love to hear him talk."

5. ____ "I met Jim, and we just chit-chatted for a few minutes."

Terms:

a. diction

b. empathetic feedback

c. mixed message

d. pitch

e. rate

f. small talk

g. timbre

h. volume/intensity

Practice in Determining Speaker Intent

Join three or four classmates and practice the following exercises. One student will read the explanation, another will read the example aloud, and a third student will feed back a response. (Note: The words in parentheses should not be read, but provide the speaker with an indication of the paralanguage to use.)

- Paralanguage strengthens or conflicts with the verbal message. It enables the speaker to express intent without really putting the feeling into words.
  "Of course, you may go to the mall (but I'd rather you wouldn't)."

- Paralanguage provides subtle messages that the words do not convey.
  "He seems like a very nice person (but I don't have enough evidence to judge)."

- Paralanguage can contradict the words.
  "I'm crazy about dogs (but don't you let that mutt near me)."

- Paralanguage helps a listener choose which message to respond to—the *content* of the verbal message or the *intent* of the speaker.
  "I don't know why you are so angry. You told me I could go."

- Paralanguage provides clues as to how the speaker really feels.
  "You said yes, but you don't really want me to go to the mall. Right?"

- Paralanguage enables the listener to dig deeper into the speaker's meaning.
  "Are you upset because you weren't invited?"

- If the listener pays attention, paralanguage can offer more accurate communication because it reveals mixed messages.
  "You said you are glad school is starting, but you don't sound glad."

How It's Said?

Join three or four classmates and practice the following exercises. Each person will read the same sentence aloud, but will emphasize a different word. The person to the left of the reader will feed back a response. Discuss how the meaning changes according to the emphasized word.

Example

- "That's my dog?" (Response: "Which one? The terrier?")
- "That's my dog?" (Response: "I thought it belonged to your son.")
- "That's my dog?" (Response: "That's no dog; it's a mop.")

Practice

- "I hit him in the eye yesterday."
- "She invited me to the dance."
- "I have fifteen dollars."
- "I haven't cracked the textbook yet."

Same Word, Different Meaning

Choose one member of the group to be the responder. The only word the responder may say is "yes." The other members of the group will ask the following questions. The object of the exercise is to see if several different meanings rather than just the affirmative are spotted through paralanguage. What messages did you hear and see? Was the answer a content-level "yes" with a subtext level "yes," or was it a mixed message? Write your observations in the space below the questions and share them with the group.

- Have you ever had a serious operation?

- Did you feel a great deal of pain?

- Did the doctor and nurses do everything to make you feel better?

- Were you required to clean your plate as a kid?

- Are you fond of brussels sprouts?

- Were you the smartest kid in your seventh-grade class?

- If you won $10,000, would you give it away to charity?

- Would you be delighted to stay after the ballgame to clean the stadium?

- Is red your favorite color?

Continue to take turns asking questions of different responders.

MAKING CONNECTIONS

Speech Communication

This exercise is designed to improve your rate and diction and provide personal growth. Speakers average 150 words a minute when they speak at a conversational rate. Time yourself as you read the following paragraphs aloud, and write your times on the lines below. Practice until it takes you one full minute to say the 149 words. Take time to speak clearly. Pause for emphasis. Use this same conversational rate whenever you make a presentation.

What a marvelous instrument your voice is! Always available, turned on at will, and never failing until you stand to speak before an audience. Then your stomach quivers with thousands of butterflies madly fluttering their wings. You notice your irregular breathing, your tight throat, and your dry mouth full of cotton. Your clammy hands dangle awkwardly, your weight shifts from one foot to the other, and when you speak, the high-pitched voice doesn't sound like yours. This is "stage fright"—a common complaint of speakers.

Yet, rejoice! Your heartbeat has speeded up, your blood is racing, and adrenaline flows through your body—all functioning to provide an exciting edge to your performance. Regulate your nervous symptoms by breathing deeply to restore a normal breathing rate, roll your head to relax your neck muscles, and massage your stiff hands. Put on a smile and speak with confidence. You are in control!

_____

_____

_____

_____

_____

_____

_____

_____

Communication Network

On separate paper, draw a series of concentric circles similar to Figure 3-1, label them, and list the names of people with whom you communicate in each ring. From personal experience, write two or three sentences regarding the changes in speech content, language styles (formal or less formal), freedom to express attitudes, vocabulary use, and so forth, at each level.

_____

_____

_____

_____

Research

Using a library, the Internet, or a perhaps your employer's human resources department, find examples of organizational charts showing the structures of large businesses. (Hint: An organizational chart is often included in a business's published annual report.) Depending on the type of chart, you may note levels of international, national, regional, and local employees, or perhaps entry-level, supervisory, middle management, senior-level, and executive employees. From the charts, what conclusions can you draw about speech communication within a business's organizational structure? Back up your answer with an example.

_____

_____

_____

_____

PROJECT

Presentation to a Small Group—Individual Speech

Prepare an informal speech to be presented to a small group of your classmates. Your purpose will be to explain something valuable that you have learned in school, at work, or from someone in your family. List five ideas here.

Select one of the ideas you listed above. Use the questions on the next page to help organize your thoughts regarding the topic. Use the sample outline on page 47 as a model for preparing your final outline. Deliver your speech informally to a small group of your classmates as you remain seated. Ask one member of your group to use the critique sheet provided on the next page to give suggestions for improvement.

Organize Your Thoughts

1. How will you INTRODUCE your topic?

2. What will be your KEY IDEA?

3. What MAIN POINTS will develop your key idea?

4. How will you CONCLUDE your speech?

CRITIQUE SHEET FOR PRESENTATION

Circle "A" (Average), "G"(Good), or "E" (Excellent) for each question.

1. Did the introduction catch attention, get the audience involved, and establish the speaker's credibility?   A G E

2. Was the speech built around the key idea?   A G E

3. Did the speaker move smoothly from one point to the next?   A G E

4. Did the speaker bring the presentation to a smooth ending with a summary and a focus?   A G E

5. Was the speaker's voice loud enough to hear easily?   A G E

6. Was the presentation free of speech errors (poor grammar, mispronunciations, and so forth)?   A G E

7. Did the speaker control nervous mannerisms, appear confident, and maintain eye contact with the audience?   A G E

Comments:

_____

_____

_____

_____

_____

SAMPLE SPEECH OUTLINE

Introduction

(Get attention)   A. Bring an alarm clock, set off alarm.

(Involve audience)   B. *Does that sound chill you? When you hear it, do you just want to roll over and play dead?*

(Establish credibility)   C. *There is probably no one in this room who hated that sound more than I did—but now that's changed.*

Key Idea

In my business career, I've learned three helpful strategies for managing time.

Development of Key Idea

Transition: (The first strategy . . .)

Main point   I. *I've learned how to organize time.*
- A. Set up lists of goals.
  1. Explain daily, short-term, long-term goals.
  2. Visual—show a goal and how to handle it.
- B. Use a tickler file.
  1. Define tickler file (file for organizing things to do that will "tickle" the memory).
  2. Explain how it works.

Transition: (The second strategy . . .)

Main point   II. *I practice cutting time.*
- A. Telephone
  1. Visual—show egg timer to limit time.
  2. Explain—cluster calls to return them.
- B. Set priorities.
  1. Example—make minor decisions quickly.
  2. Example—set deadlines.
  3. Example—handle each paper only once.

Transition: (The third strategy . . .)

Main point   III. *I make time.*
- A. For me.
  1. Say "no" when I have to.
  2. Set times that work best for me.
  3. Work standing up.
- B. By delegating to others.
  1. Trade off with friends, sister.
  2. Ask for help when needed.

Conclusion

Transition: (In summary . . .)

(Summarize)   A. *I've told you my strategies for handling time: I organize it, I cut it, and I make time for myself.*

(Focus)   B. (Show clock again.) *Now when the alarm goes off, I don't hate it.*

DECA
Full-Service Restaurant Management Role Play

Review the following role-play scenarios. You have ten minutes to prepare a strategy for each situation. You will then have ten minutes to present your strategy to the judges, who may be representing customers or business leaders. You will have five additional minutes to answer the judges' questions.

Role Play #1

You are the manager of a popular restaurant. An angry customer wants to speak to you. The customer's group was told they would be seated within 15 minutes. Forty minutes later, they were seated by a less-than-pleasant host. The meals were served cold, and the meat was undercooked. These customers have been regular patrons to your business *until now*. You must develop a management solution for these unhappy customers in order to keep them coming back to your restaurant. One of the judges for this role play is the angry customer.

Role Play #2

You are the manager of a successful Italian pizza restaurant in a growing college community. Your restaurant has been around for 70 years and is a popular landmark located near the college campus. Because your community has experienced a huge growth spurt, numerous national pizza chains have located in the community. These new restaurants have intercepted 30 percent of your business. You must present a promotional strategy to the restaurant's owners for regaining business lost to the competition.

Performance Indicators Evaluated

- Communicate a customer service solution to retain customers.
- Understand the importance of customer satisfaction.
- Develop a promotional plan for a restaurant.
- Define the competition and a marketing strategy to overcome the competition.

You will be evaluated for your

- Knowledge of customer service.
- Organized analytical skills.
- Critical-thinking and problem-solving skills.
- Communication of viable solutions.

For more detailed information, go to the DECA web site.

Think Critically

1. Why is customer satisfaction so important in today's business world?
2. How can a restaurant manager use paralanguage and empathetic listening when resolving customer complaints?
3. What type of communication would be most appropriate for each of these role-play scenarios?
4. What strategy can be used to learn more about the competition?

http://www.deca.org/

Nonverbal Codes Send Silent Messages

CHAPTER OBJECTIVES

After completing this chapter, you should be able to

- Explain the ways that nonverbal messages affect communication.
- Identify channels of nonverbal communication.
- Distinguish voluntary and involuntary movements, and explain what they may reveal.
- Recognize the importance of effective nonverbal strategies to enhance communication in the workplace and in presentations.
- Understand the importance of the appropriate use of space and time when communicating.

KEY TERMS AND CONCEPTS

overt body movements	voluntary movements	gesture
covert body movements		personal space
self-image	involuntary movements	social distance
hygiene		public distance

IDEA BOX

Make a list of six topics you could talk to the class about while *showing* them at the same time. This is called a demonstration speech. Consider the following topic categories.

Show how to assemble an object
Show how to use a product
Demonstrate the steps in a process
Demonstrate a workout routine
Teach a dance step
Share a recipe

Messages Seen, Not Heard

You've heard, "Actions speak louder than words." Is it true? If someone says, "I'll be glad to come in to work on Saturday," and the words are accompanied by a shrug of the shoulders, which message do you believe? Probably not the words, and perhaps not the tone of voice. In this case, the body language sets up a mixed message. "Glad" has little to do with an indifferent shrug of the shoulders.

We know that communication is more than mere words. It is also more than the sound of the voice as it delivers the words. Speech communication includes a whole range of *nonverbal* behaviors that influence how verbal messages are received. Nonverbal communication takes place without words. It includes **overt body movements** (easily noticed actions), **covert body movements** (slight or hidden expressions of the face and eyes), choices regarding personal appearance and possessions, as well as the use of space and time—all supporting, supplementing, enhancing, and at times, contradicting spoken words. This aspect of communication is fascinating to study, because it is often under less direct control of the speaker.

As receivers, we must be cautious about the conclusions drawn from what we observe. Remember a lesson learned earlier—*assumptions* are the cause of many communication problems. Verify your interpretation of a nonverbal behavior before acting on it. No one really knows for sure what a particular action means without asking the person who is being observed. Carefully check your inferences.

- "Her hands are shaking. She must be nervous."
- "He's driving so slowly. He must be afraid of this heavy rain."
- "Her face is flushed. She must be embarrassed."

Are the conclusions too rapid? Can there be other reasons for such behaviors?

We depend on our eyes to provide a context for what we hear. Think of the last time you were in an audience listening to a well-known speaker. Your eyes did a complete assessment as he walked to the podium. You noticed the way he moved, his approximate age, the cut of his suit, the crispness of his shirt collar, the style and length of his hair, and his appearance of ease. With these details filed in your head, you tuned in to what he had to say. Perhaps you were eagerly receptive, neutral, or reluctant to listen—and all of this *before he said a word*. You were responding to nonverbal clues.

After a bit, you may have tuned out his words as you watched him shuffle papers, fiddle with his glasses, push back his hair, or pull his hands in and out of his pockets. Unless his words were vitally interesting to you, your focus may have been on his silent messages. Your eyes—like a video camera—recorded each distracting detail. Communication is much more than the words spoken. Nonverbal messages are seen and not heard.

"My eyes have always told me more than my ears."

—Gertrude Stein

Silent Messages—Codes and Channels

Each culture has unwritten rules that generally govern the way its people behave. Perhaps you've heard the following statements.

- "Use a handkerchief."
- "Look at people when you talk to them."
- "Don't spit on the sidewalk."
- "Don't stare."

Similarly, codes of acceptable dress and manners help us learn to get along in groups and function as a society. We learn that certain things are expected of us as civilized people. Most of the time, we fit in. We express our individuality in other personal ways, such as through choice of hairstyle, clothing, accessories, and surroundings. Silent messages flow through many channels.

Physical Features

Physical distinctions are inherited as genetic gifts. We have little ability to change such features as skeletal structure, skin color, or height. We can modify them only to a minimal extent. Those of short stature may wear shoes with high heels to appear taller, body builders will work out to make more of what nature has given them, and brunettes may bleach their hair blond. But generally, our bodies can reveal clues of our family heritage and of our attitudes toward health, fitness, and self care.

Appearance

How you enhance and decorate your physical body expresses your individuality and reflects your inner self. Your clothing, shoes, jewelry, hairstyle, and personal surroundings project your **self-image**, or how you see and think about yourself. Through these choices, you send messages about how you want to be seen. Some may criticize others who color their hair or wear excessive makeup as not being themselves, but in reality these choices are expressions of personality.

You may follow fashion trends, or you may disregard codes of dress and behavior as "not being you." In businesses, however, clothing is often regulated through formal or informal policies or dress codes. Although some corporations are sticking with a long-pants look, other firms have loosened their policies to redefine "business casual" to include shorts and even flip-flops at certain times. But, even businesses with the

Our choice of hair and clothing style reflects our personality.

©Getty Images/PhotoDisc

most relaxed standards usually discourage such clothing as hot pants, spaghetti-strap tops, and saggy, baggy pants, considering them as inappropriate attire for the office. When accepting a job with a company, it is important to determine what the rules—written and unwritten—require of you in the way of appearance.

Clothing that is too conspicuous, too tight, too unusual, too casual, or too dressy calls attention to the wearer. It is a way of saying, "I'm me." Workplaces rarely have patience with individuals who choose not to meet business standards. When you go to work, the more you know about the dress code of your organization, the more assured you will be about correct appearance choices on the job. For example, a trendy new haircut that looked right for school may not fit the impression you'll want to give in your new work environment. Clear understanding of what your company expects is essential if you want to succeed.

To feel confident about your appearance in a work situation, pay attention to what others are wearing. Note the dress and appearance of the person at the next higher level, and aim for that level of professionalism. You may be promoted to that level sooner than you think.

Personal Grooming

Nothing says more about you than the way you care for yourself. Good **hygiene**—cleanliness and care of self and personal belongings—is a must. Soap and water, razor, deodorant, toothpaste, polished shoes, and laundered clothing are standard requirements for a favorable impression. In short, your personal grooming tells others how you regard yourself.

Group Identification and Status

Your association with a particular company or group is often displayed through uniforms, caps, logos on shirts, and so forth. Work clothing and gear can sometimes reveal the type of job, such as the uniforms worn by service personnel, health workers, and security people. Companies take pride in the way they identify their staff. "Designing a uniform for Air France, France's roving ambassador, that is totally open to cultures the world over is a wonderful opportunity," said designer Christian Lacroix.

In some offices and workplaces, entry-level employees and line managers wear uniforms or business casual clothing, while the upper-level managers and executives wear professional suits or dresses. This is an example of status (level or position) shown through clothing. Often, employees are nonverbally ranked in an organization by the clothing they wear. Consider how position and training are also depicted in the clothing of police officers, military members, and airline personnel.

What kind of information is provided about these individuals through their clothing and appearance?

Possessions

The car you drive (especially if you can afford the one you really want), the objects you wear or collect, the music to which you listen, the books you read, and the way you decorate your living quarters all send messages about you. These are ways you express yourself in your own space.

Voluntary and Involuntary Movement

Your posture, walk, gestures, facial expressions, and the gleam in your eyes all provide unspoken coded messages about your feelings and attitudes. Many of these movements, such as standing up straight or putting your hands on your hips, are **voluntary movements** that are under your control in that you consciously make them. Others easily notice these overt body movements. However, some movements are **involuntary movements** that you make without realizing it. The nervous way you play with a pencil or the twitch of an eyebrow may reveal something about your state of mind. The slowness of your response or the slump of your shoulders gives clues as to what is going on inside you. When you're sad, the lack of animation in your movements may reveal your mood.

These signals can be tricky to read. For example, the rate of your friend's pace or the length of her stride may be less than normal because she is reluctant to arrive at the destination. Or, she could just be exhausted. Maybe she has developed a blister on her foot. You can tell something is different, and it makes sense to ask what is going on. Such covert movements are less easily observed, but are often more revealing than overt movements. Clues are provided by physical tensions, lack of eye contact, a twist of the lips, or a frown. Often they are involuntary and revealing. Sensitivity to and awareness of nonverbal clues are communication assets to a receiver.

Posture and Positions

The way you carry yourself can also convey coded nonverbal messages. An upright posture says that you are confident, but a rigid body can convey discomfort. A slouched posture may be seen as a lack of confidence or lack of respect, while in actuality the person may be tired. A comfortable walk or sitting position conveys ease in a situation.

The way you sit in relation to another person is also a clue about your feelings. Leaning forward and facing directly toward a person can indicate a desire to communicate. When someone crosses his or her arms, sits turned away, chooses a seat some distance apart, covers the mouth or eyes, or drums the fingers restlessly, the clues all indicate an unwillingness to participate.

A word of caution—it is easy to make snap judgments about how another person is feeling, and you may be wrong. So, ask if you are concerned. Perhaps the distressing behavior has nothing at all to do with you or the present situation. The person sitting with his arms crossed may simply be cold.

Hands and Gestures

A **gesture** is an expressive movement of *any* part of the body. We often think of hand movements because they are easily seen and can effectively back up our verbal messages. Try a little experiment. Let your hands speak in each of the ways listed in the margin quotation to the left. Can you?

Usually our hands are very expressive until we get in front of an audience. It is important to include gestures when you speak so you don't look frozen. Practice can help. You can remind yourself to include planned movements by writing them in your speech note cards.

Hands probably communicate most effectively through the sense of touch. Because unwritten rules govern body contact, members of American culture are less likely to touch each other than people of other nations. When hands reach out to comfort a friend, extend a greeting, seal a bargain, or offer congratulations, these gestures can say more than words do.

> *"The hands speak by themselves—by them we ask, promise, invoke, dismiss, threaten, entreat, deprecate. By them we express fear, joy, grief, our doubts, assent, or penitence, we show moderation or profession and mark number and time."*
>
> —Quintillian

"See? That means, 'What do you clowns want?'"

Nonverbal Communication

Your interpretation of a shrug, someone's posture, a wink, or a smile may be correct. Then again, was it a shy smile or a sly smile? We read nonverbal signals as messages, and often we read them right. However, beware of jumping to conclusions. If there is a chance of doubt, verify by asking. It is embarrassing and frustrating to misread clues. If you are not sure what is meant, say so. "Does this mean you approve?"

Business relationships are more formal and impersonal than close friendships, and thus a code about touching exists. Handshakes are very important. Men and women in business shake hands automatically, indicating a meeting between equals. Women often indicate whether a handshake is appropriate from a business colleague by initiating the gesture.

Hands that are damp or limp or that grasp too loosely create negative reactions toward their owners. Firm, direct handshakes are welcomed. Practice with a friend. Try to learn what impression people get when they shake hands with you. What impression do you get of someone who has a limp handshake?

Facial Expressions

Facial expressions may be the most important way that feelings are shown. In his pioneering book, *Silent Messages,* Albert Mehrabian concluded that feelings are communicated primarily through facial expressions and secondly through tones of voice. Spoken words rated a distant third. Why might facial expressions and tone of voice convey feelings better than spoken words?

Have you ever watched a person's head shake "no" while the mouth answered "yes"? Such contradictory messages reveal inner conflict. Small, fleeting changes of the face are often involuntary, and we must watch for them to totally understand the speaker's emotional state. Think for a minute of the twitch of an eyebrow, the curl of a lip, the flaring of nostrils, or the tightening of lips. To a careful observer, these movements send messages about their owner's inner feelings. The interpretation may not be correct, so it signals a good time to feed back a statement or question about intent.

It is said, "Eyes are the windows of the soul." What is there about the movement of eyes, the intensity of a gaze, the shifting of vision, or the dropping of eyelids that provides messages? You have learned to look

Language trap

Don't say, "I should of taken the earlier flight."
Say, "I should have taken the earlier flight."

All photos ©Getty Images/PhotoDisc

What do these facial expressions and gestures communicate about these individuals?

at the eyes of another to help determine what that person is thinking or feeling. Of course, you probably know many unwritten codes about seeing.

- "Don't stare."
- "Look at me when I'm talking to you."
- "A person who wants to speak to me will look at me first—if I look away it means I don't want to talk."

Of what other unwritten rules about seeing are you aware?

Channels of Space and Time

People send silent messages using the channels of space and time. These messages are often subtle, being sent outside of the awareness of the person sending them. Consider the manager who is always late to meetings and the coworker who always gets in your face when speaking to you. What statements are they making by their actions? Sometimes it is good to become aware of distracting habits. Improved communication might result.

Space and Distance

You may never have thought of space and distance as a means of conveying nonverbal messages. For example, you have your own territory—your place at the table, your seat in class, your closet, and so on. There is also an area with invisible boundaries around you, known as *personal space,* in which others are generally not welcome. When someone stands too close to you or gets right in your face when talking, it usually makes you feel uncomfortable. Communication distance falls within three ranges.

- **Personal space**—We only permit someone special to sit or stand within 1½ to 3 feet of us for intimate conversation.

- **Social distance**—Appropriate social distance varies from 3 to 12 feet, such as the space across a desk or table where we talk with friends or business associates. It is also the distance within which we feel comfortable standing when conversing with colleagues or new acquaintances.

- **Public distance**—This range is 12 feet or more between the speaker and listeners, such as for presentational speaking.

What kinds of messages does your choice of space indicate? The closer your relationship with others, the closer you allow them to get when communicating with you. Who do you permit into your personal space? How does communication distance work in business? Some people use invasion of personal space as a nonverbal message of aggression and intimidation. What do you think it means if someone continually backs away from you while you are talking? Maybe what you are saying is making the other person feel uncomfortable. Maybe you stand close because you count the person as an intimate friend, but your friend doesn't feel quite the same way. Or maybe the reason is as simple as poor hygiene or bad breath.

If a salesperson is invited into your home, he may suggest that you sit together around the dining table. This provides a comfortable space for him to make his presentation. You might be uncomfortable about

Personal
CHECK-UP

Give an example of when you felt your personal space was invaded. Give another example of when you were aware of how important the distance was between people. Is the seating arrangement important?

COMMUNICATION AT WORK

Tien Cheng works in the office of a dentist. Her job is to clean patients' teeth, identify problems, and teach good dental hygiene. Not much conversation goes on during the cleaning process, as Tien is careful not to frustrate her patients by asking questions when she is working in their mouths. As she works, she watches for nonverbal signals from her patients. If a patient blinks or flinches, it might mean Tien has touched a sensitive spot that needs a closer look. She uses her own body language to put her patients at ease. Tien knows her own nonverbal signals are at least as important as what she says to a patient. If she moves in a pleasant, calm, confident manner, her patients are more likely to relax.

©Getty Images/PhotoDisc

FIGURE 4-1 Nonverbal channels

Physical Features	Body structure, size, proportion, height, weight, age, sex, skin color, skin texture, blemishes, and disabilities
Appearance	Choices of clothing, shoes, glasses, jewelry, makeup, facial hair, hair color, and hairstyle, as well as personal grooming
Possessions	Personal office accessories, automobile, home, furnishings, collectibles, and so forth
Body Movement	Posture in sitting, standing, or reclining; movement of torso, arms, legs, head, hands, or shoulders; and subtle movements of face and eyes
Space and Distance	Personal space, social distance, and public distance
Use of Time	Being punctual, maintaining schedules, meeting deadlines, respecting other's time, how you spend time, and so forth

having him sit next to you—especially if you are lukewarm about his product. You may feel he is invading your personal domain.

Use of Time

How does the way we use time communicate nonverbal messages? Americans are a "wristwatch society," and businesses illustrate this through time clocks, timetables, work schedules, appointment books, and calendars—often in electronic formats that may be updated with speed and efficiency. Employers have expectations as to how employees use their time on the job. An employer will expect you to

- Arrive on time.
- Keep scheduled appointments.
- Use work hours for company business, with few exceptions.
- Complete personal errands that must be accomplished during business hours in a prompt and timely manner.
- Observe allotted time for breaks and lunch.
- Leave no earlier than your scheduled time.

Your careful use of time will be important to your career. If you are continually late and keep people waiting, you will give the impression that you think you are more important and their wasted time is of no value. The same is true of someone who constantly interrupts others' conversations and workflow for his or her own needs.

Nonverbal clues, such as how you observe time, care for your appearance, and present yourself to others, send messages about how seriously you take your work and how committed you are to your job. Your peers and subordinates will watch your example. Your supervisor will appreciate being able to count on you. Customers will be impressed with your professionalism and promptness.

Being able to interpret and respond to nonverbal messages will convey an attitude of cooperation and respect—an important skill for work and life success.

CHAPTER SUMMARY

Speech communication has three aspects—the spoken words, the tone of voice, and any accompanying nonverbal movement and/or behavior. Even when not speaking, individuals send nonverbal messages through their personal appearance, hygiene, choice of possessions, posture and body positions, hand gestures, facial expressions, and even their use of space and time. We all send silent messages (both voluntarily and involuntarily), and we read the silent messages of others. When we become employees, it is important to know the written and unwritten rules for appropriate clothing and behavior on the job. To be effective communicators, it is essential to understand both the words spoken and how nonverbal behaviors affect verbal messages. Silent messages may be as relevant as speech, but care must be taken to not make assumptions too quickly. When receiving a mixed message or a nonverbal cue, question the sender.

CHAPTER REVIEW

1. Why are nonverbal messages essential in communication?
2. Why is it important to know the appropriate clothes for a job?
3. What are your feelings when talking to someone who won't look at you? Why?
4. Of all the areas of nonverbal communication, over which ones do you have the most control? The least control?
5. If someone's words, tone of voice, and body language are sending a mixed message, which do you tend to believe? Why?

CAN YOU DEFINE THESE TERMS?

Match each description with the appropriate term. Write the correct letter in the blank preceding the sentence.

Terms:

1. ___ How you see and think about yourself
2. ___ The distance within which we feel comfortable standing when conversing with colleagues or new acquaintances
3. ___ Cleanliness and care of self and personal belongings
4. ___ Movements that you make without realizing it
5. ___ An area with invisible boundaries around you in which others are generally not welcome
6. ___ Easily noticed actions
7. ___ An expressive movement of any part of the body
8. ___ Usually defined by 12 feet or more between the speaker and listeners
9. ___ Movements that you purposely and consciously make
10. ___ Slight or hidden expressions of face and eyes

a. covert body movements
b. gesture
c. hygiene
d. involuntary movements
e. overt body movements
f. personal space
g. public distance
h. self-image
i. social distance
j. voluntary movements

APPLICATIONS

The Handshake

Read the following excerpt from the article "A Taste of International Cultures for Business Students" by Rosetta R. Reed. Answer the questions that follow.

"Handshaking customs vary the world over. When Americans meet for the first time, they shake hands. However, when greeting someone from France, a quick handshake with only slight pressure is preferable, as the traditional American handshake is considered much too rough and rude. A Latin American greeting is much more exuberant—a hearty embrace is common among men and women alike. The men often follow it with a friendly slap on the back. But in Ecuador, to greet a person without shaking hands is a sign of special respect.

In India, too, the handshake is uncommon except between more Westernized individuals. The preferred greeting is the *namaste*, in which the palms of the hands are placed together and the head is nodded. Also, Indian women take offense at being touched by strangers, so one should never offer to shake their hands. The Japanese place great emphasis on formal courtesies and signs of respect. The bow, rather than the handshake, is their traditional form of greeting."

1. Under what circumstances would you greet someone with a handshake?

2. Why do you think a handshake is considered professional etiquette in the United States?

3. Why is it important to understand greeting customs when visiting a foreign country?

4. Working with a partner, act out a scenario in front of the class in which you are greeting

   ■ Your grandmother.
   ■ A new coworker.

   ■ A good friend.
   ■ Your boss's spouse.

Who's Who in Your Class?

This activity will help you to discover how you view your fellow class members and how they see you. Your perception of each other is frequently based on nonverbal communication rather than just speaking. It is important for members of the class to review each other's names for this activity. Sit in a large circle so that people can see each other. Set up name cards in front of each person if needed. As your instructor slowly reads the following questions, select the name of a class member who best fits the category. Write that person's name and the category number on a separate sheet of paper to turn in without your signature.

1. To whom would you go for help with an urgent work-related problem?

2. Who has given you the best listening response?

3. Who would be a good manager or leader?

4. Whom would you trust with a confidential business matter?

5. Whom would you like to help you organize a party?

6. With whom would you like to attend a party?

7. Who would be a good instructor for a training session?

8. Who could deliver a clear verbal message to you on the telephone?

9. Whom would you consider a serious competitor?

10. To whom would you lend your automobile?

After the papers are collected and turned in, several students may volunteer to chart the results for the class and give an oral report summarizing the results. As you listen to the report, make a profile of how your peers see you by recording below the number of votes that you received in each category.

1. Helper

2. Listener

3. Leader

4. Confidant

5. Organizer

6. Companion

7. Instructor

8. Telephone communicator

9. Rival

10. Trustworthy friend

Record your feelings about the way your classmates see you. Identify both positive and negative feelings.

MAKING CONNECTIONS

Interviewing for a Job—The Recruiter

Picture a situation at a local college. The recruiter has come to the campus to interview applicants for future employment with her company. Students are brought in for personal interviews, and, as each one leaves the office, the recruiter walks him or her to the door. Visualize the scene described below, and then answer the questions that follow.

A smiling recruiter for a large company steps to the office door, calls the next job applicant's name, and surveys the people seated in the waiting room. Each person is a prospective employee and is present for an interview. One young woman sits by herself. She has short hair and wears no makeup, and her white-collared, navy blue dress covers her knees. Her fingers snap and unsnap the clasp of the navy blue purse she holds in her lap as she returns the recruiter's gaze without smiling. Across the room slouches a college-age man in a brown, three-piece suit. His vest has rolled up on his stomach, and his left ankle rests on his right knee. His hair is straight and falls below his white shirt collar. Next to him lounges a man in matching sport coat and slacks, white socks, and loafers. His legs are spread out in front of him as he chats with a woman dressed in a rose pantsuit. Her large, gold, hoop earrings bounce as she tosses her long hair and returns the recruiter's smile.

1. Why does the recruiter look around the room at the applicants?

_____

_____

_____

2. Will the recruiter's first impressions make a difference in the interviewing and decision-making process? Why or why not?

_____

_____

_____

_____

3. Do you think the recruiter has a mental picture of the person she would like to hire? Explain your answer.

_____

_____

_____

4. What general qualities do you think the recruiter is seeking?

_____

_____

Research

Using the Internet or library, research three hand gestures or body movements that mean different things to different people. Explain the confusion that can be caused by them. (Hint: Search for "gestures" or "body language." For example, try to find out what the "okay" sign, the "thumbs-up" sign, the "V for victory" sign, and other American gestures mean in other countries.)

_____

_____

_____

_____

Geography

Assume you are being sent by your company to a country located in either Central or South America. Choose a country in one of those regions and research the customs, culture, climate, terrain, size, population, language, currency, and tourist attractions. Of what cultural differences does an American traveler need to be aware in order to avoid inadvertently offending someone in that country?

_____

_____

_____

_____

PROJECT

Demonstration Speech

For this assignment, you will be planning a speech in which a product or a process is demonstrated to the class. One of the most useful speeches given in the workplace is the demonstration speech. Salespeople use it to show features of their products to customers. The demonstration speech is also useful for trainers to show new workers the steps in the process of doing any job. This speaking assignment requires you to inventory your knowledge and skills and to select an object that you can bring to demonstrate to the class.

1. Choose a topic on which your classmates' information is limited. Your audience will be more interested if they are learning something new. Consider the members of your class and their general knowledge.

2. The object must be large enough to be seen by the whole class. If it is hard to see, the audience will lose attention and then stop listening. If you are unable to show the object, you must be able to show a large, clear diagram or photograph.

3. The object should be one that you can manipulate—take apart, put together, and hold up. Because you'll be using your hands to demonstrate, stage fright is usually reduced.

4. If you choose to talk about a process, bring the materials or ingredients and show how the process works, step by step.

5. Plan the speech a step at a time. Use the sample outline on page 64 as a model to follow. You might demonstrate a process with such steps as (a) gather materials, (b) assemble materials, and (c) finish the item.

6. Practice ahead of time. Work with the object(s). Plan to look at your audience as you demonstrate.

7. Explain how you came to know about your topic. Tell why you want your audience to know about it, or suggest what they might do with the information. Be brief, be direct, and limit yourself to five minutes.

8. Have your instructor or a student evaluate you as you speak, using the critique sheet on page 65.

SUGGESTED TOPICS Choose a topic from the list you created for the Idea Box activity at the beginning of the chapter. Or, consider a topic similar to one of the following.

- How to operate a camcorder
- How to clean a rug
- How to program an answering machine
- How to make Mexican wedding cookies (bring ingredients and samples)
- How to make pottery
- How to reconcile a bank statement (you'll need a large chart as a visual)
- How to bandage a wound
- How to make a bookshelf

SAMPLE DEMONSTRATION SPEECH OUTLINE

Materials needed: Seven flags—red, yellow, green, checkered, black, blue, white

Introduction

(Get attention)   A. (Wave checkered flag) *Almost everyone who has been to the races knows what this flag means!*

(Involve audience)   B. *Who has been to a car race or seen one on TV?*

(Establish credibility)   C. *Being a racing fan myself, I thought I'd share how the officials communicate with race drivers on the track.*

Key Idea

I'm going to describe and explain the use of these seven flags in racing.

Development of Key Idea

Transition: (First, I'm going to talk about flags that signal all drivers on the course.)

Main point   I. *Let me explain the flags that apply to all drivers.*
    A. *The green flag means the track is clear.*
       1. (Show flag.) Waved to signal start of race.
       2. Drivers read it as "go!"
    B. *The next often-used flag is the yellow flag.*
       1. (Show flag.) Waved to signal "caution."
       2. Drivers watch for stalled car, debris on track, etc.
    C. *The red flag signals "danger."*
       1. (Show flag.) Waved to signal "stop immediately!"
       2. Explain types of dangers.
       3. Describe "heart-stopping experience."

Transition: (Now that I've explained the general uses of flags . . .)

Main point   II. *Let me discuss flags used to signal individual drivers.*
    A. *Blue flag with the orange stripe is the passing flag.*
       1. (Show flag.) Waved to signal "slow driver."
       2. Signals driver to pass with care.
       3. Example—2003 Indy 500 race.
    B. *Black flag warns a driver about his own behavior.*
       1. (Show flag—unfurled and waved, furled and pointed.)
       2. Example—2005 Indy 500 race.
    C. *White flag indicates, "There is only one more lap."*
       1. (Show flag, wave it.)
       2. Each driver wants to be the first to see this flag.
    D. *Checkered flag is shaken at the winner.*

Conclusion

Transition: (Let me summarize for you.)

(Summary)   A. *Officials communicate with drivers by means of flags. Green, yellow, and red apply to all drivers. Blue, black, white, and checkered signal to individual drivers.*

(Focus)   B. *Now that you know what the flags mean, you'll understand what's going on at the races.*

CRITIQUE SHEET FOR DEMONSTRATION SPEECH

Speaker: Give this page to your instructor or student evaluator before you speak.

Evaluator: On a scale from 1-10 (with 1 being "poor" and 10 being "excellent"), rate the speaker on each of the following elements by circling the number of points awarded.

Total Possible Points: 100 (Each question is worth a maximum of 10 points.)

1. Was the introduction to the key idea carefully planned to get attention, involve the audience, and establish the speaker's credibility?   1 2 3 4 5 6 7 8 9 10

2. Was the key idea stated clearly?   1 2 3 4 5 6 7 8 9 10

3. Were the main points clear enough so that the audience could write them down or remember them?   1 2 3 4 5 6 7 8 9 10

4. Were the visual materials well planned so that the entire audience could see clearly?   1 2 3 4 5 6 7 8 9 10

5. Did the conclusion summarize the key idea and main points and focus on the desired audience response?   1 2 3 4 5 6 7 8 9 10

6. Was the speaker's voice loud enough to be heard easily, and were language and pronunciation correct?   1 2 3 4 5 6 7 8 9 10

7. Did the speaker control nervous mannerisms, appear confident, and maintain eye contact with the audience? 1 2 3 4 5 6 7 8 9 10

8. Did the speaker seem enthusiastic and well prepared?   1 2 3 4 5 6 7 8 9 10

9. Did the presentation meet the time requirement?   1 2 3 4 5 6 7 8 9 10

10. Was the goal "to tell the audience something they did not know" fulfilled? 1 2 3 4 5 6 7 8 9 10

Total Points: _____

Comments:

_____

_____

_____

_____

_____

_____

_____

FBLA Impromptu Speaking

The dynamic business world counts on individuals who effectively express thoughts without prior preparation. Effective speakers demonstrate poise, self-confidence, and command of the topic they are presenting. Leaders with solid communication skills can effectively organize thoughts into meaningful presentations or speeches without advance warning. They have a command of verbal and nonverbal communication when delivering a speech.

You will be randomly assigned a current event based on one of the following topics.

- Ethics in a Competitive Business World
- Etiquette in the Workplace
- Cultural Baggage in the Global Marketplace
- Making an Impression by How You Dress
- Success Through Effective Teamwork

You will have ten minutes to prepare a speech. You will be given one 4-by-6-inch index card that may be used to organize your thoughts. Notes may be written on both sides of the card and used during the impromptu speech. No reference materials may be used to prepare or present the speech. A microphone may not be used. The length of the impromptu speech should be four minutes. Five points will be deducted for any speech under 3:31 minutes or over 4:29 minutes.

Performance Indicators Evaluated

- Demonstrate a command of the topic through concrete examples.
- Organize thoughts into a meaningful presentation.
- Explain the business topic in a clear, concise manner with real business examples.

For more detailed information, go to the FBLA web site.

Think Critically

1. Why is ethics a hot topic in today's business environment?
2. Why are major companies hiring consultants to teach employees about etiquette and other social issues?
3. Why must business leaders be sensitive to other cultures?
4. How can a person's clothing make an impression?
5. How does a leader implement successful teamwork?

http://www.fbla-pbl.org/

Unit 2

Communicating Person to Person

Unit Objectives

After completing this unit, you should be able to

- Describe ways to reduce stage fright in presentational speaking and job anxiety at work.

- Analyze causes of communication apprehension.

- Apply appropriate verbal, nonverbal, and paralanguage communications in person-to-person conversations on the job.

- Discuss workplace etiquette and how to use tact, courtesy, and assertiveness.

- Identify causes of conflicts in professional relationships and techniques for developing solutions.

- Explain and use strategies for effective interviews.

5 Building Confidence

CHAPTER OBJECTIVES

After completing this chapter, you should be able to

- Identify the physical and psychological causes of stage fright and how to reduce them.
- Explain how communication apprehension affects job performance.
- Discuss aspects of self-image.
- Describe the role of a mentor.
- Apply the use of basic tools for professional behavior.

KEY TERMS AND CONCEPTS

stage fright	communication apprehension	self-esteem
fight-or-flight response	clichés	mentor
adrenal system	word whiskers	evaluation interview
energy potential	interpersonal skills	assertive

IDEA BOX

Make a list of five things you really like to do (your interests). Make another list of four things you know you do well (your talents or abilities). Make a third list of three things you feel strongly about (your beliefs, values, or attitudes). Don't be hasty. Compile these lists over time. Think about the categories off and on for several hours, adding to and adjusting the lists as you think of topics that apply.

Things I like to do

Things I do well

Things I feel strongly about

All About You

No one is born knowing how to speak. It takes time to know who to imitate, who to listen to, and who can be trusted. Communication with others begins with the ability to believe in ourselves. So, this chapter is mostly about you.

As a child you probably learned rules.

- "Tell the truth, even when it hurts."
- "You're only as good as your word."
- "Think before you speak."
- "Treat others as you would like to be treated."

Then you learned the hard way that these rules are broken every day. You found out for yourself that trust is the center of significant relationships and that trusting yourself means taking care of your own needs and safety. You learned to count on yourself.

It's frightening to speak before others until you know you can trust yourself to make a good presentation. The nervousness felt at appearing before an audience is called **stage fright**. Even the most skilled speakers and performers experience it, but there are ways to overcome it and even use it to your benefit.

Stage Fright

Of all the scary things that people dread, speaking in public is almost always number one. Jerry Seinfield joked that surveys have shown that fear of public speaking ranks higher in most people's minds than fear of death. Well, some folks do say they'd rather die than get up to speak. Why is it that speaking to a group is so stressful?

©Getty Images/PhotoDisc

Speaking in public can be a stressful experience, but stage fright can be conquered through preparation and practice.

When human beings are threatened by an event they regard as harmful ("What if they don't like me?") or a situation that seems uncontrollable ("What if I forget what I want to say or what if my voice cracks?"), then the inborn instinct is the **fight-or-flight response**, in which our bodies gear up to either fight or run. We would like to run and avoid the entire situation. However, most of us believe we are capable of making a speech, even if it scares us. After all, we've been speaking all our lives, so we don't run, but sometimes we do tense up and feel miserable. Here's why.

Physical Causes of Stage Fright

Your body gears up to take care of you.

1. The brain alerts your body to the speaking event just as it would warn you of physical danger. This alert signals your **adrenal system** to release chemicals to stimulate nervous and muscular systems to prepare for fight or flight.

2. These chemicals increase the heart rate and elevate the blood pressure.

3. As blood flows away from the digestive tract, the sensation of *fluttering butterflies* occurs in the midsection.

4. Increased oxygen in the blood tenses the muscles so suddenly that shoulders become tight and feet get wiggly (the body is ready to fight or run).

5. Blood circulating rapidly warms the hands and feet, which, as they perspire, feel clammy and unnatural.

6. The senses (sight, smell, and touch) become keener and more acute.

7. The breathing rate accelerates, and it may become difficult to control breath for speaking. The mouth becomes dry, and the voice may crack.

8. Toxic poisons gather, and a trip to the restroom is needed.

With all of this going on inside your body, it is no wonder the sensations are called "stage fright." However, an amazing thing happens. As a result of the body changes from the fight-or-flight response, a tremendous **energy potential** is developed. Under these conditions, a speaker can channel that energy into a dynamic, forceful speaking presentation.

Psychological Reasons for Stage Fright

If you have anxiety problems going into an interview, taking part in a discussion, or speaking in front of a group, you are not alone. But, these are not physical threats—they are psychological. Your self-image is related to the way people respond to you. You worry about what they will think of you, the content of your speech, and your delivery of the message. It frightens you to put yourself "on the line." There may be other inner conflicts as well.

"In this seminar we'll discuss a simple technique for over-coming your fear of speaking in public."

Stage Fright

Any challenging situation can cause your body to get ready for fight or flight. Speaking in public is a challenge, because most people do it infrequently and the nervousness they feel sends them into a panic. Accept the challenge. Plan what you will say, practice it orally until you're sure of it, then channel all that nervous energy into erect posture, confident eye contact, and a rich, vibrant voice. Controlled stage fright creates dynamic delivery.

- You may be assigned a speech you don't want to give. Resentment often causes anxiety.

- You may feel your knowledge of the subject is lacking. Worry can cause apprehension.

- You may feel frightened at the size of the group or the number of people before whom you will appear. Dread causes stage fright.

It is normal to be nervous about public speaking, especially when it is not something you do regularly. It is important to examine the reasons why anyone would avoid facing such situations—and people do avoid speaking. After all, much is expected of the speaker. The audience anticipates an interesting message presented in a compelling way that not only provides new knowledge and/or entertainment, but also leaves them with a lasting impression of a capable, well-prepared presenter. When you are the speaker, the pressure to live up to the expectations causes stress—something you naturally want to avoid. But, professional people who refuse to make presentations on the job often endanger their careers and put their advancement at risk. It is better to face up to the expectations and take measures to control the stage fright.

Suggestions for Controlling Stage Fright

To rescue yourself from this kind of stress, you must channel all the energy created by stage fright into disciplined preparation and practice.

- Do not talk about your fears. Focusing on the negative aspects only magnifies them out of proportion.

A speaker can channel the energy created by stage fright into a dynamic, forceful presentation.

Language trap

Don't say, "I should
have went to the
store."
Say, "I should have
gone to the store."

- Take control of your nervous energy and channel it into enthusiasm for your topic.

- Use your preparation time wisely. Research and organize your ideas. Talk them out in private. Prepare notes that will support you. Know exactly what you will say—especially the first few words. Once you are off to a good start, your nerves will calm down.

- Visualize exactly how the room will be set up. (Where will you sit? Will there be a lectern to stand behind? Where will you put your notes? What will you do with your visual materials to ensure everyone can see them?)

- Practice visualizing how the audience will look to you as you stand in front of them. (How many people will be there to listen? See them in your mind.)

- Mentally walk to the stand, put your notes out, look at the audience, pause, breathe deeply, and smile.

- Practice giving your presentation with any visual aids, especially those that involve technology, to ensure you can integrate the aids smoothly as you speak. You may discover you need an assistant.

Remember, the more prepared you are, the more confident you will be. If you channel your nervous energy to focus on your ideas and deliver what you have practiced with passion and care, your audience will listen with interest and will be impressed by your earnest desire to communicate.

Communication Apprehension

Stage fright is probably a main source of anxiety for you right now. There is a term that covers many fears relating to communication. Have you ever been called to the principal's office, dreaded an interview, felt shy about speaking to a romantic interest, or felt miserable because you didn't know what to say to someone? These are all situations that you will face with some degree of discomfort. The name for it is **communication apprehension**. How do you recognize this larger and more general anxiety? Try answering the following questions.

1. When you are uncomfortable, do you tend to speed up, talk rapidly, and come on strong?

2. When you are nervous or fearful, do you find your voice getting higher?

3. When you are depressed, tired, or sad, does your voice tend to trail off?

4. When you are excited, do you speak loudly and dominate the conversation?

5. When you lack confidence in what you're saying, do you tend to speak too softly?

6. Can you feel your throat muscles tighten when you are angry and don't want to show it?

7. Do you reveal a lack of confidence by repeating "right?," "I guess," "know what I mean?," or "like" (i.e., **clichés** or overused expressions)?

8. Do you punctuate your conversation with frequent "uh," "ah," or "um" sounds (i.e., **word whiskers**)?

Personal CHECK-UP

Describe a speaker whom you personally admire. Name him or her. What qualities caused you to choose that person? Be specific.

COMMUNICATION AT WORK

Hair stylists and manicurists hear a variety of stories as their customers are having their hair and nails done. Nikki Rin owns Eclectic Beauty Salon and interacts with both her employees and her customers. She believes that it is important to know when to talk, when to listen, and when to allow tranquil silence. Her goal is to provide a pleasant atmosphere in which customers are comfortable and relaxed. Nikki coaches her employees on how to start pleasant, appropriate conversations with their customers. She teaches them to take their cues from the customers. If a customer is talkative, just listen to him or her talk. If a customer is quiet, don't try too hard to force a conversation. Above all, Nikki and her employees are courteous and friendly to all customers. Nikki knows that the success of her business depends upon her customers' desire to come back.

©Getty Images/PhotoDisc

9. Do you try to hide your feelings by giggling or making jokes?

10. Do you feel yourself boasting or stretching the truth when you feel a strong need for acceptance?

11. Do you say something negative about yourself so that someone will reassure you?

12. Do you frequently soften your disagreement by saying, "Well, I agree with you, but..."

13. When you are unsure, do you repeat yourself over and over?

14. When you disagree, do you find your foot wiggling, your fingers tapping, and so on?

Perhaps you have noticed these annoying behaviors in others, but it is hard to recognize them in yourself. Over the course of several days, watch carefully to observe these behaviors in other people. When you begin to notice communication apprehension translating into nervous habits in others, you'll also become more aware of your own behavior. Check yourself and, if you find you are doing any of these things, ask yourself why. What anxiety do you have? Try to make changes to correct the habit(s). Enlist a good friend to help you. Pencil tappers, head scratchers, cliché users, conversation dominators, nail biters, and so forth all fit into the communication apprehension mode. You do not have to stay in this mode. As you become aware of behaviors to eliminate, your improved communication skills will boost your confidence and your professional image, adding to your success in your chosen field.

> "When I speak, I learn about myself. When I listen, I learn about others."
>
> —Stella Briskin

Self-Image

We have talked about negative behaviors that are caused by communication apprehension, but let's get positive here. We need to talk about **interpersonal skills**—those behaviors you need in order to develop relationships with other people. But, before you get to know someone else, it is wise to know yourself—your interests, talents, and values. The Idea Box activity at the beginning of the chapter gave you a picture of yourself. Your inventory of interests, abilities, and values can help you reach some understanding of the motivations that drive you. Such awareness of yourself will help you focus your talents toward future dreams and goals. This means making the most of your *potential* for success.

Believe in your ability to use your gifts. The diligence with which you practice your talents and participate in varied activities will translate into skills for future jobs. One way to elevate your image is to be positive. If you have realized behaviors that indicate your nervousness when communicating with others, you can do something about it.

- Be aware of your mannerisms.
- Change or eliminate such distractions.
- Do not downgrade your self-image.

Language trap

Don't say, "I'm going to get me a snack." Say, "I'm going to get a snack for myself."

Such statements as, "Oh, I haven't anything to contribute because I don't do anything well," are damaging to your **self-esteem** (the way you value yourself). You are a worthwhile human being with all the struggles, ups, and downs that life provides. Handling the "downs" successfully will lift your confidence and allow you to speak with assurance.

Make a list of your assets right now. Write down all of the positive personality qualities that you know you have. To get started, you may choose words that apply from the following list, but you should also include words that aren't listed here but that truly describe you.

cheerful	ambitious
cooperative	dedicated
friendly	tolerant
tenacious	patient
independent	courteous
perceptive	resourceful
enthusiastic	poised
efficient	dependable
emotionally stable	helpful
honest	pleasant
responsive	energetic
loyal	conscientious

Your list provides positive feedback that you are indeed a person who is interesting to be around. Post that list on the bathroom mirror or wherever you can see it often as a constant reminder of your good qualities.

Finding a Mentor

Do you have a person in your world who you admire very much? Is there someone who takes a special interest in you, encourages and supports you, and applauds your successes? This person might be a teacher, friend, neighbor, or anyone with whom you can develop a close, supportive relationship. Even on the job, employees seek out a **mentor**—an experienced, knowledgeable person who offers guidance and advice to help them reach their goals.

If you find a mentor, you will have someone to turn to for counseling during tough times. That person will offer a listening ear, and you have to choose to trust him or her. If your mentor is firm, caring, and consistent, you'll find yourself dealing with your feelings out loud, analyzing your behavior, and, with your mentor's help, setting up plans for improvement. Such guidance is invaluable as you work to increase your self-esteem, develop your interpersonal skills, and build new relationships.

> **"A mentor is someone—man or woman—who is genuinely interested in helping you move ahead in your career; someone who is supportive, non-judgmental, can help you build your knowledge and abilities through creative discussion, and can provide encouragement at critical points in your career."**
>
> **—Annie Moldafsky**

A mentor can offer guidance and advice to help you reach your potential.

Personal CHECK-UP

Describe an incident when you were criticized and apply the questions listed (at the right) to the situation.

Handling Criticism

While in the process of building your confidence, you may face some tough situations. Think of a time when you were criticized—by a parent, a teacher, a supervisor, or one of your friends.

- How did you feel?
- What was your response?
- Did you learn anything from the criticism?
- Did you use the criticism constructively for personal improvement?

Handling criticism is an extremely difficult communication skill in any situation. In the workplace, you will likely encounter regular criticism from supervisors and coworkers, often in the form of an **evaluation interview**. Most companies require these regularly scheduled "check-ups" on employees. The points to be considered deal with such issues as being punctual, being reliable, getting along with fellow employees, and accomplishing assigned duties. Even if your overall rating is high, you may feel somewhat surprised to score lower in some areas. Remember, no one is perfect, and it is an important part of the process to pinpoint areas for improvement. Everyone experiences criticism, but it is important to deal with it professionally, positively, and respectfully.

Becoming angry, defensive, or hurt will not help. Instead, remember that criticism should not be taken personally, but should be perceived as a learning experience and an opportunity to improve your skills.

Always try to handle criticism respectfully and in a positive, professional manner.

Knowing how to respond positively to criticism can make a difference between being promoted and being fired. When receiving criticism, remember to do the following.

- Listen carefully to the criticism being given.
- Confirm your understanding by asking specific questions and paraphrasing.
- Explain your actions if needed, but show a willingness to change or adjust your behavior.
- Together, create a plan for improving your performance.

One more point—think twice before you criticize others. It does little to boost your confidence to tear into someone else. Be sure that you have a legitimate complaint. If you must convey a criticism, focus your comments on the behavior rather than on the person. If you give constructive feedback in the spirit of offering help, your criticism will be more willingly received and acted upon.

"Great Spirit, Grant that I may not criticize my neighbor until I have walked a mile in his moccasins."

—Indian Prayer

Building Confidence

To prepare for the future, strengthen your positive view of yourself. Your self-image consists of positive and negative pictures of your own abilities, skills, talents, and accomplishments. People reveal how they see themselves and think of themselves by what they say. With a negative self-image, an individual will likely say things indicating a low self-esteem.

- "Oh, it was nothing." "Do you really like my outfit?" "Oh, anybody could do a high dive like that." (Unable to accept praise or give recognition to others)

- "It's not my job." "Nobody would help me." "Mary started the project, and then walked out." "Well, it's not my fault." (Defensive about accepting blame)

- "I've heard better ideas." "It's OK if you like that sort of thing." (Cynical or suspicious attitude)

- "Oh, gee—I'm just a natural klutz." "I've never been good at math." "I blew it—as usual" (Putting self down)

- "Well, he was just lucky." "She got the job because her mother works here." (Sneering at others)

- "I don't know why I have to go. I always have a rotten time." "I'm not buying a raffle ticket; I never win anything." (Pessimistic, negative, or hopeless attitude)

If you should hear yourself making similar statements, don't immediately decide that you are always defeated when you think about your abilities. Just try to catch your comments before you say them aloud. Better yet, try not to even think them. If you really feel like saying something negative, write it down in a journal or notebook so that you can remember it and later analyze it. Keep a healthy attitude about your talents and abilities to build your confidence.

What kinds of thoughts and statements strengthen your self-image and build confidence? People who are well balanced make **assertive**, positive statements—they are firm and confident without being harsh or disagreeable. You hear such statements frequently, and you can learn to say them too.

- **Focus on other people**—"If it wasn't for Jane, we'd never have made the deadline." "Let's listen to Carmen. She has a great idea."

- **Honest apology**—"It was my fault. Please forgive me." "Sorry I performed that procedure incorrectly. I know how to do it correctly now."

- **Able to handle diverse relationships**—"My boss and I play golf on the weekends, but I always call her Ms. Gray at work." "Don't forget to include Kwanzaa in the holiday celebration this year." "Would you like a hand with all those boxes, Dr. Anderson?"

- **Able to take risks**—"I really don't understand. Will you go over it again, please?" "Would you be willing to consider a new procedure?"

- **Able to empathize**—"I'm not sure I agree with this decision, but I can understand why it is important to your group." "I'm upset about the error, but I can see why you set it up that way."

Learn these methods of responding positively. Practice making such positive statements to increase your communication skills and to build your confidence.

CHAPTER SUMMARY

Public speaking is ranked as a top fear in survey results. It can prompt the fight-or-flight response, setting off a chain of physical reactions that speakers must learn to control. The resulting energy potential can be channeled into a dynamic, forceful speaking presentation. A number of psychological factors also contribute to stage fright, including a poor self-image and inner conflicts of resentment, worry, and dread. A natural reaction is to avoid the situation (run), but professional people need to be able to make presentations in order to advance and grow in their careers. Nervous energy can be channeled into preparation—research your facts, organize your thoughts, prepare your notes and visuals, and practice giving your presentation while visualizing your audience and setting. The better prepared you are, the more confident you will be. Communication apprehension is a term used to cover a wide range of communication anxieties. These anxieties often manifest themselves in nervous habits. To reduce these worries, speakers are encouraged to examine their self-image, identify their positive traits, boost their self-esteem, select a mentor for guidance, and react positively to criticism. Choosing to make positive statements and avoiding negative ones can help build confidence.

CHAPTER REVIEW

1. Of what value can stage fright be to a speaker?
2. Name some ways the physical body gears up in stressful situations.
3. How is self-image related to building confidence?
4. How does a person's self-esteem reveal itself through speech?
5. Of what value can a mentor be in developing confidence?

CAN YOU DEFINE THESE TERMS?

Match each description with the appropriate term. Write the correct letter in the blank preceding the sentence. Some terms will not be used.

Terms:

1. ___ The nervousness felt at appearing before an audience
2. ___ The larger and more general anxiety covering many fears relating to communication
3. ___ In response to a threatening situation, the inborn instinct in which our bodies gear up to either fight or run
4. ___ Overused expressions
5. ___ Releases chemicals to stimulate nervous and muscular systems to prepare for fight or flight
6. ___ Frequent "uh," "ah," or "um" sounds punctuating conversation
7. ___ Behaviors needed to develop relationships
8. ___ Regularly scheduled "check-ups" on employees

a. adrenal system
b. assertive
c. clichés
d. communication apprehension
e. energy potential
f. evaluation interview
g. fight-or-flight response
h. interpersonal skills
i. mentor
j. self-esteem
k. stage fright
l. word whiskers

APPLICATIONS

Refereed Discussion

Work in groups of five or six people. First, select a trusted member of the group to sit outside the discussion circle and serve as a referee. The job of the referee is to stop the discussion if the "discussion rule" is not followed. Read the following topics. Vote for one to use in this discussion. Try to give personal examples to prove or disprove your statements. Express your feelings freely about the subject.

Topics

- What are some ways of reaching a person who will not listen to what you say?
- How can you encourage a person to speak freely about himself or herself?
- At work, how can you get a boss or supervisor to listen to your ideas?
- How does a person's attitude affect his or her listening?
- Give some examples of how personal bias interfered with listening accuracy.
- If you are criticized and feel defensive, how do you respond without cutting off communication?

Discussion Rule

No one may speak on the subject unless he or she summarizes what the person just before has said. The previous speaker must agree that the summary is accurate.

Referee Report to Group

How many times did you have to remind members of the group to summarize?

Did the members listen and summarize accurately in your opinion?

Individual Report

How did you feel when someone accurately summarized or rephrased what you said?

Did the discussion rule encourage or hinder your participation?

How can someone listen carefully to another and yet give reasoned argument to the discussion?

Handling Criticism

Working with a partner, role play the following situations. One of you should read the comment, and the other should respond appropriately to the criticism, practicing the steps offered in the chapter.

A. "Brian, this paper doesn't even deserve the "C" I gave it. You missed the point entirely, and you misspelled more words than you spelled correctly."

Response: (oral)

B. "Tyrone, when appointments are scheduled too close together, I simply don't have enough time with each customer. When other customers have to wait, they end up being angry. I've showed you the proper times to allow for our different salon services. Why are we having this problem?"

Response: (oral)

C. "You've let four defective engines pass through your inspections this week, Helen. I'm not going to cover for your mistakes. If you can't get it right, maybe you should move to a different department."

Response: (oral)

Discuss

1. What techniques did you try when responding to the criticism?

2. How effective is the criticism given in each scenario?

3. If the criticism is not effective, explain how it could be changed to be more helpful. If you think the criticism is effective, explain why.

Further Criticism and Response

List several critical comments that you have heard. Were they effective? What response would you give to each?

MAKING CONNECTIONS

Communication

Some colleges and companies require applicants to submit a one-page essay describing the applicant's interests, abilities, and values. Use the information you have developed in this chapter to provide a positive picture of your self-image. Be sure your spelling and writing are your very best. Jot down ideas for your one-page essay here.

_____

_____

_____

_____

_____

_____

Communication

If there is a concerned, supportive adult in your life who has helped you and offered you guidance toward your goals, write a description of this individual. Make clear how the mentor relationship serves your academic, career, and/or personal needs.

_____

_____

_____

_____

_____

_____

_____

_____

PROJECT

Ceremonial Speech

Ceremonial or courtesy speeches are regularly presented at both business and social events. They are carefully planned to suit the individual, the audience, and the occasion. The speeches are brief, clearly and originally worded, and practiced (if notice is given) until the delivery is spontaneous and sincere.

Suggested Types of Ceremonial or Courtesy Speeches

- **Speech of Introduction**—This speech creates audience interest in the main speaker and provides biographical details about the speaker. The speech also seeks to link the speaker with the needs of the audience. Focus on the speaker or subject.

- **Speech of Presentation**—These words accompany a gift, prize, award, or trophy and express appreciation or congratulations. Explain the significance of the award, the qualifications of the honoree, and the reasons why the award is being presented.

- **Speech of Acceptance**—When a gift or award is presented, a gracious response is needed. Acknowledge the award and what it represents, and express sincere gratitude for the honor. Share credit with others, relate personal involvement with the group, and share feelings of appreciation.

- **Speech of Welcome or Farewell**—A speech of welcome generates goodwill, notes common bonds, and helps the audience feel proud to welcome the newcomer. A speech of farewell is extended to a person who is leaving. Mixed feelings are expressed. Reflect on past experiences and look forward to future meetings or new challenges. Wish the honoree success.

Assignment

Select a particular audience and occasion and build a ceremonial speech of your choice. Use an interest-getting device, such as a quotation, an analogy, or a short story. Be brief but sincere. Use the sample speech below as a model. Practice your speech out loud several times. Explain the audience, setting, and occasion to your class, and then deliver your speech using only a single note card with a few phrases for reference. Jot down preliminary ideas and notes here. Have your instructor or a student evaluate you as you speak using the critique sheet on the next page.

SAMPLE SPEECH OF ACCEPTANCE

The audience: 27 sales representatives and their spouses.

The setting: A dinner in a hotel banquet room.

The occasion: Annual awards ceremony, dinner, and announcement of Salesperson of the Year.

If you have ever watched a cat as it hunts for a bird, you know that only one bird can be caught at a time. If the cat tries to catch two or three birds at once, it won't even get a feather.

Tonight, in accepting this award for Salesperson of the Year, I have to thank my cat for letting me observe him. He taught me to take care of one customer at a time, close the deal, and then go out for bigger game.

Now that all of you know my secret, I hope you all will join me in selling your way to a fortune—or at least to this gratifying award of Salesperson of the Year! Thank you very much.

CRITIQUE SHEET FOR CEREMONIAL SPEECH

Speaker: Give this page to your instructor or student evaluator before you speak.

Evaluator: On a scale from 1–10 (with 1 being "poor" and 10 being "excellent"), rate the speaker on each of the following elements by circling the number of points awarded. Under comments, provide both words of praise and suggestions for improvement.

Total Possible Points: 100 (Each question is worth a maximum of 10 points.)

The Verbal Message

1. Did the speaker identify the audience, setting, and occasion prior to the speech?   1 2 3 4 5 6 7 8 9 10

2. Did the speaker present adequate information, such as who the speaker is, why the award is given, and so forth?   1 2 3 4 5 6 7 8 9 10

3. Did the speaker effectively represent the spirit of the audience and occasion?   1 2 3 4 5 6 7 8 9 10

4. Did the speaker include one of the requirements (quotation, analogy, or short story)?   1 2 3 4 5 6 7 8 9 10

5. Did the length of the speech suit the occasion?   1 2 3 4 5 6 7 8 9 10

6. Was the conclusion effective (i.e., did it lead to a climax, create anticipation, and so forth)?   1 2 3 4 5 6 7 8 9 10

The Nonverbal Message

7. Was the speaker enthusiastic, poised, and communicative?   1 2 3 4 5 6 7 8 9 10

8. Was the speaker's voice loud enough, interesting to listen to, and free from language and pronunciation errors?   1 2 3 4 5 6 7 8 9 10

Effectiveness of Communication

9. Did the speaker maintain interest?   1 2 3 4 5 6 7 8 9 10

10. Did the speaker fulfill the purpose of the assignment?   1 2 3 4 5 6 7 8 9 10

Total Points: _____

Comments:

_____

_____

_____

_____

_____

FBLA Job Interview Role Play

You are applying for a position as an event planner at Clear Communication Event Planners, Inc. The job description calls for an individual with strong communication, organizational, and leadership skills. Fringe benefits for this position include health insurance, a pension plan, sick leave, paid holidays, and paid vacations. Salary will be based upon experience and education.

This event involves

- a letter of application and a resume
- a job application form
- interviews

You must prepare a one-page letter of application, and your resume should be limited to one or two pages. You will complete a job application form with the use of your resume and a one-page reference sheet. No other reference materials may be used. The letter of application, resume, and job application should be put in a file folder with the applicant's name on the tab of the folder.

Your initial interview with a business leader (judge) will last ten minutes. Finalists from the first round of interviews will have a second, 15-minute interview. Students will be hired based upon the top scores totaled for the letter of application, resume, job application, and interviews.

Performance Indicators Evaluated

- Prepare a letter of application and business resume that are worthy of generating results.
- Neatly, completely, and accurately fill out a job application form.
- Demonstrate strong interviewing skills necessary to win a job.

For more detailed information, go to the FBLA web site.

Think Critically

1. What personal qualities should the job applicant highlight for this position? Why?
2. Why should a candidate research the company before going on a job interview?
3. What can the job applicant do to reduce communication apprehension before the interview?
4. Give some examples of assertive, positive statements to make in a job interview.

http://www.fbla.org/

6 Developing Interpersonal Skills

CHAPTER OBJECTIVES

After completing this chapter, you should be able to

- Identify guidelines for engaging in appropriate business conversations.
- Discuss the social skills necessary in a business setting.
- Explain how to recognize unspoken organizational protocols for appropriate behavior.
- Describe causes of conflicts in the workplace.
- List the stages of conflict.
- Discuss common methods of dealing with conflict.
- Explain six rules for negotiating resolutions to conflicts.

KEY TERMS AND CONCEPTS

dyad	passive response	territory
directive questions	assertive response	conflict
nondirective questions	protocols	ego conflicts
aggressive response	etiquette	

IDEA BOX

Make a list of common behaviors in others that bother you. To get you started, some common irritants are listed below. Select and adapt from the list, then add ideas of your own. Also describe some ways for dealing with the irritating behaviors.

Borrowing something without asking permission
Blaming mistakes on others
Arriving late
Expecting special favors
Having the inability to apologize
Taking credit for others' work
Pushing one's own responsibilities off on someone else

Interpersonal Communication

The smallest communication unit, called a **dyad**, is a group of two, such as you and one other person. Important communication takes place in dyads.

- A recruiter talks to you about your job application.
- Your boss calls you on the carpet for an error.
- A mentor offers you valuable advice.
- A person who sits behind you in accounting class becomes a lasting friend.

You have learned much about language and improving self-confidence and presentation skills before a group. Now you will study specific communication skills and behaviors that are important for creating positive *interpersonal relationships* on the job.

Business Conversations on the Job

When you begin a job in a workplace, it is likely that your new coworkers will be strangers to you. Starting up a conversation can feel threatening if you are not experienced at taking the lead. Conversations can die within 30 seconds. If you are expected to work with someone, you will have to talk to him or her. You will both be more comfortable if you make a friendly effort at the start. Begin with small talk, and look for the right conditions for establishing common ground.

Conditions Needed for Communication Success

Successful communications on the job will only develop· in an environment where participants are willing to meet the appropriate conditions.

- **Risk**—You must be willing to take a chance and risk rejection.
- **Positive communication climate**—Both parties must be interested in communicating.
- **Openness**—Each person must be receptive and responsive.
- **Listening**—Each person must listen for both the content of messages and the underlying intent.
- **Withholding of judgment**—Criticism and personal prejudices must be kept to yourself. Avoid making assumptions.

It takes sensitivity to properly become acquainted with another person, and it takes patience and trust to build a communication relationship. On the job, too much openness—saying whatever you think with little concern for the other person's feelings—can destroy any hope of closer understanding. Until you know people well, it is best to keep conversations somewhat impersonal and focused on the job.

> *"Alone we can do so little, together we can do so much."*
>
> **—Helen Keller**

Social Skills for Business Success

You can practice social behaviors right now that will make you a valued and likeable employee in your professional future.

Initial Contacts and Good Impressions

INTRODUCE YOURSELF Extend your hand, establish eye contact, and say your name clearly. The other person will give his or her name. Repeat it and file it in your head for future reference. Remembering names is a courtesy that leaves a good impression, indicating respect for another person. Can you name everyone in your communication class? One trick is to associate a person with an applicable adjective that begins with the same letter to help you recall the name. This will be your private code that is not to be shared, of course. Some examples are as follows.

- **a**ttractive **A**nne
- **s**ilver-haired Mrs. **S**anchez
- **i**ntelligent Mr. **I**ngersoll
- **b**ookkeeper **B**ertha

LEARN CORRECT TITLES ALONG WITH NAMES When you address professional adults, use their appropriate titles—Mrs., Dr., Ms., Miss, or Mr.—in addition to their last names. Be aware that some professions and specialists, such as those affiliated with the military, government, or church, have prescribed forms of proper address. If you need to use these titles, listen for them or ask someone who works in that particular field to identify the correct titles.

If you are invited to use a first name, do so. Many workplaces today are less formal, and employees even call the upper-level managers by their first names. In some traditional offices, however, senior staff members speak to junior employees on a first-name basis, but not the other way around. When you join a company, ask your superiors how they would like to be addressed.

INTRODUCE PEOPLE TO EACH OTHER This is a graceful skill that is appreciated both socially and professionally. Try to do it with poise and enthusiasm, without head ducking and feet shuffling. If you are uncertain about the proper way to handle an introduction, use these traditional guidelines.

- When introducing a male and female, name the female first.
  Suzanne Smelser, this is Jerry Boyd. Jerry, Suzanne.
  Sonia Medina, this is Dr. Allen Heinz.

- When introducing a younger person to an older person, name the elder first.
  Mrs. Watkins, this is my sister, Nancy.

Being able to make introductions with poise and enthusiasm is an important interpersonal skill.

©Digital Vision

- Use titles of position in introductions.
  Mayor Azor, this is Dr. En Hong Yang.

- Name the person of higher status, position, or rank first.
  Dr. Ramsdale, this is a new member of the Purchasing Department, Jon Delgado.

- Introduce a fellow employee to a customer or client by identifying the client first.
  Mrs. Sheng, this is our other salesperson, Joe Anderson.

- If it is not clear which rule applies to your situation, state the person you know better last.
  Jeffrey Ramirez, I'd like you to meet my good friend, Jean.

Simple Courtesy

REMEMBER THE VALUE OF PLEASE AND THANK YOU Use these words frequently. The habitual use of these words will give your conversations a tone of courtesy and respect.

DON'T INTERRUPT A SPEAKER Cutting off someone during a conversation says that you have been waiting for your opportunity to speak rather than listening. Instead, pay careful attention to what is being said. When the speaker is finished, offer feedback, such as paraphrasing, to show that you have understood the speaker's message before you move on to what you would like to say. Make your recently acquired communication skills count in your favor.

CHOOSE APPROPRIATE TOPICS FOR CONVERSATIONS Try to be aware of current subjects by reading newspapers and listening to broadcast news. This will allow you to initiate interesting conversations on current topics. Being able to actively participate in such conversations can boost your morale.

Emphasize the difference between fact and opinion. With facts, quote your source. *"The Wall Street Journal* says that manufacturers of hybrid cars have increased production." Take responsibility for your opinion by saying, "From what I know, I think . . ." or "In my judgment . . ." Be careful not to get involved in a controversial topic with someone you don't know well. Politics, religion, and personal beliefs can ignite heated arguments and hard feelings. Steer away from these, especially with someone you have to face at work every day.

AVOID NEGATIVE JUDGMENTS Be cautious about making critical comments about your friends, your job, or your coworkers. Nothing spreads more quickly. Negative statements may bounce back at you with connotations you did not intend. Messages often become distorted and embellished as they are repeated. If you must say something negative, do so privately to the person it concerns.

Thoughtful Consideration of Others

WORD QUESTIONS CAREFULLY Questions that can be answered "yes" or "no" are called **directive questions**. These are specific and very useful when you must have a positive or negative answer. **Nondirective questions** are *open-ended questions* that allow you to probe gently to get the information you need. They also permit the responder to decide how best to answer. Try asking nondirective questions starting with one of these *journalistic* words.

- Who? *Who has helped you in your career?*
- Where? *Where did you find that file?*
- What? *What did you learn from that situation?*
- Why? *Why did you choose that supplier?*
- When? *When did you cancel the project?*
- How? *How would you describe your leadership style?*

By wording a question in this way, you often open doors to answers that give you information you might not otherwise get. It is difficult to know how far to go when asking questions in casual conversations. Sometimes simply a quizzical look will clue the speaker that you are listening and would like to hear more. He or she will either pick up your hint and share more, or ignore it if the details are too private. But, there are out-of-bounds questions that should always be avoided. Examples are, "How old are you?," "How much do you make?," and "Do you like the manager?" It is rude to ask questions like these outright and put someone on the spot, especially with matters that may be none of your concern.

Language trap

Don't say, "Two of the new patients was in the waiting room." Say, "Two of the new patients were in the waiting room."

USE ORDINARY LANGUAGE In general conversation, it is considerate to use language that is understood by the other person. Avoid using street slang, technical jargon, uncommon abbreviations made with acronyms or shortened words, and offensive language that includes racist slurs, cursing, or sexual connotations. A skilled communicator soon knows just what is appropriate by paying attention to the other person. Be careful also of language that labels people stereotypically as if those of the same nationality, age, occupation, gender, or religion are all the same. Careless use of words can damage relationships.

Asking nondirective questions and listening carefully will allow you to get information you need from a conversation.

©Digital Vision

CHOOSE CAREFUL RESPONSES Stressful work situations can cause communication to spring out of control. It is to your advantage to provide a calm but firm response that maintains interpersonal relationships. Here are three responses to the query, "Will you trade shifts with me tomorrow?"

- An **aggressive response** is a reaction that is unnecessarily harsh and forceful. Threatening gestures punctuate the statements.

  My gosh, this is the third time you've asked me to trade with you. Can't you ever do what you're assigned to do? No, I won't trade shifts. I can't believe you are asking me!

- A **passive response** is a reaction that is weak and lacks energy. In this situation, a passive responder would probably avoid eye contact and accept the trade without protest, even if miserably unhappy about it.

  Okay, I suppose I could do it.

- An **assertive response** is a reaction that communicates your preferences and feelings in a firm but positive way. This is the best way to show your true feelings without being offensive. Keep your voice in a normal tone and establish good eye contact.

  I would rather not trade shifts with you because it would cause me to have to reschedule all of my appointments.

LISTEN WELL AND PROVIDE FEEDBACK In conversation, you form the ties that bind your personal relationships. Skills in speaking, listening for both content and intent, giving feedback by paraphrasing to show that you understand, and sending and reading nonverbal messages all contribute to positive daily interactions on the job.

Personal CHECK-UP

Make a list of specific communication skills that you can apply in business situations.

Business Etiquette

Any business you work for will have its own organizational culture within the larger framework of society. The company will have established **protocols** or *norms* of behavior that you are expected to learn and follow. Some may be clearly written or orally explained, whereas others are just part of organizational culture that you will have to pick up through observation over time. Your knowledge and practice of these written and unwritten codes along with proper **etiquette**—accepted social behavior—will smooth your progress toward business success. Some common organizational protocols involve space and seating, personal territory, and perceived inconsiderate behaviors.

Space

The location and size of workspace can indicate power and status in organizations. Powerful people are allotted larger offices with windows away from public places. An office can tell much about the personality and work habits of its occupant. Think of a jumbled mess, organized clutter, or bare surfaces with only a telephone and a single folder. The office resident may have the desk facing the entrance, saying, "I have an open door policy and am easily accessible." But, the computer or telephone may be on the credenza so that, even when the door is open, the resident's back to it clearly says, "Don't interrupt, I am busy."

Seating arrangements in business are used to advantage when people who need to cooperate are seated next to each other at a table. Competitors often are seated to confront each other face-to-face across a surface. The most important person often sits at the end of a rectangular meeting table, whereas the middle of the seating area is for those of lesser importance. When seats are not assigned, it is interesting to watch where people choose to sit.

Territory

Each person's workspace becomes an invisibly identified **territory** for that individual. Certain codes of behavior regarding territory exist, based on courtesy and regard for others. A supervisor may walk into a subordinate's territory unannounced. But, you should knock on your boss's door and wait to be invited to enter. Always ask first if you need to use someone's computer or borrow a pen and memo pad. These items become viewed as personal possessions, and ignoring the courtesy of requesting permission can cause hard feelings.

Inconsiderate Behavior

There are unwritten behavioral rules in workplaces that you will not find in an employee manual or have explained to you during your orientation and training. You must pick up on them through observation and experience. Pay attention, and observe the behavior of the people around you to get an idea of what is acceptable and what is unacceptable. If you are in doubt, ask. Breaking these unspoken rules can send a message that is unprofessional.

During work hours, it may be perceived as inconsiderate to eat at your desk, smoke, chew gum as you talk, bring soft drinks and food into meetings, read magazines, write personal letters/e-mails, make personal phone calls, surf the Internet for nonwork-related reasons, play music, or speak so loudly that people around you are distracted. Every workplace has a different level of tolerance for such behaviors. To be safe, do not indulge in them unless you observe that it is acceptable that others are doing so or someone in authority tells you it is okay.

Courtesy and awareness of the rights of others are signs of maturity and professionalism. Begin now to visualize your success in a career by adopting the kind of behavior that will advance you up the ladder. You can start today to build your reputation as a dedicated, loyal, honest, and conscientious person.

Conflicts at Work

In social and family situations, it is important to be able to resolve disagreements effectively. In the workplace, unresolved issues with customers, coworkers, or supervisors can damage working relationships, leading to reduced morale and productivity. It can even affect your chances for career advancement.

You are not able to choose your coworkers and supervisors, so you must learn how to tolerate and get along with everyone—even those with whom you disagree. If you aren't careful, tiny irritations can explode into destructive, time-consuming situations that cause misery. Employees sometimes exhibit defensive, manipulative, intimidating, or devaluing behaviors that cause pain to others and create unhealthy working conditions. Knowing how to recognize and deal with problem situations before they get out of control is a valuable skill.

The word *conflict* may connote something unpleasant for you, as it does for many people. Generally, it occurs when one person's behavior interferes with someone else or threatens others. Behavior that is different from yours can confuse and anger you. Luckily, effective ways to cope with conflict and change situations for the better are available.

"If you have learned how to disagree without being disagreeable, then you have discovered the secret of getting along—whether it be in business, family relations, or life itself."

—Bernard Meltzer

Causes of Conflict

Conflict can be defined as a clash of differing attitudes, behaviors, ideas, goals, or needs. The exercise of one interferes with another, and a struggle occurs. Review the following causes of conflict. Some are more serious than others.

- **Simple disagreement**—You said this, another said that, and neither of you agrees. A basic argument over a simple fact can often be settled by looking up the information, calling a reference source, or asking an expert. Or, the two of you may simply agree to disagree. You part friends, and that's all there is to it.

- **Attack on self-concept**—Sometimes you are told—or worse, you overhear—a comment that belittles your sense of self-worth. You want to spring to your own defense. **Ego conflicts** can be damaging to personal and professional relationships because they are perceived as individual attacks on our abilities or on who we are. In these situations, tell the careless speaker how the comment made you feel. Also, consider the speaker's intentions. Often, an apology and/or clarification of intended meaning will prevent the incident from escalating into conflict. If the comment was intended as constructive criticism, try to take an objective view and accept the comment in the spirit it was intended. If you feel the speaker is mistaken, gently explain your viewpoint. If further understanding of the situation warrants, don't hesitate to apologize yourself.

- **Perceived conflict**—We sometimes make "something out of nothing." If you believe that two of you have equal responsibility for achieving a goal, you may be upset if you are struggling to do the job and your coworker is not helping. When you feel betrayed, angry, or confused by the actions of another, express how you feel. "I was counting on you to help get these newsletters stapled today." The other person may then explain that she had gone to get the stamps so the newsletters could be mailed quickly. It turns out that no conflict really exists.

Knowing how to manage conflict effectively is important in maintaining work relationships.

- **Value conflict**—You have your set of standards and others have theirs. None are better than the others—they are simply different and based on different life experiences. Sometimes these standards collide over relatively minor events. It is best not to engage someone in a conflict over values. Values can rarely be changed. If Shirika is collecting money for a gift for Andrea's new baby, and you are opposed to gifts for colleagues, you should politely decline to participate, but send Andrea your best wishes. Shirika and your other coworkers should respect your decision. If they allow themselves to be hurt by your lack of participation, conflict may erupt. You may need to explain your previous unpleasant experience that caused your policy decision.

Conflict Stages

Morale in the workplace may become low if conflicts are not handled well. Eruptions of strong feelings can be destructive and can cause workers to be distracted from the tasks that must be done. Stress will increase, causing cooperation to become even more difficult. Any tense situation usually goes through a damaging cycle that is characterized by the following stages.

1. A conflict develops between two people.
2. Others get involved by taking sides.
3. People begin keeping score.
4. Someone demands a showdown.
5. Destructive threats are made.
6. Constructive activity, such as discussing the problem and possible solutions, begins to take place.

It is wise to prevent a disturbance from building into a destructive cycle. Negative behaviors will not help. *Avoiding* the problem by ignoring it or running away from it will not resolve it. *Delaying*, or putting off recognition of the problem, will only permit it to escalate. And of course, the most hostile and useless way of handling conflict is to do so with *aggression*—trying to force someone to accept your ideas or behavior. Both verbal and physical aggression can harm the climate of the workplace and result in miserable working conditions.

Methods of Settling Conflict

How do you handle disagreements? Make a list of actions you have taken. Compare your list to the following methods.

1. **Confrontation**—If handled in an open communication climate, this can be a "win–win" approach in which two people can work out their differences. This means facing the

COMMUNICATION AT WORK

Like most doctors' offices, the one where Anita Millwater works is usually a calm, quiet place. Conflicts do occur, however, and Anita has to deal with them. As a physician's assistant, Anita leads patients from the waiting room to the examination rooms. She often must endure complaints from patients about how long they've had to wait. Anita knows that the best approach is to make a brief, sympathetic reply, and then get right down to business. Some patients become frustrated or angry about their bills or how their insurance company is handling their claims. In many cases, patients simply aren't aware of the proper procedure to follow. Anita calms them down by patiently explaining the process. By staying calm herself, she reassures patients that a solution to their problems exists.

©Getty Images/PhotoDisc

Personal CHECK-UP

Explain the five methods of solving conflicts. When would each be appropriate? Identify a particular situation of each and suggest a solution.

problem, being willing to admit feelings, and being open to areas of agreement and suggestions for a solution. Good feelings can result if both parties give a little in order to achieve common ground.

2. **Competition**—This approach is a contest between rivals that results in a "win–lose" situation in which one person comes out on top, leaving the other with a sense of failure. This method may temporarily end the conflict, but hard feelings may continue and may eventually resurface with even more problems.

3. **Compromise**—In this "lose–lose" approach, both people give up something of lesser importance to gain a higher priority. For compromise to work, both people must be willing to give up a lower-priority item. Compromise can end in good feelings.

4. **Accommodation**—This is a "smoothing" approach, known also as "win–yield." One person yields to the other, giving in quickly with little discussion. This approach often leaves the yielding person with a sense of failure while the winner feels little accomplishment.

5. **Avoidance**—This is a "win/lose-refuse" approach in which one person simply withdraws, refusing to participate in resolving the issue but enjoying a sense of control. The other may be a winner but often feels the loss of the relationship.

Negotiating Techniques

Some basic negotiating techniques can help you resolve differences with coworkers and supervisors in a positive way that will benefit both you and your employer. Experts in the art of negotiation suggest six rules for resolving conflicts successfully.

1. **Listen**—Listen carefully to be sure you understand the situation. If the other person doesn't seem to be listening to you, you need to set the example and be the first to listen well.

2. **Understand the other person's point of view**—Once you listen, verify your understanding by asking questions and paraphrasing. This will show your willingness to understand the other person's position.

3. **Focus on the problem, not the person**—Do not approach problems by pointing fingers and placing blame. This puts others on the defensive. Coworkers will waste time and energy defending themselves, passing blame, and/or covering their tracks instead of finding a resolution. Hard feelings result when others feel they are being attacked. Simply state the problems you are experiencing and seek collaboration for resolving them. Show an understanding of the other person's situation and needs and an overall willingness to come to an agreement. By doing so, you can build, maintain, and even improve relationships.

4. **Satisfy the interests of both sides**—Identify your interests and help the other side identify its interests. Recognize what you have in common and look for a solution in which both parties' needs are met.

5. **Invent new options for solving problems**—When you spend time identifying the interests of both sides, you will think of several new ways to solve the problem. Be open to considering new options.

6. **Reach an agreement based on what's fair**—Seek to determine a standard of fairness that is acceptable to both sides. Weigh the possible solutions and choose the best option.

© 1996 Ted Goff

Dealing with Differences

We don't always agree with the people around us, but such situations need not turn into arguments. Taking a confrontational approach can give you a reputation for being pushy or difficult. Instead, try negotiating rather than arguing. Or, try removing the cause of the disagreement or friction. Through negotiation and compromise, you can work with others to reach agreements and find solutions.

CHAPTER SUMMARY

Specific communication skills and behaviors are important for creating positive interpersonal relationships on the job. When making initial contacts, make a mental note of the contact's name, use correct titles, and follow proper etiquette for introductions. Choose appropriate topics for workplace conversations, avoid negative judgments, and word questions carefully. Nondirective questions allow you to probe gently for information. Companies have their own cultures and protocols for proper behavior. You must pick up on unspoken behavioral norms through observation and experience. Clashes in the workplace may arise because of simple disagreement, attack on self-concept, perceived conflict, and value conflict. Rules for negotiating resolutions are to listen, understand the other person's point of view, focus on the problem and not the person, find a way to satisfy both interests, invent new options, and seek a standard of fairness for both sides.

CHAPTER REVIEW

1. What conditions must be present for a communication relationship to be established? Suggest what might happen if one of these conditions is not met.

2. Name a specific time when someone introduced you so well that you felt appreciated. What was special about the introduction?

3. Think about three recent conversations you have had. Give examples of simple courtesy that kept communication moving ahead.

4. Pinpoint the cause of a conflict of which you are aware or have experienced. Was specific negative behavior present? How did it affect the conflict?

CAN YOU DEFINE THESE TERMS?

Match each description with the appropriate term. Write the correct letter in the blank preceding the sentence. Some terms will not be used.

Terms:

1. ____ A reaction that is weak and lacks energy

2. ____ Accepted social behavior

3. ____ The smallest communication unit, made up of a group of two

4. ____ Open-ended questions that allow you to probe gently to get the information you need

5. ____ Norms of behavior that you are expected to learn and follow in the workplace

6. ____ A reaction that is harsh and forceful

7. ____ Arise from the perception of an attack on our abilities or on who we are

8. ____ Questions that can be answered "yes" or "no"

9. ____ A reaction that communicates your preferences and feelings in a firm but positive way

10. ____ An employee's invisibly identified workspace

a. aggressive response

b. assertive response

c. conflict

d. directive questions

e. dyad

f. ego conflicts

g. etiquette

h. nondirective questions

i. passive response

j. protocols

k. territory

APPLICATIONS

Question and Response Types

Write a statement illustrating each of the listed terms below.

1. assertive response

2. nondirective question

3. directive question

4. aggressive response

5. passive response

Introductions

Working in groups, practice introducing the following people through role play. Be sure to follow the guidelines for proper introductions.

- Dr. Pamela Houston and Mr. James Villegas
- Your 16-year-old brother, Fred, and your college professor, Dr. Hector Martin
- Governor John Smith and your neighbor, Mrs. Michelle Morgan
- Your friend, Jamal, and your friend, Helen
- Your boss, Brenda Kwan, and a new employee, Carmelita Evans

Initiating Conversations

Working in groups, each of you must imagine a conversation with someone you do not know well, such as a cashier in a grocery store, a new colleague at work, or a new neighbor. Each person must write a situation and a list of topics other than the weather that would be appropriate for the conversation. Be creative! Fold up the written ideas and place them in a hat. Pair up. Each person must draw an idea from the hat and initiate the described conversation with his or her partner through role play.

Conflict Management

Part I. Work in groups. Read the following statements aloud. Match each to one of the five methods of handling disagreements: confrontation, competition, compromise, accommodation, and avoidance. Describe the way each statement may leave the recipient feeling.

1. "Well, my department will work overtime to meet the June deadline, but you've got to contact the dealers and change the distribution orders."

2. "Look, I understand your problems, and I know we don't agree about how fast we can get the product on the market. Since we do agree on the importance of a June shipment, what steps can we eliminate from the production process?"

3. "If you are going to make that decision, just leave my department out of your plans."

4. "Well, I'll go along with the date you want for shipping just because it's so important to keep to the schedule. But in order to meet that deadline, my department will have to use the old packaging instead of our new cartons."

5. "Listen, my department can't be ready to ship that merchandise by next month and that's final. Make other plans."

Part II. Discuss an issue of controversy in your school about which there may be strong feelings in your group. Make statements about the topic that fit into each method of handling conflict.

Confrontation

Competition

Compromise

Accomodation

Avoidance

MAKING CONNECTIONS

Business Protocols

Work with a partner. Read aloud the parts of Ms. Benson and Richard Chin in the following conversation. Ms. Benson is vice president of the Mervin County Bank. Richard is a new customer service representative who has been working at the bank for three days. The setting is a private meeting in Ms. Benson's office. After reading the conversation, answer the questions that follow.

Ms. Benson: Richard, what are you wearing? Do you think you are dressed appropriately for work?

Richard: What do you mean, Ms. Benson? These are my favorite jeans.

Ms. Benson: But is it proper attire for working in the customer service office?

Richard: You're going to tell me . . . Do we have a dress code here? It wasn't in my employee handbook.

Ms. Benson: I'm afraid I'm going to have to make some suggestions, Richard. It's my job.

Richard: What do you want me to do? Go home and change?

Ms. Benson: I want you to think carefully about the bank's image, Richard. I don't expect to have to speak to you about this again.

Discussion Questions

1. Richard obviously didn't understand some of the bank's protocols. How could he have avoided his mistake?

   _____

   _____

2. What do you think will be the outcome of this conversation? Why?

   _____

   _____

3. Which rules for participating effectively in conversations did Richard break? Which rules did Ms. Benson break? Working with a partner, rewrite the conversation so that it follows the rules, and then read it aloud with your partner.

   _____

   _____

   _____

4. Whose responsibility is it to ensure that employees are not conflicting with the image the business wants to project? Should businesses have formal, written dress codes? Be ready to defend your position to the class.

   _____

   _____

Business Research

For employers who value ability over appearance, body decorations are not a problem. Personnel decisions aren't influenced by visible tattoos or piercing, say 25 percent of those surveyed in a recent study by the Chicago outplacement firm, Challenger, Gray & Christmas. But, nearly half of employers in a National Association of Colleges and Employers survey said nontraditional appearance would sway their hiring decisions. Complete your own research as instructed below.

1. Research the dress codes of five businesses. Summarize your findings in a two-page essay. Provide your sources of information in correct bibliographic form.

2. Interview several business people you know and find out how dress codes have changed in their companies through the years. Include former and current attitudes on business casual attire, political or cause-related T-shirts and buttons, sandals, shorts, halter tops, bare midriffs, jeans, and sweatshirts. Give an oral report to the class.

PROJECTS

Competitive and Cooperative Behaviors—Can You Agree?

In this activity, you will identify different behaviors as competitive or cooperative. Complete this exercise individually first. In the blanks at the left, mark the item "O" if you consider the statement to apply to a cooperative behavior, "X" if you consider it a competitive behavior, or "?" if the behavior could apply to both or neither situations. Then, join a group of four or five classmates. Review the entire list with your group. Place a checkmark in the right-hand column for those items on which the group does not agree. For checkmarked items, discuss your different viewpoints. Can you come to agreement? If so, write the agreed answer and the reasoning behind it in the space below the statement. If not, write reasoning for all opposing viewpoints.

Individual's Answer		Group Disagreement
_____1.	Wants to beat someone else at a particular task.	1. _____
_____2.	Enjoys winning.	2. _____
_____3.	Doesn't hesitate to ask questions if the task is not understood.	3. _____
_____4.	Can change own mind without loss of self-esteem.	4. _____
_____5.	Is considered friendly, good-natured, and helpful.	5. _____

_____6.   Has high self-image.   6. _____

_____7.   Is willing to discuss the views of another.   7. _____

_____8.   Listens well and is interested in others.   8. _____

_____9.   Can pull ideas together to make them work.   9. _____

_____10. Is receptive to new ideas.   10. _____

_____11. Often puts profit, prize, or position before people.   11. _____

_____12. Will point out errors to others.   12. _____

_____13. Loves to receive praise and encouragement.   13. _____

_____14. Is willing to talk, lead, and take responsibility.   14. _____

_____15. Works to eliminate communication barriers.   15. _____

_____16. Trusts others to do their part.   16. _____

_____17. Can follow directions.   17. _____

_____18. Accepts group decision when different from own   18. _____
           ideas.

_____19. Feels the need to live up to the expectations of   19. _____
           others.

_____20. Is ready and able to challenge.   20. _____

_____21. Feels the need to be superior.   21. _____

Individual's Answer		Group Disagreement
_____ 22.	Doesn't admit defeat but tries again.	22. _____
_____ 23.	Blames mistakes on others.	23. _____
_____ 24.	Takes deep satisfaction in accomplishment.	24. _____

Communication Barriers

In this communication exercise, the class will practice giving and receiving instructions in one-way and two-way communication. Two speakers will set up varying degrees of barriers to communication. The class will note the effects of the barriers on the results. The third speaker will provide for two-way communication. The class will compare the results to the previous experiments.

Materials needed: box of paper clips, paper, and pencils

A speaker will create a design with five paper clips and describe it to the audience. Each member of the audience will then draw the design as it is described. Students may use a paper clip as a pattern/stencil for their drawings.

Instructions

A. One volunteer is needed to be the first speaker. This student will follow these instructions.

- Stand with your back to the audience.

- Arrange five paper clips in a pattern on a flat surface. Do not let the audience see it.

- Describe the paper clip design so that each member of the audience can draw the pattern described.

- Do not look at the audience. Do not use gestures. Do not answer any questions.

- When finished, check the students' papers and count the number of students who have drawn the exact design described.

B. A second volunteer will repeat the experiment using these instructions.

- Stand facing the audience, but arrange the paper clip pattern (making a different one) so that it cannot be seen.

- Describe the paper clip design so that the students can draw the pattern described.

- You may use gestures and watch the audience while talking. You may not answer any questions or correct errors.

- When finished, check the number of accurate designs.

C. A third volunteer will repeat the experiment using the following directions.

- Stand facing the audience, but arrange a different pattern of paper clips in a position where it cannot be seen.
- Describe the new pattern.
- Use gestures. Encourage the students to ask questions. Answer questions. Watch the students' efforts and help them.
- Check the papers for accuracy.

Discussion Questions

1. What barriers existed between the speaker and the audience in each of the settings?

2. What feelings did the barriers cause for the speakers? For the receivers?

3. How do one-way and two-way communication differ? Which is more effective? Why?

4. How does this communication exercise fit with the strategies of solving conflicts in business?

BPA Presentation Management Team Event

Effective communication is essential in the workplace. Business professionals understand the importance of good listening skills, teamwork, professionalism, ethics, etiquette, and the proper use of electronic forms of communication. Hidden agendas and body language can have negative effects on business communication.

Your team of 3–4 members is challenged to prepare and deliver a presentation using desktop technology. The presentation must explain and promote effective communication in the workplace.

Your presentation will be evaluated for effective use of current desktop multimedia technology. No VCR or laserdisc is allowed during the presentation. Charts and other graphics should be incorporated into the presentation. The student must secure a release form from any individual whose name, photograph, or other information is included in the presentation.

You will have ten minutes to set up your multimedia presentation. You will then make your presentation, which must be between seven and ten minutes in length. Judges will have an additional five minutes to ask questions.

Performance Indicators Evaluated

- Show effective use of current desktop multimedia technology.
- Show effective use of space, color, text, and graphics in presentational design.
- Demonstrate teamwork and group dynamics.
- Define professionalism as it relates to communication in the workplace.
- Describe effective listening skills.
- Explain the power of body language.
- Explain the disruption caused by conflicts in the workplace.
- Describe appropriate and inappropriate forms of communication in the workplace.

For more detailed information, go to the BPA web site.

Think Critically

1. Why is listening an important aspect of communication?
2. Give an example of body language that indicates insincerity.
3. How is effective teamwork disrupted by conflicts?
4. What are some appropriate and inappropriate forms of communication in the workplace?

http://www.bpa.org/

Interviewing Effectively

7

CHAPTER OBJECTIVES

After completing this chapter, you should be able to

- List and explain the characteristics of business interviews.
- Discuss the roles of interviewer and interviewee.
- Describe a variety of types of business interviews.
- Identify strategies for successful job applicants.
- Describe interviewer strategies for easing negative discussions.
- Explain how to prepare for an interview.

KEY TERMS AND CONCEPTS

interview	employment interview	performance appraisal
interviewer	training session	reprimand interview
interviewee	counseling interview	problem-solving interview
climate	informational interview	exit interview

IDEA BOX

Imagine that tomorrow you will have an opportunity to interview anyone in the world of your choice—alive or dead, famous or not so famous. Imagine further that you will be limited to only five questions. Decide whom you would want to interview, and think about what you would like to ask. Make a list of five carefully worded questions. Each question must begin with one of the following.

Who

What

When

Where

Why

How

107

One-to-One Business Communication

Speech communication is basic to human relationships, and business success is built as you interact daily with others, one by one. Between two people at work, speech exists for two important reasons.

1. **To do the work**—to be productive, meet the goals of the company, and earn income.

2. **To establish and maintain relationships**—to get along with others.

As previously discussed, communication relationships must be established under certain conditions, and certain "rules" of courtesy apply. These same rules apply in the workplace. But, workplace conversations are different from social conversations because advance preparation is required, a specific time and place may be established, participants play specific roles, and certain goals must be accomplished. The effective communication skills that you have learned will lead to success in an important type of workplace conversation—the interview.

Interviews—Conversations at Work

Interviews are not just for filling job positions. An **interview** is a conversation—formal or informal—with one of a number of business purposes, including employment seeking, information gathering, employee evaluation, or new policy explanation. In the workplace, interviews are used to accomplish a number of goals, but they all have the same basic characteristics.

Characteristics of Interviews

INTERVIEWS HAVE SPECIFIC GOALS They may be formal or informal discussions, but interviews always have at least one specific goal.

- To gather information.
  "Why would you like to work for our company?" "Could you give me a status report on your project?"

- To give information.
  "I'd like to tell you about the guarantee that goes with our new product."

- To persuade another person by changing that person's beliefs or actions.
  "I'd like to talk to you about a possible transfer to our Dallas office."

- To work together toward the solution to a problem.
  "I've asked you to meet with me to iron out a problem in this department."

TWO OR MORE PEOPLE ARE INVOLVED Usually, an interview is a *dyad*—a one-to-one communication encounter with two participants. Some types of interviews involve business people of different levels.

Personal CHECK-UP

What are some common goals of interviews?

- Both people may be members of the same company with the same status level, such as two managers.

- Both may be employees of the same company with different positions and levels, such as supervisor and employee.

- Participants may be from different organizations, such as a sales manager and a distributor.

- One person may be from inside the company and the other from outside, such as a human resources manager and a job applicant.

EACH PERSON HAS A ROLE Sometimes roles shift between participants or roles are shared. In more formal situations, such as employment interviews, the roles are typically as follows.

- The **interviewer** is the person who plans the meeting, sets the goals, asks the questions, and generally controls the direction of the conversation.

- The **interviewee** is the person who answers questions, provides information, and helps achieve the goals of the meeting.

TIME AND PLACE VARY AND ARE ESTABLISHED IN ADVANCE Generally, an interview meeting is set up by appointment for a certain day and time. Often, the meeting takes place in the office of one of the participants. The physical setting, including the seating arrangement, lighting, and distance between people, can help set the **climate**, or tone, of the meeting.

Types of Interviews

You will be involved in a variety of interviews in your professional life. Consider the following types of one-to-one business situations.

Employment Interviews

The **employment interview**, or job interview, is the first one-to-one business conversation you will have. Your goal is to secure an entrance into the job market. The first time you encounter an employment interview, you will be the interviewee, and the personnel director, recruiter, and/or your prospective boss will be the interviewer(s). This type of interview can be a high-pressure situation. It is important because your future may depend on it, so you might feel apprehensive.

You may not be the only one who feels tense during the meeting. Remember that the interviewer has the important task of selecting a person who will perform the duties of the job and fit well into the work team and whose skills will benefit the company. The interviewer will be under a great deal of pressure to select the best applicant. This means you will have to answer some tough questions, so the recruiter can picture you in the job for which you are applying. You will want to

A successful employment interview can secure the job you want.

do some advance preparation. For starters, have answers ready for commonly asked questions such as the following.

- "Tell me about yourself."
- "How do your abilities fit our job requirements?"
- "What are your biggest weaknesses? Strengths?"
- "Why are you the best candidate for this job?"

Figure 7-1 lists additional suggestions for a successful job interview.

Training Sessions

Once you are hired, you will be instructed in specific company policies and told what is expected of you on the job. This may be done for several new employees at once in a training class, or you may be turned over to a fellow employee for individual training. The two of you will meet in a one-to-one **training session** to go over procedures and to orient you to new surroundings. The trainer's role is to provide information, and your role is to ask questions and repeat instructions to ensure your understanding. Most organizations have an ongoing commitment to training and development, so you can expect to participate in these types of sessions throughout your employment.

Counseling Interviews

When you reach a point at which you need special help on the job, request an interview with your supervisor. The purpose of this type of meeting, called a **counseling interview**, is to give/seek guidance and advice. You will need to make the situation clear and express your feelings honestly. Your supervisor will work with you to review possible solutions and to set goals. You may simply need more training. If the situation is more serious, you may even need to discuss different work assignments or a different job.

FIGURE 7-1   Strategies for Successful Job Applicants

Job interviews are based on effective communication. The successful candidate in today's competitive job market must do the following.

Present a positive attitude.

- Know and understand the requirements of the position.
- Show evidence of the qualifications being sought.
- Show enthusiasm toward the company and the open position.
- Indicate previous research on the company by citing experts, web sites, library sources, and so forth.
- Identify with the employer's interest in building company goals.
- Stress a desire to start a career, not temporary employment.

Present yourself favorably.

- Take an active part in the interview, talking at least half of the time and initiating comments and questions.
- Listen closely and sense the interviewer's expected responses.
- Appear confident by wording questions in the first person. *"When would you expect me to start?"*
- Summarize qualifications and interest in the position positively and assertively.
- Push for commitment from the interviewer regarding when a hiring decision will be made.

Communicate effectively.

- Ask specific questions about policies, employee turnover, structure, and so forth.
- Speak fluently and directly, providing supporting material to prove your main points.
- Use technical terms to indicate familiarity with the position.
- Explain in short, simple sentences using concrete examples, interesting descriptions, and accepted rules of grammar.
- Keep constant and focused eye contact with the interviewer.
- Articulate distinctly and vary your rate and volume of speaking.
- Sit comfortably, gesture meaningfully, and lean slightly forward to communicate.

Informational Interviews

Suppose you need to interview an expert for specific information. Examples of an **informational interview** include asking the business manager questions about accounting practices and interviewing an employee for an article you are writing for a company newsletter. As the interviewer, you will need to ask for an appointment, make clear your goals, and prepare a list of questions to ask. You will need to listen well, write down or record answers, and draw further information by asking questions based on the answers you receive. Ask permission to use a tape recorder for detailed information. Remember to request permission to quote your interviewee.

As a computer programmer, Mark Haydon hasn't had much trouble finding a job. He has switched jobs several times to keep his career moving. Mark knows that interviewing for a job is not just spending an hour answering questions in an uncomfortable suit. Sometimes interviewers pose problems during the interview and ask how he would solve them. Mark has learned that he needs to be able to think quickly and express his ideas clearly and briefly. Early in Mark's career, computer programming was a solitary job. Employers hired him for his technical skill, and he and his computer did the work. Now, workplaces are much more team oriented. Mark has to explain to his interviewers how he uses such skills as negotiation, conflict management, and team building to successfully complete team projects.

If you have expertise in a certain area, others may ask to interview you. As the interviewee, be courteous, answer questions carefully and thoroughly, and help the interviewers gather the information they need to reach their goals.

Evaluation or Appraisal Interviews

Many companies conduct performance appraisals to formally evaluate their employees' job performance. A **performance appraisal** is a meeting between an employee (interviewee) and direct supervisor (interviewer) to discuss how well the employee performed job duties over a specific period of time—usually six months or one year. These performance evaluations are opportunities to receive guidance, give feedback, review career plans, and set goals. Topics may cover a variety of subjects—punctuality, attitude, deadline achievement, goal attainment, expectations, and relationships with others. Positive changes in your work habits may be suggested. When negative beha-viors must be addressed, advance preparation and a cooperative attitude will help the performance appraisal go smoothly. Figure 7-2 presents interviewer tips for appraisal interviews.

Reprimand Interviews

At some time, you may be called into a **reprimand interview**, a one-to-one meeting in which some undesirable behavior or problem with your work is brought to your attention. A private office with a closed door is usually the setting for such an interview—no one likes public criticism. In difficult situations of this kind, both the interviewer and interviewee may be ill at ease. Both parties will need skill and patience to tactfully approach the problem, acknowledge the improper actions, and work out strategies for improvement. In a reprimand interview, it is best to remember that the criticism being given is about work performance and is not meant to be a personal attack. Hurt feelings can be avoided if both parties are cooperative and professional.

> "If there is any one secret of success, it lies in the ability to get the other person's point of view and see things from his angle as well as your own."
>
> —Henry Ford

FIGURE 7-2   Interview Strategies for Supervisors

Soon, you will be on the manager's side of the desk and responsible for reviewing the job performance of your employees. Interviewees probably will not like hearing some of the negative things that you will need to address, such as excessive tardiness, missed deadlines, poor job performance, and so forth. You will not enjoy this part of your job, either, but you may use the following guidelines to make the meetings less painful.

- Remember that your goal is to have a smooth-running operation with highly motivated employees.
- Set the tone of the meeting. Arrange the meeting in a neutral but private location. Select a convenient time for both parties. Start on a positive note, assuring the employee that you are interested in his or her progress.
- Plan the points of the agenda. List the employee's strengths on the job. Work your way to the problem areas or points in need of improvement. Together, work on solutions.
- Conduct the meeting as a dialog. Ask questions to encourage the employee to talk about personal goals, immediate projects, and concerns. Listen attentively. Offer useful feedback.
- End on a positive note. Set specific goals for changes in job performance. Schedule a date for a follow-up meeting.

Problem-Solving Interviews

A **problem-solving interview** is often the basis for airing concerns. If you should ask for this type of interview, it is important to provide clearly worded explanations of the conditions causing your distress. Express concerns in a professional manner. Focus on the problem and not on the person. Pointing fingers and exploding with anger will only put the other person on the defensive. It is best to listen calmly to the other person's point of view and be ready to propose solutions and suggestions for change that can satisfy both parties. If both parties are flexible and open to other opinions and suggestions, together you can work out a solution to the problem.

"Problems can become opportunities when the right people come together."

—Robert Redford

Exit Interviews

An **exit interview** is an informational interview that takes place when an employee leaves a position in a company. Conducted by the human resources department, this meeting gives the employee an opportunity to express views about the organization and working conditions. This is the time to share concerns or suggestions about your job situation. If you are being released from your position, the interviewer will explain the reasons to you. Regardless of the circumstances, you should always leave a position gracefully. Be honest about your views of the company, but do not to be overly critical or emotional. You may need that employer as a reference or want to return to work there one day. You will want to leave the employer with a favorable impression.

Ongoing training and counseling interviews help employees gather information they need to perform well in their jobs.

The Key to a Successful Interview—Preparation

When you meet to talk with someone you know and like, the situation is usually relaxed, the atmosphere is friendly and non-threatening, and the flow of communication is easy and spontaneous. When the meeting is over, both participants feel good about the meeting because you have achieved mutual goals. Such an interview style requires planning and is successful only when both members are prepared for both roles—interviewer and interviewee. The following suggestions will help you become a more effective participant in a business interview.

Know the Details of the Meeting

If you are initiating the interview, determine who, what, when, where, and why before you make the appointment. If you are asked to meet with someone, go through the same steps. Be sure of the location and how to get there. If the meeting location is unfamiliar to you, do a practice run beforehand. Allow yourself plenty of time to arrive before the meeting, and know how much time you will have for the interview.

Learn What You Can About the Other Participant

Seek information that will enable you to think of the other interview participant as a person and a partner in meeting a goal. If you have not met before, make sure you find out the person's name, title, job duties, company, office location, and so forth. This information will help you initiate friendly conversation and ask meaningful questions.

Think Through the Interview in Advance

If you are meeting in the other person's "territory" (office), imagine what it will be like to sit in the meeting. How much distance will there be between you and the other person? Visualize how the person will see you. Think of how you can help ensure the wise use of time available during the meeting. Make sure you know what the goals are, and consider how to conclude the meeting to your mutual satisfaction.

Plan the Topics You Want to Discuss, and Prepare Answers to Questions

Write down the things you want to ask. Leave space to jot down important answers as they are explained to you. Anticipate the questions you will be asked and think through your answers. If you are applying for a position, you can prepare by responding to the questions listed on page 110 and the additional ones that follow below. Practice answering each of these questions aloud. Try recording them and listening to your answers. Rephrase your answers to make them as clear as possible. Don't memorize your answers, but give yourself practice in verbalizing clearly what you already know.

- "How would you describe yourself?" (Select several appealing things about your background, interests, and personal skills. Phrase the information in three to five positive sentences.)

- "Do you like routine work? Regular hours?"

> **"When you're prepared, you're more confident. When you have a strategy, you're more comfortable."**
>
> —Fred Couples

A cooperative attitude and professional conduct will help difficult interviews go smoothly.

- "Do you plan to continue your education? What field are you planning to study?"
- "Tell me about your hobbies or what you do with your spare time."
- "What is your greatest weakness?" (The interviewer wants to know whether you can be objective about your shortcomings and whether you know yourself well enough to have overcome some failings.)
- "What subjects did you like best in school?"
- "What business and personal communication skills have you learned in your classes?"
- "Why do you want to work for our company?"
- "Do you have any questions?" (Be prepared with several questions that show you have researched the company and the position for which you are applying.)

Be Physically Prepared

To know that you look neat and well groomed gives you a sense of poise and confidence. Conservative business attire is a requirement for an employment interview. This means coat and tie, dress shirt, dress trousers, and dress shoes for men. Women should wear a business suit or dress with appropriate hosiery and sensible dress shoes. Avoid buying something new for the occasion, because you may be uncomfortable in something you haven't worn before. Heavy jewelry, cosmetics, and fragrances can be distracting and should be avoided. Good personal hygiene is a must, and hair should be clean and tidy. For other types of interviews, looking your best will give you an air of confidence, but you can adjust your dress according to the occasion and environment.

> "*Dress and conduct yourself so that people who have been in your company will not recall what you had on.*"
>
> **—John Newton**

© 2002 Ted Goff

"And another thing, I don't like people who ask me a lot of questions during job interviews."

Interviews

A business interview is a conversation between two people for a specific purpose. Typically, the participants take turns playing the roles of interviewer and interviewee. Even at a job interview, don't expect to be answering all the questions. Show that you are knowledgeable and interested by asking some questions of your own. Maintain a friendly but formal attitude no matter how informal the interviewer may be. Your professional attitude should be reflected in your clothing as well as in your behavior.

Be sure to bring with you any materials that you may need. For an employment interview, this could include a copy of your resume, references, samples of your work, a pen, and a notebook. You may also need to show identification, proof of citizenship, or your diploma. For other interviews, be sure to bring something with which to take notes or record the information. Also, bring along documents or samples of your work that you may need to refer to during your discussion.

Be Mentally Prepared

If you are interviewing for a position, it is essential that you know as much as you can about the company—its size, location, products or services, and so forth. If you are meeting to conduct business and are expected to have certain information available to present, be sure you spend enough time preparing so that you understand the information and why it is needed. Set aside private time in which you can practice presenting the information and answering questions orally. Always get a good night's sleep before an important meeting.

Set the Interview in the Proper Perspective

Accept the fact that for an employment interview, a reprimand interview, or an important meeting, you may be somewhat anxious or apprehensive. This is likely to be the case if the results of the interview affect your future, and it is totally normal. Remember, however, that it is not a life-or-death matter, but merely communication between two human beings. Be prepared, and try to stay focused and calm.

Expect the Interviewer to Take the Lead

An interview situation cannot be diagrammed like a football play. You will need to be alert and aware as the other person gives you verbal and nonverbal clues. If you are the interviewee, the interviewer will indicate where you are to sit and what the interview style will be, as well as when the meeting is concluded. If you are interviewing another person to get information for a report and are in that person's office, remember that you are a guest. But even as the guest, it will be up to you, as the interviewer, to take responsibility for beginning the interview, setting the style and pace, and concluding the meeting.

Carry Your Share of the Conversation

Whichever role you play in an interview, the other participant cannot know what you are thinking if you do not speak. It is not necessary to volunteer information that is not requested, but it is important to be a responsive, involved, and active participant. Listen carefully and use your paraphrasing skills to determine content and intent. Most interviewers are seeking more than "yes" or "no" answers. Expect indirect questions that require explanations and questions mirroring your answers that require further information.

Language trap

Don't say, "Oscar and Rita has been treated for their injuries." Say, "Oscar and Rita have been treated for their injuries." or "Oscar and Rita were treated for their injuries."

Personal
CHECK-UP

Name five things you can do to prepare for an interview.

Know Questions That Are Prohibited

In preparation for an employment interview, know that interviewers are forbidden by the Equal Opportunity Commission to ask personal questions that do not relate to the job you are seeking. You do not have to answer questions about personal life, religion, race, physical attributes, age, or national origin. For example, the following questions are off limits.

- "Are you married?"
- "Do you have children?"
- "What church do you attend?"
- "What is your height and weight?"
- "What is your date of birth?"
- "Are you a naturalized or native-born citizen?"

You can be asked for proof of high school graduation and whether you are over the minimum age for workers. If you are asked a question that feels too personal, you may politely ask, "Is it necessary for you to know that?" or "Do I have to give that information?" Questions related to your past jobs, stability, motivation, resourcefulness, and ability to work under the direction of others are also permitted.

Follow Up

After an employment interview, take the initiative to write a thank-you letter to the interviewer. For other interviews, it is sufficient to telephone or e-mail your appreciation for the meeting and to summarize any decisions that were made or duties that were assigned. Be sure to follow through on anything you promised to do as a result of the meeting and to report back in a timely manner. Whether the interview was successful on your terms or not, you can count it as valuable experience gained. Take some time to think about how you might have prepared better, questions you wish you had asked, and explanations you might have worded more clearly. Learn from the experience and plan to do even better the next time.

©Digital Vision

No matter what the outcome, interviewing is a valuable experience from which to learn and grow.

CHAPTER SUMMARY

Interviews are typically conversations between two people for the accomplishment of a specific business purpose. The goal of an interview meeting may be to gather or give information, to persuade another person, or to work toward the solution to a problem. Interviews are of a variety of types, including employment, training, counseling, informational, appraisal, reprimand, problem-solving, and exit interviews. The key to a successful interview is preparation. In advance, know details about the meeting, learn about the other person and/or the company, plan questions and responses, have appropriate attire ready to wear, and practice any presentations you will be giving. The interviewer should take the lead, but the interviewee should carry an appropriate share of the conversation. Follow up an employment interview with a formal thank-you letter. For other interviews, express appreciation and summarize your understanding of the outcomes of the meeting. Be sure to follow through on any commitments made in the meeting.

CHAPTER REVIEW

1. What is the difference between a social conversation and an interview? What rules and skills apply to both?

2. Describe in detail the roles of the interviewer and the interviewee.

3. What is the purpose of an employment interview? An evaluation interview? A problem-solving interview?

4. Which kinds of interviews have you experienced? Identify three aspects of the meetings that you would like to improve upon in future interviews.

CAN YOU DEFINE THESE TERMS?

Match each description with the appropriate term. Write the correct letter in the blank preceding the sentence. Some terms will not be used.

Terms:

a. climate
b. counseling interview
c. employment interview
d. exit interview
e. informational interview
f. interview
g. interviewee
h. interviewer
i. performance appraisal
j. problem-solving interview
k. reprimand interview
l. training session

1. ___ An informational interview that takes place when an employee leaves a company

2. ___ A conversation with a business purpose

3. ___ Answers questions, provides information, and helps achieve the goals of the meeting

4. ___ Plans the meeting, sets the goals, asks the questions, and controls the direction

5. ___ A meeting regarding some undesirable behavior or problem with your work

6. ___ A meeting between employee and supervisor to discuss how well the employee performed job duties over a specific period of time

7. ___ A business conversation with the purpose of giving/seeking guidance and advice

8. ___ The tone of the meeting affected by the physical setting

Fair Employment Interview?

Read the following poem about an interview by British poet Ursula Askham Fanthorpe. What kind of mood or climate has she created? Respond to the questions that follow the poem.

You Will Be Hearing From Us Shortly

You feel adequate to the demands of this position?

What qualities do you feel you

Personally have to offer?

Ah

Let us consider your application form

Your qualifications, though impressive, are

Not, we must admit, precisely what

We had in mind. Would you care

To defend their relevance?

Indeed

Now your age. Perhaps you feel able

To make your own comment about that,

Too? We are conscious ourselves

Of the need for a candidate with precisely

The right degree of immaturity.

So glad we agree

And now a delicate matter, your looks.

You do appreciate this work involves

Contact with the actual public? Might they,

Perhaps, find your appearance

Disturbing?

Quite so

"You Will Be Hearing From Us Shortly" by U. A. Fanthrope appears in *Collected Poems 1978–2003* (Peterloo Poets, 2005). Printed with permission.

Questions

1. What does the title mean? Is it familiar to you?

2. What are the words or phrases that sit to the right (*Ah, Indeed, So glad we agree, Quite so*)? Why do you think the author put them there?

3. What do you know about the interviewer from the poem? What do you know about the interviewee?

4. Why do you suppose the interviewer is conscious of "the need for a candidate with precisely the right degree of immaturity"? What does this statement mean?

5. Why would the public find "appearance disturbing"?

6. Reread the whole poem. How do you feel about the situation presented?

7. With a partner, rewrite the poem as an actual interview. Make sure the interviewer's questions follow the rules presented in the chapter. Write complete responses for the interviewee. Conduct your interview for the class.

Reprimand Interview

Read the following summary of a reprimand interview and respond to the questions that follow.

My name is Edward Kleinhaus, and I work as a federal fire fighter on a military installation. My duties include regular rotation as dispatcher in the Fire Department Communication Center.

After being newly trained in the Communication Center, I failed to follow procedure in a dispatching sequence, which delayed a support unit's response to an emergency by approximately five minutes. No serious consequences occurred at the site of the emergency as a result of this error.

I was called into my supervisor's office at the end of my shift. I was handed a written reprimand stating my substandard performance during the stated emergency. My supervisor then briefed me on the seriousness of making an error as dispatcher and that my employment would have been terminated if the situation had been life threatening. I acknowledged my supervisor's statements and signed the written reprimand.

My supervisor then asked me if I was having any problems at home. I responded by saying that there was a lot on my mind as I was trying to organize my wedding, go to school full time, and work in a new position. My supervisor responded, "Don't bring your problems to work. Leave them at home."

Questions

1. What do you think was the goal of this interview?

2. From the summary you read, do you think the goal was achieved?

3. What mistakes, if any, did each participant make in the interview process?

4. With a partner, rewrite the conversation that took place during this interview. Then, act out the scene with one person playing Edward and the other playing the supervisor. Make sure you follow the suggestions presented in the chapter.

MAKING CONNECTIONS

Interviewing Applicants

Interview three people to gain information about how their job interviews compared to information in this chapter. Discuss climate, goals, roles, participation, and courtesy. Jot notes here.

_____

_____

_____

_____

_____

_____

Interviewing a Prospective Mentor

Interview someone who is in your desired career field. Ask for advice on how to get into the business, which educational courses to take, how to avoid common career pitfalls, and so forth. If this person is not willing or able to be a continual mentor for you, ask for names of people that he/she would recommend and find out how to approach those individuals. Take notes. Report your findings.

_____

_____

_____

_____

_____

_____

PROJECTS

Asking Questions

Working with a classmate, take turns reading the examples of communication stoppers and communication promoters. After one person reads the question, the other person must tell how the question makes him or her feel and then provide an answer.

Communication Stoppers

1. Puts the other person on the spot.
   "You haven't held any job for very long, have you?"

2. Tells the other person the answer he or she wants.
   "I'm expecting a good turnout from our department. Jane, will you be going?"

3. Asks for either "yes" or "no."
   "Are you going to apply for the job or not?"

4. Probes further than necessary.
   "Did you get a failing grade like the rest of us did?"

5. Arouses defensive behavior.
   "You didn't turn your report in on time again, did you?"

Communication Promoters

1. Is an open-ended question.
   "How did you feel when that happened?"

2. Clarifies the purpose.
   "Because we are considering a promotion for Thelma, we'd like your opinion of her work."

3. Starts from common ground.
   "Do you know about our retirement policy, or would you like a brief explanation?"

4. Comes from what the other person has already said.
   "Can you explain that a bit further?"

5. Focuses on what the person is feeling about what she or he is saying.
   "I wonder if you are feeling disappointed that your office staff does not appreciate your extra efforts."

Recognizing Communication Stoppers

Review the following list of questions. Enter "S" if the question is a communication stopper and "P" if the question is a communication promoter. Rewrite the communication stoppers to make them promoters.

____ 1. What happened at work today?

____ 2. How was your day?

_____ 3. What did you do to the fax machine?

_____ 4. Tell me about yourself.

_____ 5. What grade did you get?

_____ 6. Will you give me an example of that?

_____ 7. I think the other employee is absolutely wrong. What do you think?

_____ 8. Don't you love the new lobby decorations?

Role Playing an Interview

Working in small groups of three or more, you and a classmate will assume the roles of interviewer and interviewee. Other members of the group will serve as observers who will critique the interview.

1. In preparation for your turn in assuming the role of interviewee, select three questions of your choice from the lists on pages 110 and 115–116 and write them on a slip of paper.

2. Take a minute to think through the answers to these questions. Determine how you would reply if a prospective employer were to ask these questions.

3. Give your list of questions to your interviewer. Select one observer to be in charge of filling out the critique sheet on the following page. The observers should listen and watch carefully and take notes during the interview.

4. To start the role-play interview, the interviewer should introduce himself or herself and engage the interviewee in small talk to establish rapport. Then, the interviewer should ask one question from the list of three. The interviewee should answer as though in an actual interview situation.

5. The interviewer may ask follow-up, secondary questions based on the answer to the primary question. A skillful interviewer listens intently to the reply and asks the next question based on that reply. When the interviewer has completed exploration of a primary question, the interviewer may move on to the next question on the list.

6. Once all three questions have been discussed satisfactorily, the interviewer should terminate the interview in a skillful manner.

7. Review and discuss the feedback provided by the observers on your critique sheet.

8. Group members may then exchange roles and repeat the exercise. Continue until all in the group have assumed each role one time.

CRITIQUE SHEET FOR INTERVIEWEE

Interviewee: Give this page to your student evaluator before the interview.

Evaluator: On a scale from 1–10 (with 1 being "poor" and 10 being "excellent"), rate the interviewee on each of the following elements by circling the number of points awarded. Then, provide words of praise and suggestions for improvement in the comments section at the bottom of the sheet.

Total Possible Points: 100 (Items 2 and 3 count double the assessed value when calculating the total score.)

1. You are evaluated on the use of these speech tools.

   a. Perception—You understood the question, were prepared to present insight into yourself, and were able to see the interviewer's point of view.   1 2 3 4 5 6 7 8 9 10

   b. Language—You chose appropriate words, were fluent in expressing what you wanted to say, and were careful to find common language.   1 2 3 4 5 6 7 8 9 10

   c. Speaking—You were clearly audible to the whole group; seemed spontaneous, communicative, and enthusiastic; were descriptive and concrete in your answers; and used correct grammar and diction.   1 2 3 4 5 6 7 8 9 10

   d. Listening—You focused on the interviewer's questions and listened to and interpreted secondary questions well.   1 2 3 4 5 6 7 8 9 10

   e. Feedback—You used paraphrasing and clarifying questions to ensure understanding of the interviewer's secondary questions.   1 2 3 4 5 6 7 8 9 10

   f. Nonverbal Communication—You handled your voice and body so as to appear poised and in control. You paid attention to nonverbal clues from the interviewer.   1 2 3 4 5 6 7 8 9 10

2. You actively participated and carried an appropriate share of the conversation. (Double value)   1 2 3 4 5 6 7 8 9 10

3. You created a favorable impression through the way in which you presented yourself. (Double value)   1 2 3 4 5 6 7 8 9 10

Total Points: _____

Comments:

_____

_____

_____

_____

_____

_____

BPA Advanced Interview Skills

Opportunity for advancement is the reward earned for proven skills, dedicated work ethic, and accomplishment in the workplace. The up-to-date career portfolio serves as an important marketing tool when applying for a job or promotion.

Assume that you have been a dedicated bank teller at Charter Bank for six years. The bank hired you as a paid intern during your last two years of high school. After two years of work experience, you were promoted to lead bank teller, and you maintained that position throughout college. You will be receiving your business management degree in two months with a GPA of 3.8.

Charter Bank is building a new branch in your community, and you are applying for the manager position. You must create a resume, application letter, and career portfolio that highlight your strengths and accomplishments. The application letter should be addressed to Mrs. Connie Wichman, Human Resource Department, Charter Bank, 7786 Red River Street, Austin, TX, 78701. You will have the opportunity to sell your qualifications in a 15-minute job interview.

Performance Indicators Evaluated

- Demonstrate knowledge of job search skills.
- Apply technical writing skills to produce an application letter and resume.
- Demonstrate the ability to create and effectively use an employment portfolio.
- Demonstrate effective communication skills.
- Discuss an understanding of work ethics and environment.
- Define how your qualifications fulfill the needs of the management position.
- Demonstrate interpersonal skills.

For more detailed information, go to the BPA web site.

Think Critically

1. Why are high school and college internships important for career development?
2. What strengths and accomplishments should you highlight in your career portfolio?
3. What personal qualities should you highlight during the interview to land the manager position?

http://www.bpa.org/

Group Communication

Unit Objectives

After completing this unit, you should be able to

- Explain the factors that affect group dynamics.
- Identify ways in which groups make decisions.
- Differentiate between task-oriented and process-oriented speaking.
- Distinguish between positive and negative group behaviors.
- Identify the differences between informative and persuasive presentations.
- Apply the principles of debate.
- Demonstrate problem-solving and critical-thinking skills.

8. Speaking in Groups

CHAPTER OBJECTIVES

After completing this chapter, you should be able to

- Explain basic parliamentary procedure.
- Describe the two general types of meetings.
- Identify factors that affect group dynamics.
- Explain the various ways in which groups make decisions.
- Recognize the difference between task-oriented and process-oriented roles of group members.
- Describe common leadership roles in group meetings.
- Discuss leadership styles in terms of the degree of leadership control.

KEY TERMS AND CONCEPTS

socializing process	give-and-take meeting	process-oriented roles
parliamentary procedure	dynamics	autocratic style
main motion	consensus	persuasive style
one-way meeting	hidden agenda	democratic style
agenda	task-oriented roles	permissive style

IDEA BOX

Make a list of groups—both formal and informal—with which you meet at various times. Choose from the categories listed below. Then, focus on one of the groups and identify its goals—why do you meet? Think of one decision the group recently made. How did the group arrive at this decision? Did you participate in the interaction?

Clubs	Governing boards
Associations	Student government
Support groups	Professional unions
Committees	Work teams
Task forces	Sports teams

Group Speak

In studying speaking, you have learned about one-to-many presentations and one-to-one interactions, but it is equally important to consider how to interact with others in groups. Knowing how small groups operate will add an edge for success when communicating in a group situation.

Social Groups

Human beings like to gather and socialize—visit, chat, and laugh. Informal social groups are gatherings to celebrate, eat, have fellowship, or just talk. Social groups can be of almost any size and have no set rules for speaking.

Action Groups

Like interviews, group meetings are usually called for a purpose. People come together for common projects—citizens join action committees, elected officials meet to make laws, and members of interest groups team up to ensure their views are heard. Community members convene to support special activities, such as planning an awareness campaign or organizing a fundraiser. In size, action groups may vary from four or five to several hundred people. Action group meetings are held to achieve a goal, discuss an issue, propose a solution, or brainstorm new ideas. Because several individuals are involved, the talk is different.

When group members meet for the first time, they go through a **socializing process**—a time for getting acquainted and learning about each other. As a new member of a group, you may be uncomfortable until you discover the group's goals and how you can contribute to them. Don't be impatient with this sometimes slow introductory process. Listen to both the content and intent of the messages. Be honest when you express yourself, but be tactful and show respect for other points of view. Your listening skills must be highly focused as you pay attention to what others think and say. You will busily knit together the verbal messages to find out how people stand on the issues, what points of view they represent, and how you fit in. You may not say much in the beginning, but this is normal.

Action groups differ from social groups in that they have a specific goal to accomplish or problem to solve.

Rules for Conducting Meetings

When a large number of people are meeting, it is important to make sure each person has an opportunity to contribute. Some formal procedure is needed to ensure fairness. As in meetings of our Congress, state legislatures, and other important business groups, leaders of these sessions use parliamentary procedure to provide opportunity for everyone to be heard. **Parliamentary procedure** is a set of rules and practices used by large groups to maintain order during meetings. You will want to carefully review the basic principles in Figure 8-1 so you understand the premise of the procedure when you attend such a meeting. Specific terminology used to set up action (called a *motion*) is carefully followed. You will want to learn the appropriate expressions, such as "I make a motion to invite the guest speaker to our next meeting."

Basic Procedures

When a group member wants to open a topic for discussion, the member does so by getting permission to speak and then stating the

FIGURE 8-1 **Basic Principles of Parliamentary Procedure**

A meeting run according to parliamentary procedure is orderly and business-like. Group members are free to voice their opinions, but there are certain ways in which they should do so. Following is a brief summary of the basic principles presented in *Robert's Rules of Order*. Familiarity with these six basic principles will provide the foundation for understanding parliamentary procedure.

1. *Parliamentary procedure ensures equality.* All group members have equal rights, privileges, and responsibilities.

2. *The majority rules.* In most cases, the majority—or half the voting members plus at least one more—carries the vote. An exception can be made if a two-thirds or three-quarters majority is called for in connection with a particularly important or critical issue.

3. *The rights of the minority are protected.* No penalties are suffered for disagreeing, and everyone is allowed to speak, regardless of his or her opinion.

4. *One issue or question is discussed at a time.* A decision must be made on the issue at hand before another can be introduced.

5. *One person speaks at a time.* One person is recognized by the chairperson, or given permission to speak, at a time. If others want to speak, they must wait for the chairperson to recognize them.

6. *Free debate takes place.* Discussion can continue until the members choose to stop it. Debate on an issue can be limited or cut off only if two-thirds of the members agree to it.

topic. Another group member must voice approval by saying, "I move to accept this proposal." Yet another group member must approve by saying, "I second the motion." At that point, the issue is open for full discussion. An issue or question that is under discussion is called a **main motion**. It is usually a proposal (made and seconded) for some kind of action. Following discussion, the membership must vote on the motion. All group members vote on paper or by a show of hands. The chairperson then announces the outcome of the vote.

Personal
CHECK-UP

List four of the six basic principles of parliamentary procedure.

Other Kinds of Motions

During the discussion of a main motion, *subsidiary motions* may arise. These motions provide ways for handling the main motion. A group member might suggest changing the wording of the motion, establishing a committee to study the motion, postponing discussion until a later date, or calling for an immediate vote on the motion. All of these suggestions constitute a subsidiary motion, which a majority must approve.

Incidental motions relate to the normal course of business that takes place during discussion of a main motion. An incidental motion might be, "Mr. Chairman, I move to suspend the rules in order to hear our guest speaker at this time." Or, a group member who disagrees with the chairperson or who believes that the chairperson has made a mistake might say, "I appeal from the decision of the Chair."

As you can see, there are certain ways to say and do things within the structure of parliamentary procedure. It may take awhile to feel comfortable participating in meetings run in this way. The brief discussion provided here will help you know what to expect.

Group work sessions may be informal or formal, spontaneous or planned far ahead.

Types of Meetings

The purpose for which people meet often determines the rules of group conduct. There are generally two types of meetings—one-way situations in which a leader runs the session with little opportunity for interaction, and give-and-take sessions in which participants are expected to contribute. Whether business meetings are called conventions, seminars, committees, task forces, forums, or executive sessions, work groups meet to carry out company goals.

ONE-WAY MEETINGS A one-way meeting is called by a leader, such as a company supervisor, to provide information to others, such as subordinate employees, about business issues, benefits, or procedures. As leader, the supervisor provides an agenda—a planned list of items to be covered. The leader *presides over,* or conducts, the session and makes clear when it is appropriate for others to ask questions, contribute ideas, or give feedback. Some one-way meetings are less formal, with members taking turns to speak freely, although the group leader maintains control and manages the discussion.

GIVE-AND-TAKE MEETINGS For job-oriented problems or planning situations, coworkers may meet as work teams to combine their expertise. In a give-and-take meeting, group members are expected to speak up, listen, disagree, express their views, compromise, and reach consensus. Such groups, often called *task forces,* must develop leadership, contribute ideas and information, work out individual roles, and make decisions based on discussion. Within such a group, employees with a mixture of skills and knowledge may also have a variety of status levels and positions. For example, the group may include managers, engineering specialists, researchers, project directors, executives, and ground-level technicians. If many members of high status are within the group, you may feel intimidated about speaking up. You must remember that each person is present because of specialized know-how or a unique perspective to offer. Your input is valuable, and all team members are expected to contribute.

Even when employees from the same company assemble to work on a task force, they must go through a socializing process. An adjustment period for getting acquainted occurs as participants find ways of relating to each other. This early communication sets up patterns of behavior so that people can work smoothly together. This process is essential if interaction within a unified group climate is expected.

Factors Affecting Group Dynamics

If two heads are better than one, then certainly four to nine voices sharing ideas can be even more productive. Groups are important decision-making bodies that affect our lives. Learning to speak productively in a group meeting is a skill you will use all of your life. The more you know about how groups operate, the more comfortable you will feel about speaking up, sharing your ideas, and discussing issues.

Language trap

Don't say, "That's a very unique idea."
Say, "That's a unique idea."

Dynamics is a term that refers to physical forces causing energy and motion. As applied to a group of people, **dynamics** refers to the way people function together and interact with each other to make decisions or reach goals. Many factors affect group dynamics.

- **Size of the group**—The number of people present makes a difference. With a small number, members can interact with each other in face-to-face situations. Members get to know each other more quickly, and generally a more casual and open dialog develops. As group size increases, the more difficult the process becomes. More formal lines of communication must be established to maintain order and ensure everyone is heard.

- **Time**—Work groups need a block of time in which to work. Each employee takes time from individual responsibilities to serve in the group. If employees are not freed sufficiently from regular responsibilities to take time to engage in the process, they may feel pressure to produce a decision too rapidly and without proper consideration.

- **Place**—Critical elements in building a good working climate are the setting for the meeting and the arrangement of space. The room should be easy to locate and provided with proper lighting, heating/cooling, comfortable chairs, presentation tools, and so forth. If members are to participate as equals, a round table works best so that seating doesn't reflect status. Also with a round table, all members can more easily see and interact with each other. If the table is rectangular, members will tend to sit according to company position and status and interaction may become more formal.

- **Participants**—The people who form the group may themselves be the greatest force affecting the dynamics. The process of group interaction is complex. Pulling out ideas, discussing implications of each, comparing them to group goals, arriving at consensus, and getting along with others is a difficult set of tasks to juggle. Some people handle the process well, and others do not. Ineffective group participants may be misinformed, may listen poorly, may differ loudly in their opinions, or may be ill at ease and refrain from speaking. How well individual members are able to adapt and interact affects the group as a whole.

A round table helps all group members feel that they are equal participants who have valuable ideas to contribute to the group.

Personal
CHECK-UP

How can working
in a group be more
productive than
working alone?

- **Task**—The task at hand and members' attitudes toward it will affect the group dynamics. Everyone must fully understand the job to be done and the agenda. Some members may have volunteered to be part of the group because they feel passionate about the issue being addressed. Others may have been appointed and feel indifferent or even resentful. Still others may have selfish motives, concerned only about how being a part of the group or the group's decision will affect them personally.

- **Training**—How well members have been educated in techniques for team building and group decision making will also affect the group dynamics.

Group Decision Making

Group decisions can come about in a number of ways.

NEGATIVE DECISIONS When someone offers a suggestion for a solution or action and it is ignored by others, the idea dies for lack of support. Often, no further comments are made, and the group moves on, leaving the originator feeling rejected. While a suggestion may not in itself be a good idea, it could spark an idea from someone else. It is important that all ideas be encouraged. Negative decisions must be handled in such a way that the person who offers an idea doesn't lose self-confidence, or that person may never speak up again.

ONE-PERSON DECISIONS If an individual who is respected and trusted offers an idea, group members may not voice an objection, so a decision is made. This can also happen when an individual with recognized authority or prestige makes a statement or announcement. If no one disagrees, the decision is finalized.

TWO-PERSON DECISIONS When one person proposes an idea and another warmly supports it, it may become a group decision. The enthusiasm of the two members may be enough to prevent any objection. A decision slides through.

MAJORITY VOTE A decision made by a show of hands or voice vote is quickly finalized. The decision is made by the majority of votes. This method is widely used and accepted. However, it is important to allow ample opportunity for all views to be clearly expressed before voting and to show respect for those who were on the losing side of the vote. If some members are constantly on the losing side or are put down for their views, those members may withdraw from further discussions.

CONSENSUS TAKING **Consensus** means a harmonious agreement of all members. A feeling of cooperation must exist, and time must be taken for each person to share his or her views, provide additional information, question others, or add persuasive arguments. Full agreement requires adjustments in people's thinking, changes of attitude, and compromises—all of which may take time. It is important that members not feel threatened or rejected in the process of reaching a consensual decision.

"A compromise is the art of dividing a cake in such a way that everyone believes that he has the biggest piece."

—Ludwig Erhard

Negative Group Behaviors

All of us like to believe that decisions are logical, analytical, and based on sound reasoning and factual evidence. But, we also know that while people can be logical, they are also emotional, subjective, sensitive, and whimsical. This means behaviors may revolve around self-interest and frustrated needs. Because of this, an individual may come to a meeting with a **hidden agenda**, or a set of needs that are different from those of the group and its goal. These motivations may spring from the need for recognition, acceptance, or control. For example, someone who feels unimportant or unrecognized may constantly disrupt the work of the group in order to gain attention. Several negative roles can disrupt group work.

- The *withdrawer* does not participate or acts indifferent or bored.

- The *competer* clowns for attention, distracts the group from its task, aggressively takes control, or monopolizes the discussion.

- The *side-stepper* refuses to stick to the topic, interjects personal topics, argues minor points, or rejects responsibility.

- The *blocker* attacks the ideas of others or puts down their efforts as invalid or without value.

Consider your own behaviors. Should you recognize yourself here, consider what you can do to put your hidden agendas aside so that they don't get in the way of your group work. If you are frustrated by another's display of negative behaviors, try to figure out what the individual lacks and offer a constructive comment to fill the need.

Group behaviors are expressed through body language as well as through people's words. What kinds of communication do you see taking place in this photograph?

Member Roles

What should you do in a group? What should you say? As a group member, it is important that you play a part in the communication. A *member's role* is the behavior that the individual takes on in relation to other group members and to the group's task. When members take on the kinds of behaviors that get the assignment done, they are assuming **task-oriented roles**. When members take on roles that serve to smooth interactions and maintain relationships, they are assuming **process-oriented roles**. Both types of behavior contribute to a team effort.

Task-Oriented Roles

Are you someone who likes to know exactly what is supposed to be done and wants to "get on with it"? If so, you are task oriented. A task-oriented person may take on one or more of the following roles in moving a group toward a decision.

- An *initiator* starts communication, sets up procedures, defines terms, organizes ideas, and suggests solutions.

- An *information seeker* asks for factual material based on knowledge or experience.

- An *information giver* provides answers and sources of information for the group.

- An *opinion seeker* asks questions to gauge how members think or feel about a topic.

- An *opinion giver* states beliefs based on experiences and qualifies them as opinion.

- A *summarizer* pulls together ideas, restates general points, and tests group opinions.

- A *coordinator* clarifies ideas, rephrases, gives examples, and shows relationships.

COMMUNICATION AT WORK

In an increasingly complicated world of prescription drugs, pharmacy technicians like Albert Tavenor must communicate precisely with medical professionals as well as with customers. Albert works in a task-oriented role of information seeker when he confers with a doctor about a patient's prescription. If Albert knows the patient is taking a drug that counteracts the new medicine, Albert is an information giver. He serves as an initiator because he is willing to start the communication process. As a summarizer, Albert emphasizes the dosages and possible side effects, repeating this important information if necessary to be sure the message is understood. Albert also assumes a process-oriented role of climate maker when he provides friendly service to his customers.

©Getty Images/PhotoDisc

Process-Oriented Roles

A process-oriented person, on the other hand, wants to know more about the individuals on the team and draw contributions from all participants. The process-oriented person may take on one or more of the following roles to smooth the group process.

- A *harmonizer* avoids conflict, patches up misunderstandings, and reduces tensions.

- A *climate maker* creates a friendly, encouraging atmosphere.

- A *gatekeeper* brings others into the discussion, asks about feelings or reactions, and encourages others to speak.

- A *standard setter* sets the model for good listening and speaks to help the group remain objective.

Note that no one assigns task and process behaviors to a specific person. The descriptions simply indicate the verbal messages and observable actions that spring spontaneously from people interacting together. A single group member may take on many roles or serve a variety of functions during the course of a group discussion.

Leadership Roles

Many groups have a designated leader. A leader is responsible for calling meetings, setting the time and place, and preparing agendas. In business, employees may be group leaders because of their status or position, their knowledge level, or their personal qualities. During a meeting, the leader's roles may include

- Calling the meeting to order.
- Stating the purpose of the meeting.
- Helping to set group goals.
- Distributing information.
- Keeping the group focused on the topic.
- Working to resolve conflicts.
- Summarizing to help clarify issues.
- Dismissing the meeting.

Leadership Styles

People who lead meetings use a variety of approaches, ranging from strong to minimal control. The style of leadership can be determined by assessing the leader's level of control.

AUTOCRATIC STYLE A leader who uses the **autocratic style** exerts high control, makes decisions, and tells others what to do and how to do it. This efficient method minimizes wasted time, sets up a tight structure, and makes it easy to delegate details. The autocratic style gets results, but resentment can develop if people have no opportunity to interact or express feelings.

Personal CHECK-UP

What are some process-oriented behaviors you have observed that helped a group work more smoothly?

"Does anyone else have an opinion that should be kept to themselves?"

Team Players

You know about dynamics—the active, energetic forces at work in a group. When people are engaged in a group task, even a few egos can prevent the job from getting done. People who refuse to take leadership roles, who will not participate in membership roles, and/or who participate only out of self-interest prevent a team from accomplishing its goals. Learn to apply your strengths to help your group or team get its work done. The spotlight may not shine on you, but it may very well shine on your team.

PERSUASIVE STYLE A leader who exerts **persuasive style** may make a decision and then work to move the group to accept the decision, rather than forcing the decision on the group. The leader may initiate discussion, but members are expected to express viewpoints and concerns, contribute suggestions, and ultimately make a group decision. Members are usually more satisfied with the results of the decision because they have had the opportunity to air concerns, express their opinions, and offer input.

DEMOCRATIC STYLE A leader who uses **democratic style** may start the meeting, but members are expected to initiate discussion, suggest procedures, and make decisions. Members actively participate, decide on common efforts, evaluate results, and assume responsibility for decisions. The democratic leadership style may consume more time and rely on membership participation, but members are usually satisfied with the goals accomplished. Members tend to take more ownership of group decisions when actively involved in the decision-making process.

PERMISSIVE STYLE If a leader uses **permissive style** and offers little guidance, the discussion may drift and the group may never decide on common goals. If members are unwilling to make decisions or accept responsibility, little will be accomplished. Under a permissive leader, group members must step into roles that push the task forward and make the process work. If they do, agreement and a sense of accomplishment will result.

It would be a lonely business world if people did not interact on the job. Don't be surprised to find yourself employed in a position where your manager expects you to be a member of a decision-making group. Your knowledge of how work groups operate will help you contribute productively. Furthermore, your understanding of membership roles will help ensure that your group meets its goals.

> "The nice thing about teamwork is that you always have others on your side."
>
> —Margaret Carty

CHAPTER SUMMARY

Groups may form simply to socialize in an informal manner, or they may organize to accomplish a specific action. Parliamentary procedure is followed in large, formal groups to maintain order and to ensure that all have an opportunity to be heard. There are generally two types of meetings—one-way meetings in which one person presents information, and give-and-take meetings where people interact to share information and make decisions. The dynamics of group interaction are affected by the size of the group, the time allotted, the physical setting, the participants themselves, the task at hand and attitudes toward it, as well as team training. Styles of decision making are negative, one-person, two-person, majority vote, and consensus taking. Member roles can be categorized as task-oriented to get the assignment done or process-oriented to smooth group interaction. Leadership styles include autocratic, persuasive, democratic, and permissive, depending upon the amount of control the leader exerts.

CHAPTER REVIEW

1. Why is the socializing process important for a group?
2. List factors that affect group dynamics.
3. Briefly describe three ways in which groups make decisions.
4. What may cause individuals to display negative group behaviors?
5. How is an autocratic style of leadership different from a democratic style?

CAN YOU DEFINE THESE TERMS?

Match each description with the appropriate term. Write the correct letter in the blank preceding the sentence. Some terms will not be used.

Terms:

1. ___ A type of meeting called by a leader to provide information to others
2. ___ The way group members function together and interact with each other to make decisions or reach goals
3. ___ Roles assumed by group members that serve to move the task along and get the job done
4. ___ An individual's set of needs that are different from those of the group and its goals
5. ___ A planned list of items to be covered
6. ___ A harmonious agreement of all members
7. ___ Roles assumed by group members that serve to smooth interactions and maintain relationships
8. ___ Style in which the leader exerts high control, makes decisions, and tells others what to do
9. ___ An issue or question that is under discussion
10. ___ A set of rules and practices used by large groups to maintain order during meetings

a. agenda
b. autocratic style
c. consensus
d. democratic style
e. dynamics
f. give-and-take meeting
g. hidden agenda
h. main motion
i. one-way meeting
j. parliamentary procedure
k. permissive style
l. persuasive style
m. process-oriented roles
n. socializing process
o. task-oriented roles

APPLICATIONS

Assuming Task- and Process-Oriented Roles

TASK-ORIENTED ROLES The following member roles involve task-oriented behaviors relating to the job at hand and how it can be accomplished. Along with the description of each role is an example of what that individual might say to other group members. In the space below it, write another example.

1. An initiator starts communication, sets up procedures, defines terms, organizes ideas, and suggests solutions.
   "How can we find out about these student organizations?"

2. An information seeker asks for factual material based on knowledge or experience.
   "I'm sure the special activities director has a list. Does anyone know what the director's office hours are?"

3. An information giver provides answers or sources of information for the group.
   "I'm pretty sure Ms. Conroy has office hours starting at noon. She is usually there until five o' clock, when most of the special activities are over."

4. An opinion seeker asks questions to gauge how members think or feel about a topic.
   "Do you think just getting a list is enough? Shouldn't we contact all the organization chairpersons?"

5. An opinion giver states beliefs based on experiences and qualifies them as opinion.
   "Don't forget, we all have the same assignment. If everyone goes the same route, we'll just be repeating each other. My opinion is that we should be more original. We all have friends in various organizations. Why don't we check with them and then quote them in our report?"

6. A summarizer pulls together ideas, restates general points, and tests group opinions.

   "Okay, we can contact Ms. Conroy, approach the groups themselves, or go through our friends for information on how their organizations operate. What do you think, gang?"

7. A coordinator clarifies ideas, rephrases, gives examples, and shows relationships.

   "We are not sure if we need in-depth coverage of all types of school organizations, including athletic, music, science, political, and so forth. Are we also supposed to include the clubs that are mostly social? Is our goal to get a general overview of student organizations or a close look at a handful of clubs?"

PROCESS-ORIENTED ROLES The following member roles involve process-oriented behaviors that serve to increase team spirit, fill needs for recognition, and provide positive feedback. Along with the description of each role is an example of what that individual might say to other group members. In the space below it, write another example.

8. A harmonizer is someone who avoids conflict, patches up misunderstandings, and reduces tensions.

   "Kunio and Jared have good ideas. Let's try to work both of their suggestions into our plan."

9. A climate maker creates a friendly, encouraging atmosphere.

   "I'm looking forward to hearing what your buddy Chuck tells you about team meetings, Theo."

10. A gatekeeper brings others into the discussion, asks about feelings or reactions, and encourages others to speak.

    "You've been pretty quiet, Angelo. How do you feel about our plan?"

11. A standard setter sets the model for good listening and speaks to help the group remain objective.

    "It seems as if we're on the right track. Lila, could you go over that explanation one more time?"

Identifying Task- and Process-Oriented Roles

Some statements made by group members are task oriented and help to move the job along. Other statements are process oriented and help to involve all members and build team spirit and group unity. Read the statements below. Mark a "T" before the task-oriented statements and a "P" before the process-oriented statements.

_____ 1. "You haven't said anything, Ann. Do you agree with us?"

_____ 2. "That's a good idea, LaToya."

_____ 3. "We have considered the problem carefully. Are we ready to set up criteria for the solution?"

_____ 4. "Rodrigo, will you write these suggestions on the board?"

_____ 5. "Belinda, I don't think you have given Sue a chance to make her point."

_____ 6. "Are you saying that these are the long-term goals we should consider?"

_____ 7. "Mr. Herrera, will you give us the sales figures for the past six months?"

_____ 8. "I am inclined to go along with Andy on this issue."

_____ 9. "You sound as if you are unhappy with these suggestions."

_____ 10. "I can think of several solutions to this problem, but they will not meet any of the criteria we have set."

_____ 11. "What was that statement from *Business Week*?"

_____ 12. "Are we ready to make a recommendation?"

_____ 13. "What do you think, Mr. Washington?"

_____ 14. "What a great idea, Kirk! I never thought of it like that."

_____ 15. "Are we ready to vote?"

_____ 16. "Are you saying that there are two separate and distinct causes of this problem?"

_____ 17. "It seems as though we all agree on these two points. Right?"

_____ 18. "You seem to be supporting Matilda's idea, Reggie."

_____ 19. "Should we start by discussing the third point?"

_____ 20. "Wait a minute, Dante. I don't think that is what Jose means."

_____ 21. "Let me rephrase what we have said so far."

_____ 22. "How are we going to tackle this issue?"

_____ 23. "I don't know if we could start the plan that soon. What would the shipping department say, Elena?"

_____ 24. "You are suggesting that we put the plan into effect at the same time we inventory the warehouse?"

_____ 25. "Let's move on to the next point."

Self-Evaluation of Team Skills

To examine where you are right now in speaking successfully in group situations, take the following self-test. For each of the statements, circle the answer that best explains how you respond in a group situation.

1. I make an effort to be supportive and encouraging to other team members, even if I don't agree with what they are saying.

   Often　　　　　Sometimes　　　　　Occasionally　　　　　Never

2. I listen closely to what others say, and I ask for clarification if I am not sure what they mean.

   Often　　　　　Sometimes　　　　　Occasionally　　　　　Never

3. When another member of the group is disruptive or puts down other members' suggestions, I suggest a better approach.

   Often　　　　　Sometimes　　　　　Occasionally　　　　　Never

4. If I am critical of another member, I avoid personal remarks and concentrate on behaviors.

   Often　　　　　Sometimes　　　　　Occasionally　　　　　Never

5. If some members of the group are not participating in the discussion, I try to draw them out.

   Often　　　　　Sometimes　　　　　Occasionally　　　　　Never

6. I feel free to express my ideas and opinions.

   Often　　　　　Sometimes　　　　　Occasionally　　　　　Never

7. I am able to help people resolve their differences by getting them to listen to one another.

   Often　　　　　Sometimes　　　　　Occasionally　　　　　Never

8. I am able to find the common ground when two people disagree, and I can help them understand each other.

   Often　　　　　Sometimes　　　　　Occasionally　　　　　Never

9. I help keep the group on track by pausing to summarize what has been accomplished or agreed upon and what remains to be done.

   Often　　　　　Sometimes　　　　　Occasionally　　　　　Never

10. I observe the group's process and note when the discussion moves away from the group's purpose or goal.

    Often　　　　　Sometimes　　　　　Occasionally　　　　　Never

Add up your score. Give yourself 4 points for each "Often" answer, 3 points for each "Sometimes" answer, 2 points for each "Occasionally" answer, and 1 point for each "Never" answer. If your total is 35–40, you likely have excellent team skills. If your total is 25–34, your team skills are probably good, but you have room for improvement. If you scored below 25, you still have some work to do to become a successful team member!

MAKING CONNECTIONS

History

The rules of parliamentary procedure have a long history. Research to find out when and where they began, why they were started, and how they have changed.

_____

_____

_____

_____

_____

_____

_____

_____

Psychology

Research the phenomenon of groupthink. Write a short report explaining what it is and how it occurs. Provide one historical example of its negative effects. What, if anything, can you do to prevent it from occurring in groups in which you are involved?

_____

_____

_____

_____

_____

_____

_____

_____

PROJECTS

Competitive Container Corporations

In this activity, you will have the opportunity to practice communicating in groups. The class will divide into groups of seven to nine people to form small corporations that will develop a new product. The task of each corporation is to design and build "the world's best container" made of paper. Each group will select one member to assume the role of observer for the group and one member to serve as a sales representative. Your instructor will select three students who will not be part of the corporations, but will serve as judges for the entire class. Once assigned to a group/ role, follow the appropriate set of instructions on page 145, 146, or 147.

INSTRUCTIONS FOR GROUPS

1. Select one member to be an observer who will move outside the group and follow the instructions to observers on the next page.

2. You will need one set of the following materials—five sheets of heavy construction paper of various colors, two pairs of scissors, glue or paste, a stapler and staples, and cellophane tape.

3. You will have 30 minutes to construct the best possible container using only the materials specified. Do not begin until your instructor gives the okay.

4. The container will be judged on the basis of four criteria: (1) capacity, (2) aesthetics (design elements and attractiveness), (3) sturdiness, and (4) sales pitch.

5. Select one member to be a sales representative whose responsibility will be to take the container to the front of the room and present the finished product to the class and the judges. The sales representative will have three minutes to make a sales pitch.

6. While the judges add the individual scores and compare notes, listen as the group's observer provides feedback to the group based on the observations made.

7. Listen as the judges announce the results of the competition.

8. Answer the following questions.

   a. What effect did the time pressure have on your group?

   b. What kinds of behavior produced the actual container made by your corporation?

   c. What methods did your corporation use to resolve conflicts and lead to more effective production?

   d. How did your corporation discover individual talents that could be used in designing and building your container?

   e. How did you feel about competition between corporations?

   f. What were your personal feelings about winning or losing? How did you feel toward the judges?

INSTRUCTIONS FOR OBSERVERS

Use these questions as a guide for observing your group. Make notes on a separate sheet of paper as you observe. Try to answer most of the questions. Be prepared to make an objective oral report to your corporation after the sales pitches.

1. What kind of group decision (one-person, two-person, majority, or consensus) resulted in your selection as the observer? Speculate on why you were chosen. Ask for feedback from the group on this point.

2. What kind of decision making did the corporation use to choose its sales representative?

3. Who emerged in leadership roles? What behaviors did you note in the leaders?

4. What behaviors did you observe that indicated group cohesiveness (ability to work together)? Were there tensions? Was there withdrawal?

5. Which students assumed task-oriented roles and pushed to get the container designed and built?

6. Which students took on the process-oriented roles of soliciting input from others, repeating good ideas, supporting suggestions, and creating a friendly climate?

7. Whose ideas were used for the basic design of the container?

8. What kinds of behaviors helped in the creative aspects of the task (consider imagination, artistic ability, physical dexterity, and so forth)? Which students contributed in this way?

INSTRUCTIONS FOR JUDGES

You have been selected as an impartial panel of judges. Try to be as fair and objective in your decision as you can. Judge each container on the basis of (1) capacity, (2) aesthetics (design elements and attractiveness), (3) sturdiness, and (4) sales pitch. While the teams are building their containers, meet with the other judges and decide what proportional value each of the four criteria will have. You may give the sales pitch more value than capacity, for example, or rate them the same. Consider how you will determine each container's sturdiness.

Use the forms below to rate each group's container and sales pitch. You will each provide a separate rating for each category on a scale from 1–10. Total the ratings for each category, and then multiply each total by any assigned weight to compute the score for each category. Then, you will total the category scores for an overall total score. If there is a tie, resolve it through discussion. The corporation receiving the highest total from all the judges is the winner. The judges must announce their decision to the class.

Group: _____

Criteria	Ratings (Scale of 1–10)				Weight (Percentage)	Score (Ratings Total × Weight)
	Judge 1	Judge 2	Judge 3	Total		
Capacity						
Aesthetics						
Sturdiness						
Sales Pitch						
					Overall Total Score	

Group: _____

Criteria	Ratings (Scale of 1–10)				Weight (Percentage)	Score (Ratings Total × Weight)
	Judge 1	Judge 2	Judge 3	Total		
Capacity						
Aesthetics						
Sturdiness						
Sales Pitch						
					Overall Total Score	

Town Meeting

In this project, you will assume the role of a citizen of your town other than yourself. From that citizen's point of view, you will present in a town meeting what you perceive to be the "three most important goals for our town." As a group, you will discuss each citizen's presentation and arrive at consensus on the most important goals.

Instructions

1. Divide into groups of 10 to 12 members. Select a citizen role to play from the following list. Each person in your group must choose a different role.

   - The president of a local utility company
   - A teacher representing the public school teachers
   - A person representing a minority ethnic group
   - An active member of a labor union
   - The owner of a small business in the downtown area
   - A senior citizen over age 65
   - A middle-aged, lifelong resident of the community
   - A foreign student (short-term resident)
   - A retired military person
   - The manager of a chain store located in a suburban shopping area
   - An agricultural or environmental representative
   - A representative of the town's biggest industry
   - A social worker who works with people in a low-income housing area
   - The director of the local symphony orchestra
   - An elected official or any other representative of a group that exists in your town
   - An unemployed, homeless person
   - A young, single mother earning minimum wage

2. If possible, interview a person who fits the role in real life to get that person's perspective.

3. On the day of discussion, each group will conduct its own town meeting. Each citizen will make a brief statement to the group, introducing himself or herself in the citizen role and identifying three goals for the town and why they are important.

4. Each group will discuss the proposals and decide which three goals to recommend to the city council.

5. One member of each group will report the goals (listed by priority) to the class.

Questions

1. Did you find it difficult to step into the shoes of another person and present views that are different from your own?

2. What citizens from your group made the best presentations? Why?

3. What kinds of behaviors helped your group arrive at a consensus on selecting the three goals to present?

FBLA Emerging Business Issues

Together with one or two of your class-mates, work as a team to research one of the following emerging business issues. Find both affirmative and negative arguments for your topic. Be prepared to give a five-minute presentation from each viewpoint.

- High Salaries for Professional Athletes
- Fighting Terrorism Around the Globe
- Airlines Cut Back Customer Services
- Human Medical Makeovers

Ten minutes before your presentation time, you will draw to determine whether you will present an affirmative or negative argument. You will then have five minutes to finalize your presentation. Each presentation may last no more than five minutes. Presentations exceeding the time limitation will receive a five-point deduction. The judges will have five additional minutes to ask questions. Be prepared to defend your affirmative or negative argument.

Performance Indicators Evaluated

- Demonstrate research skills by citing credible sources of information.
- Define the purpose of the speech.
- Demonstrate an understanding of the topic.
- Communicate information backed by facts and examples.
- Demonstrate sound reasoning, analytical skills, and organizational skills.
- Present information with confidence.
- Demonstrate effective teamwork.

For more detailed information, go to the FBLA web site.

Think Critically

1. What group techniques from this chapter did you use to complete the assignment?
2. What group member roles did you and your team members play in completing the assignment?
3. How could your group have worked more effectively?

http://www.fbla.org/

Group Interaction

CHAPTER OBJECTIVES

After completing this chapter, you should be able to

- Identify three general purposes for speech presentations.
- Develop a purpose sentence and turn it into an appropriate thesis statement for a speech presentation.
- List and describe forms of informative speaking.
- Define three strategies used in persuasive speaking.
- Explain the rules and procedures for formal debate.
- Distinguish propositions of fact, policy, and value used in debate.
- List and describe steps in the problem-solving process.

KEY TERMS AND CONCEPTS

informative speaking	training	assertion
persuasive speaking	emotional appeal (pathos)	proposition
thesis statement	speaker appeal (ethos)	constructive argument
reports	logical appeal (logos)	cross-examination
briefing	debate	rebuttal

IDEA BOX

List each of the speeches you have given in this class. Jot down the key idea for each one. From the following list, determine the area of purpose that most closely applies to each speech.

To inform
To persuade
To entertain

Speaking with a Purpose

If you are like most people, you do a great deal of talking and listening in groups. In small, interactive groups, you probably do not consider in advance what you will say—your speech is a part of the general conversation with little planning. In a formal speaker–audience situation, the speaker has a specific purpose in giving a presentation, and careful planning is needed to ensure the purpose is effectively realized. Purposes of speech presentations can be divided into three general areas.

- **Informative speaking**, in which the speaker knows more about a topic than the audience and endeavors to share information in which the audience has interest.

- **Persuasive speaking**, in which the speaker tries to change listeners' thinking or urge them to take some kind of action.

- **Entertainment**, in which the speaker is invited to share humorous stories or provide remarks commemorating a person or event.

Stating a Purpose

Once you have chosen a speech topic, you will want to clarify your purpose. Do this by stating in one sentence what your topic is and what you want to accomplish. For example, "I want to demonstrate how to make Mexican wedding cookies." This is a *purpose sentence* for an informative speech. A purpose sentence for a persuasive speech might be, "I want all of our employees to have easy access to the necessary databases."

> **"A purpose statement is a note to yourself outlining what you hope to accomplish."**
>
> **—Ron Adler**

Creating a Thesis Statement

Turn your purpose into a **thesis statement** or key idea. Doing this simply involves restating your "I want" sentence into a specifically worded form that needs to be developed or explained. For example, the informative purpose sentence could become, "There are four steps to making Mexican wedding cookies." The persuasive purpose sentence might become, "To be productive, employees must have access to needed resources." When you word your sentence this way, the pattern for developing your idea becomes clear. Your thesis statement should be chosen with care, be repeated throughout your presentation, and resonate with the listeners.

Informative Speaking

Information is knowledge gained through communication, research, instructions, observation, and so forth. Types of information include the following.

- **Facts**—that which actually exists, something known to have happened, truth known through actual observation, and verifiable data.

- **Statistics**—the collection, analysis, and interpretation of numerical data.

- **Evidence**—that which tends to prove or disprove as grounds for belief.

- **Testimony**—the current opinion of respected experts.

The goal of informative presentations is to tell others what they do not know in a way they can understand. Informative presentations rely on accurate data collection, reliable research, and careful statements of observation. Informative speaking can take on a variety of forms, including reports, briefings, and training.

Reports

Essential to the business world, **reports** are organized presentations of factual information. They supply the results of investigations, testing, travel, or research projects. An oral report formally or informally conveys this information to people who need to know it. It is especially important for the speaker to acknowledge the source of the information—where it came from, who said it, or where it was found. Providing credit to outside sources helps an audience accept new information.

Reports come in many different types.

- **Statistical reports**—use more numbers than words.

- **Fact-finding reports**—present data based on research.

- **Research reports**—present the discovery of new information through searches, surveys, testing, or experimentation.

© 2004 Ted Goff

"It wasn't my fault. Someone put the wrong information in my notes, memos and letters to the customers."

Information

Information that's inexpensive or easy to acquire may be appealing, but it may not be what you need. And it may not be what your audience needs or wants to hear. Make sure that your information is appropriate to the topic and accurate. Use reliable, up-to-date sources, and keep track of them—you may need to refer to them again. If you use other people as sources of information, make sure they speak from their own experience and not from hearsay or speculation.

- **Progress reports**—present the status and work completed to date on a project at intervals until it's finished.
- **Analytical reports**—identify a problem, analyze data, cite a solution, and offer recommendations for action.
- **Technical reports**—convey information among specialists with similar training.

Briefings

A **briefing** is a short meeting in which precise instructions, a summary of goals, or essential information is given, often in preparation for an upcoming event. For example, fighter pilots are briefed before a mission and salespersons are briefed before they go out to sell new products. Whereas reports tell what has happened, briefings are about what will happen or what is expected. Briefings may fill in gaps of information for some and update information for others. Briefings are usually informal presentations with a great deal of interaction between the speaker and listeners. Such important presentations are delivered orally to provide open channels for feedback and questions.

Training

Training is the delivery of "how to" information in the form of instructions, explanations, or demonstrations. Training presentations are carefully organized to lead listeners step-by-step to a higher level of understanding. They usually begin with and build upon a common level of listeners' knowledge. These sessions are most helpful when the speaker and listeners can interact, allowing questions to be answered, and if appropriate, allowing supervised, hands-on practice.

Evaluating Effectiveness

Remember, the goal of informative speaking is to tell others what they do not know in such a way that they will understand. To check the effectiveness of your informative message, try to devise ways to obtain feedback—ask the audience questions, encourage comments, and involve the listeners in active participation.

Persuasive Speaking

Most speeches use information for more than just understanding. Persuasive techniques use selected information to help change an audience's views or behavior. This strategy is the basis of advertising and public relations. Sparkling television ads drum on your consciousness day in and day out. Designed to persuade a particular audience, advertising introduces a product—not just to inform customers, but to stimulate them to act on the information. Go buy it! Try it! The magic product will make you slimmer, stronger, healthier, and more beautiful.

Persuasive Purposes

Persuasion is one of the most important functions of language. By speaking persuasively, an individual can influence the words, ideas, or behaviors of other human beings. Much of what we see and hear is persuasive. As persuasive presentations seek to sway us, they have three different purposes.

- **To stimulate**—Sometimes, a speaker simply wants to stir up an audience to think differently, to open themselves to a new idea, or to reflect on an unusual concept.
- **To convince**—Through logical evidence and reasoning, a speaker may seek to change an audience's beliefs or attitudes.
- **To move to action**—A speaker proposes a particular way to behave and lays out a plan for the audience to follow.

SALES PRESENTATIONS One kind of persuasive business presentation is a *sales presentation*. During a sales talk, the speaker wants to move listeners to buy, subscribe, sign up, or act in a specific way. To create an audience need or desire for a product, sales speakers almost always show the item and demonstrate its qualities. For an audience, seeing the actual object doubles the impact of hearing about it. Well-planned visual aids are valuable assets to a business presentational speaker.

> **"A speech is designed to get audience reaction, to make the audience a partner in the enterprise."**
>
> **—Percy H. Whiting**

PROPOSALS In another type of persuasive business presentation—a *proposal*—the speaker seeks a favorable response for an idea or suggestion. When presenting and supporting a proposal, speakers must make the presentation seem sensible to the audience. They must anticipate opposing views and have answers ready when objections arise.

GOODWILL TALKS A *goodwill talk* may be a presentation delivered outside the company to represent its views, improve its reputation, or establish a positive attitude toward company policies. Goodwill talks can also be motivational speeches delivered within the company to stimulate enthusiasm for company goals or policies.

FIGURE 9-1 Speech purposes may vary

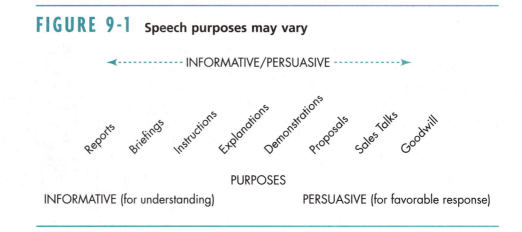

Speakers use three strategies to achieve persuasive purposes.

- Emotional appeal (pathos)
- Speaker appeal (ethos)
- Logical appeal (logos)

Emotional Appeal (Pathos)

In an **emotional appeal (pathos)**, a speaker plays on audience members' personal needs for survival, good health, safety, appreciation, and recognition. Consider current advertisements. Sparkling television commercials launch their appeals with color, movement, dance, and celebrities. A speaker must rely on vivid language, personal anecdotes and stories, descriptions, and comparisons. By personalizing the benefits of the proposal, the speaker can win acceptance for it.

Speaker Appeal (Ethos)

With **speaker appeal (ethos)**, an audience may accept a message simply because of the speaker's personal qualities and attractiveness. If a speaker has *credibility*, or appears believable, that may be all that is needed. Credible speakers display the following characteristics.

- **Competence**—The speaker is thoroughly prepared with evidence, personal illustrations, and facts backed by cited sources of information. The speaker is willing to explain difficult ideas or concepts, thereby building belief in the speaker's expertise.

- **Trustworthiness**—The speaker comes across as sincere with no selfish motives in terms of the outcome of the proposal. A trustworthy speaker communicates in a caring way and works to build a *rapport,* or a harmonious relationship, with listeners.

- **Poise**—Standing erectly, making eye contact, and projecting the voice all clearly contribute to the appearance of poise and confidence. The speaker talks fluently but with control. The speaker's mannerisms, posture, gestures, and ideas all get positive responses.

- **Enthusiasm**—The speaker seems friendly, outgoing, and spontaneous, as well as excited about the ideas presented and the opportunity to speak to the group.

Logical Appeal (Logos)

With **logical appeal (logos)**, you appeal to listeners with critical thinking and sound reasoning. Suppose you wanted to convince an audience to join you in signing a petition on an issue. You would first think critically to generate ideas, discover reasons, explore possible consequences, and imagine future events. The logical side of your mind would busily determine which ideas fit your purpose and which should be discarded. Then, you would employ the powerful tool of language to provide logical reasons for why these strangers should sign.

Personal
CHECK-UP

When you try to persuade a friend of something, which of the three strategies do you find most comfortable to use? Cite a personal example.

"An audience will forgive a speaker almost any lack if he is manifestly earnest about his proposal."
—James Winans

Principles of sound reasoning will help in a logical appeal—fitting ideas together, seeing one event as cause of another, perceiving one concept to be more significant than others, and recognizing similarities and differences. A cause and effect may seem straightforward at first, but to convince an audience, you must take into account what they know and believe. You might acknowledge what is readily observable and can be pointed to, and then lead the audience to recognize coincidence and alternate causes that exist.

Two techniques help to develop reasoning—question making and debate. You have already learned about question making. Remember, open-ended questions are valuable because they lead to higher-level, abstract thinking. "How would you feel . . . ?" "What if you . . . ?" These questions make both the questioner and the audience treat subject matter in new ways.

Debate

Debate is the discussion of an issue through the consideration of opposing arguments. In *formal debate,* a prescribed set of rules and times is followed. There is first an **assertion**, or a claim that something is true. It is given in the form of a statement to be argued called a **proposition**. A debate has two sides—the *affirmative side* that supports the proposition or claim, and the *negative side* that attacks the proposition. During debate, each side will present a **constructive argument**, or logically planned presentation in support of its view.

Beginning debaters must keep the following guidelines in mind.

- Assertions must be supported with valid evidence.
- Sources of information must be accurate and documented (title, author, and date).
- Chains of cause and effect must be logical.

The negative side will have an opportunity to ask questions, called a **cross-examination**. The negative side will give its constructive argument in support of its opposing viewpoint, followed by the affirmative side's opportunity for cross-examination. Then both sides, in turn, may give a **rebuttal**—a speech that serves to refute or disprove the other side's arguments. The rebuttals are followed by a second round of cross-examinations and final rebuttals.

Formal debate teams are usually made up of two people on each side of the argument. Each side must listen closely to the other. Debaters should learn about both sides of a proposition in order to effectively defend their positions. The person holding the negative position does more than refute the affirmative position—he or she presents a constructive argument on the opposite side of the proposition.

Skilled judges evaluate formal debates, and either the affirmative or negative side is chosen as the winner. The judges look for several things.

"*A clear statement is the strongest argument.*"

—English Proverb

- An argument supported by facts, examples, and proofs
- Accurate statistical analysis
- Related cause and effect
- The reliability of the information sources
- The relevancy of the information to present circumstances and the current state of knowledge

Debate may also occur in other settings. It may be defined as a formal discussion of a motion before a deliberative body according to the rules of parliamentary procedure. Or, it may be an informal discussion of a question by members of a group. In any setting, propositions are stated and argued to assist with decision making. Propositions may be statements of alleged fact, policy, or value.

PROPOSITIONS OF FACT With a proposition of fact, you assert that something has actually happened or actually exists. For example, "Our recent ad campaign is paying off in increased profits." For such a statement, you would determine what data are required to prove the alleged fact, such as actual sales figures before and after the campaign started. The opposing side might offer alternative reasons for the increased sales and show data gathered from surveys that show negative consumer responses to the ads.

PROPOSITIONS OF POLICY Propositions of policy relate to the design and implementation of actions, rules, laws, or regulations, such as those determined by governmental agencies. Laws that involve spending, order keeping, and domestic concerns are questions of policy, whether

©Digital Vision

Debates can be as formal as a competitive team event or as informal as a discussion among business colleagues.

national or local. For example, "Should the U.S. government exercise secret wiretapping during wartime?" A policy debate may also be over issues involving decisions for future actions. For example, members of a fund-raising organization might ask, "Should we raise funds by selling door-to-door, or should we conduct a telephone campaign?" The argument focuses on the best way to proceed.

PROPOSITIONS OF VALUE Propositions of value are judgments about the qualities of persons, events, ideas, places, or things. For example, "Does John Martin Andress deserve a promotion over other employees?" Propositions of value may be based on opinions and attitudes and grounded on accepted truths. "Should tax money be used for medical research?" These debates use less emphasis on statistically based evidence and more on social, political, and humanistic values.

Problem Solving

Working in groups to resolve a problem can be most productive when all participants agree upon a pattern of step-by-step discussion as a guide. Here, both informative and persuasive speaking fit into a rigorous discussion when the climate and leadership permit. The problem-solving process includes the following steps.

1. **Analyze the problem.** The general topic will need to be narrowed down or divided into several aspects. The statement, "How can we encourage more people to be blood donors?" does not clarify the problem. It could be restated as, "Voluntary donors are not filling the requirements for needed blood," or "People are afraid of giving blood." Asking the following questions can help to clarify a problem.

COMMUNICATION AT WORK

After graduation from his community college, Juan Martinez joined the Alumni Association and volunteered to help with various projects. Before long, he found himself as head of the fundraising committee. He is often called upon to "say a few words" at luncheons and banquets all around town. His goal, of course, is to raise money for the college. Juan approaches his different audiences in a variety of ways. For an audience of fellow alumni, he reminds them of the value of their education and uses emotional appeals, calling up fond college memories. For other audiences, he uses businesslike appeals to convince listeners that supporting the college is a worthwhile community investment for everyone. At a recent senior citizen event, Juan was so poised and believable that the group was motivated to create a scholarship for deserving students.

©Getty Images/PhotoDisc

a. Whose problem is it?
b. What are the basic causes?
c. How do we know something needs to be changed?
d. What are the symptoms?
e. What effects are created by the problem?

2. **Set up criteria for an ideal solution.** To defuse disagreements about solutions, take a few minutes to define the ideal solution—which of course does not exist. Describe how all would like the situation to be resolved. Ideally, the solution will
a. Not cost more in time and money than the problem.
b. Be practical to put into effect.
c. Reduce the major causes of the problem.
d. Satisfy everyone involved.
e. Not create greater problems than the one it solves.

3. **List possible realistic solutions.** Brainstorm possible solutions. From the list that results, select two or three of the most practical solutions for further discussion.

4. **Evaluate chosen alternatives against the criteria.** It is likely that all alternatives will have merit and that no one alternative will meet all criteria. By comparing the selected solutions against the criteria, the pros and cons of each can be weighed.

5. **Select a solution to recommend.** If the problem is carefully analyzed and the group agrees on the most important criteria that must be met, members can agree upon a solution.

©Digital Vision

Groups that follow the steps in the problem-solving process will find effective solutions that benefit all involved.

CHAPTER SUMMARY

A speech presentation requires careful planning in order to achieve the desired purpose—to inform, persuade, or entertain. Informative presentations may be in the form of reports, briefings, and training sessions. Persuasive speaking seeks to change listeners' attitudes or behavior. Persuasive strategies may take the form of emotional (pathos), speaker (ethos), or logical (logos) appeals. Emotional appeal plays on audience needs and personalizes the benefits of the proposal. Speaker appeal is based on the credibility of the speaker. Logical appeal calls on critical thinking and sound reasoning. Debate is the discussion of an issue through the consideration of opposing arguments. In formal debate, a specific set of rules and timing is followed. The proposition to be argued may be one of fact, policy, or value. In a debate, judges declare a winner based on logical reasoning and the presentation of relevant facts supported by credible sources. The group problem-solving process includes analyzing the problem, setting up criteria for an ideal solution, listing possible realistic solutions, evaluating alternatives against the criteria, and selecting a solution to recommend.

CHAPTER REVIEW

1. Write a purpose sentence, then turn it into a thesis statement.
2. Name three forms of informative speaking.
3. List three purposes of persuasive speaking.
4. What characteristics do credible speakers display?
5. What do judges look for when choosing the winner of a formal debate?

CAN YOU DEFINE THESE TERMS?

Match each description with the appropriate term. Write the correct letter in the blank preceding the sentence. Some terms will not be used.

Terms:

1. ___ The speaker endeavors to share information in which the audience has interest
2. ___ The discussion of an issue through the consideration of opposing arguments
3. ___ The speaker tries to change listeners' thinking or urge some kind of action
4. ___ A logically planned presentation in support of one's view of a proposition
5. ___ Organized presentations of factual information
6. ___ A speech that serves to refute or disprove the other side's arguments
7. ___ The delivery of "how to" information in the form of instructions, explanations, or demonstrations
8. ___ A statement to be argued
9. ___ A claim that something is true

a. assertion
b. briefing
c. constructive argument
d. cross-examination
e. debate
f. emotional appeal (pathos)
g. informative speaking
h. logical appeal (logos)
i. persuasive speaking
j. proposition
k. rebuttal
l. reports
m. speaker appeal (ethos)
n. thesis statement
o. training

APPLICATIONS

Questions of Fact, Policy, or Value

Propositions are stated and argued to assist with decision making. It is helpful to know whether you are dealing with facts and information, a matter of policy, or a question of opinion and values. Working with your group, study the examples below. Then read the numbered questions, discuss them, and identify each as a question of fact (F), policy (P), or value (V).

Examples

- A question of fact can be answered "yes" or "no" based on factual evidence.
  "Are our present prevention measures working to reduce our shoplifting problem?"
- A question of policy asks for a policy change or a better plan.
  "Shall we take further measures to reduce shoplifting in our store?"
- A question of value asks the worth of a method.
  "Which method will do a better job of stopping our shoplifting losses—hiring security guards for all exits or putting sensor clips on merchandise?"

Questions

_____ 1. Would it be more profitable to raise the price or to cut production?

_____ 2. Is the skateboard fad on its way out, or shall we continue production?

_____ 3. Shall we continue with our late closing time or try opening the salon on Sunday?

_____ 4. What percentage of our profits was derived from our overseas operations?

_____ 5. Which of these two individuals will be more valuable to our school—a risk taker with creativity or a talented administrator?

_____ 6. How much will we save if we recruit volunteers to serve dinner at the homeless shelter rather than hiring paid staff?

_____ 7. Is it worthwhile for us to change our policy and start buying plumbing supplies in bulk?

_____ 8. How can our construction company implement the new safety regulations?

_____ 9. Do we have the resources and assets to become a franchised operation?

_____10. Shall we restrict the operation of our campus bookstore?

Purpose Sentences to Thesis Statements

What is it you want your audience to know, think, feel, or do when you have finished your presentation? The answer is a purpose sentence that will help keep your preparation on track. Read the following purpose sentences and identify them as either informative (I) or persuasive (P). Then, in the space below each sentence, restate it as a thesis statement. Remember, thesis statements are memorable statements that will catch an audience's attention, focus on the main idea or purpose, and bear repeating several times in a speech. Be brief, be simple, but be creative.

___ 1. I want to convince the employees that buying company stock is a wise financial move for them to make.

___ 2. I want to persuade the audience to take their clothes to Sun Dry Cleaners next time.

___ 3. I want to describe the uses of Fiber Seal to the audience.

___ 4. I want to stimulate class members to consider working for city government.

___ 5. I want members of my audience to sign up for a free flying lesson.

___ 6. I want to demonstrate the way to test blood sugar level.

___ 7. I want to explain the steps in preparing a resume.

___ 8. I want to convince the audience that gas engines can be converted to propane fuel.

___ 9. I want our employees to invest in paging services.

___10. I want to demonstrate how to analyze a financial statement.

 Famous Lines

If someone asks, "What did he talk about?," can you answer with a clear, ringing, memorable phrase from the speech? You can if the speaker chooses to use or repeat a phrase that resonates with the listeners. Identify the speakers of the following memorable statements. Use the Internet to locate the speeches that aren't familiar to you.

1. "Ask not what your country can do for you . . ." _____

2. "I have a dream." _____

3. " . . . the only thing we have to fear is fear itself." _____

4. "It takes a village." _____

5. "Mr. Gorbachev, tear down this wall!" _____

6. "Just say no." _____

7. "Duty, honor, country." _____

8. "I consider myself the luckiest man on the face of this earth." _____

9. " . . . the chance for a just peace for all peoples." _____

10. "One small step for man, one giant leap for mankind." _____

11. "Four score and seven years ago, . . ." _____

12. " . . . but as for me, give me liberty or give me death." _____

MAKING CONNECTIONS

History

In the area of debate, you will frequently hear "Lincoln–Douglas" debates mentioned. The reference is to the famous arguments between Abraham Lincoln and Stephen Douglas. Use the Internet to discover information about the confrontations between the two men; their topics, style, and propositions; and so forth. Plan an oral report to your class. Jot notes here.

_____

_____

_____

_____

_____

_____

_____

Political Science and Technology

Presidential candidates are often involved in debates with their opponents. Research the rules of presidential debates and compare them to the rules of formal debate described in the chapter. Also, explain how the growth of technology has affected the ways in which presidential debates have been conducted over the years.

_____

_____

_____

_____

_____

_____

_____

PROJECTS

Problem-Solving Discussion

Working with a group, take 20 minutes to decide on a problem to discuss and solve. For example, "How can we encourage more people to be blood donors?" You will have research time to prepare for your discussion. You will have 30 minutes to work on solving your problem, so it should be one that has no clear answer and will encourage a good deal of discussion. Write your topic in the form of a question and submit it to your instructor. Do not discuss solutions to the problem at this time.

Thirty-Minute Discussion

You have 30 minutes to discuss your topic in your group. Your teacher or a class member will evaluate your discussion, using the critique sheet on the following page. Write your topic and the names of group members on the board or on a flipchart. Organize your discussion as follows.

- **10 minutes**—Identify the problem. Define terms as needed. Identify causes, symptoms, and effects of the problem. Whose problem is it? Be specific about why the issue is a problem. For example, "Lack of blood donors has caused a dangerously low blood supply in area hospitals."

- **5 minutes**—Set up criteria for an ideal solution. Think of how you would like the problem to be solved if the ideal solution could exist. Each group member should be prepared to contribute ideas. One person should write the ideas on a chalkboard or flipchart.

- **2 minutes**—Brainstorm possible solutions and list them on the board or flipchart.

- **10 minutes**—From the list, select two or three of the most practical solutions for further discussion. Compare them to the criteria you established for the ideal solution. Discuss the strengths and weaknesses of each one.

- **3 minutes**—Make a final group decision as to which solution the group will recommend.

Process

- Sit around a table so that all group members face each other.
- Establish a comfortable climate.
- Share the recording of information on the board or flipchart with other group members rather than having just one person do it.
- Try not to make negative judgments about others' ideas without first stating a positive attitude.
- Paraphrase each other's statements to check understanding.
- Try to move the discussion along, but give everyone a chance to contribute. Draw out the quiet group members. Recognize the ideas of others. Listen to each other.

GROUP CRITIQUE SHEET—PROBLEM-SOLVING DISCUSSION

Give this form to your instructor or evaluator before the group discussion.

Subject of Discussion_____

Possible Points: 100 (Each item is worth 5 points.)

Knowledge and Content

_____   Stated topic clearly.

_____   Presented adequate and relevant information.

_____   Gave thoughtful consideration to topic; cited sources.

_____   Stayed close to the topic.

_____   Had a sense of direction in handling material.

Emotional Climate

_____   Was animated and lively when speaking and reacting.

_____   Used good verbal and nonverbal interaction.

_____   Brought satisfying resolution to clashing ideas.

_____   Showed positive attitudes toward members' contributions.

Involvement and Participation

_____   Shared the speaking roles evenly.

_____   Cooperated in leadership and participant roles.

_____   Showed interest in presenting and supporting ideas.

_____   Asked questions, paraphrased, listened to each other.

Use of Time

_____   Moved the discussion along.

_____   Kept within the limits of time but was not pressured.

_____   Differentiated between problem and solutions.

_____   Used the criteria as a basis for judging solutions.

Achievement of Goal

_____   Understood the group goal.

_____   Was prepared to participate and discuss.

_____   Arrived at a solution through consensus.

_____   **Group Total**

Practice Debate

You will be part of one of four groups. Your group will be given a value proposition relating to the solutions recommended in the previous group discussion or one that the instructor chooses. Half of your group will take the affirmative position, and the other half will take the negative position. You will construct arguments supporting your position using theories, examples, facts, and statistics. These will be presented in three-minute speeches. You may use the outline form on the next page to prepare your speech. Each speaker will be cross-examined by a member of the other side, and each side will have an opportunity for rebuttal.

Suggested Times

3 minutes   Affirmative Constructive Argument

2 minutes   Negative Cross-Examination

3 minutes   Negative Constructive Argument

2 minutes   Affirmative Cross-Examination

2 minutes   Affirmative Rebuttal

3 minutes   Negative Rebuttal

2 minutes   Affirmative Cross-Examination

2 minutes   Negative Cross-Examination

1 minute   Affirmative Rebuttal

JUDGES Class members may act as judges and declare winners. Judges should take notes on the lines below during the debate and be able to justify their decisions.

_____

_____

_____

_____

_____

_____

_____

_____

_____

_____

_____

_____

_____

OUTLINE FORM FOR AN INDIVIDUAL DEBATE SPEECH

Topic _____

I. Introduction

(Attention Step) A. _____

(Definition of Terms) B. _____

(Thesis Statement) C. _____

II. Body of Speech

(Fact One) A. _____

(Example) 1. _____

(Statistics) 2. _____

(Fact Two) B. _____

(Example) 1. _____

(Statistics) 2. _____

(Fact Three) C. _____

(Example) 1. _____

(Statistics) 2. _____

III. Conclusion

(Summary) A. _____

(Call to Action) B. _____

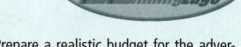

DECA Advertising Campaign

Together with one or two of your classmates, prepare an advertising campaign of any length for a real product, service, company, or business of your choosing. You must select the media for the campaign and determine an appropriate advertising budget.

Your campaign will be limited to a total of ten written pages. Visual aids are permitted. You will have fifteen minutes to present your campaign to prospective clients/advertisers (judges). The judges will be allowed an additional five minutes to ask questions. The presentation will be judged for effectiveness of persuasive speaking, presentation skills, and response to the judge's questions.

Performance Indicators Evaluated

- Develop objectives of the advertising campaign.
- Prepare a realistic budget for the advertising campaign.
- Design an effective advertising campaign.
- Demonstrate continuity and logical order in the advertising campaign.
- Communicate your campaign using persuasive language.
- Demonstrate group problem-solving skills.

For more detailed information, go to the DECA web site.

Think Critically

1. What type of appeal (pathos, ethos, logos) would you recommend using in this advertising campaign? Why?
2. What visual aids would be good support materials for an advertising campaign?
3. What strategy should team members use to ensure a smooth presentation?

http://www.deca.org/

Communicating with an Audience

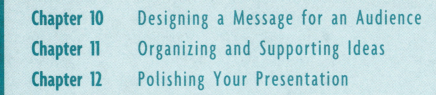

Unit Objectives

After completing this unit, you should be able to

- Describe the steps in preparing a speech presentation.

- Explain the process of and need for audience analysis.

- Identify sources of information used to develop a topic.

- Recognize organizational patterns and supporting materials for speeches, and explain how to use them.

- Develop effective visual aids that add interest and meaning to a presentation.

- Identify styles of speech delivery.

- Demonstrate appropriate body language and gestures to use in a well-delivered speech.

- Describe strategies for handling question-and-answer sessions.

10 Designing a Message for an Audience

CHAPTER OBJECTIVES

After completing this chapter, you should be able to

- Differentiate between general speeches and business presentations.
- Identify the first steps in speech preparation.
- Discuss the purpose and use of a clustering list.
- List the questions to ask yourself when preparing an audience analysis.
- Describe sources of information for a speech presentation.
- List criteria for evaluating Internet sources.
- Explain the importance of properly referencing and crediting sources of information.

KEY TERMS AND CONCEPTS

clustering list	personal esteem	electronic database
audience analysis	self-actualization	search engine
physiological needs	periodicals	plagiarism
social needs	index	

IDEA BOX

Not every audience is the same. Think of the demonstration speech you gave to your classmates. Would you give it the same way if you were asked to deliver it to one of the groups listed below? What kinds of changes would you make? Could you use the same information? What would you do to make your speech more appealing to the new group?

A class of grade school students
A group of senior citizens
A political convention
A group of tour agents
A baseball team

Successful Speaking

Language trap

Don't say, "Ya'll" or "you guys" in formal speech situations. Say, "You" or "all of you."

Remember the discussion on stage fright? One of the basic fears of any speaker is the possibility of not connecting with the audience. No one likes to be seen in a bad light or to feel failure. Knowing how to prepare an effective oral presentation will eliminate that fear. One of the best ways of preparing is to design your speech for the particular audience that will be addressed.

A successful speaker has something to say—a purpose. A speaker should not just be filling time so the civic group, for example, can have a luncheon program. Ideally, the speaker has a specific and useful message designed for the particular group of listeners. It would not be fair to have a captive audience spend time listening to someone who is rambling with no sense of direction. A prepared speaker has a purpose and can write it down. Before a speaker settles on a purpose, several things should be considered in relation to the situation, audience, and topic.

Differences in Speaking Situations

The word "speech" can be used as a general term for communicating orally in any situation. However, "speech" can take on more specific connotations, especially when combined with certain other words.

INFORMAL SPEECH When asked to "give a speech," it usually means that you will stand before a group of people and talk to them or perhaps with them. It is often thought of as a *talk* when the setting is informal. The audience may be a group of people who meet regularly—some of whom you know, whereas others may be strangers. You may be speaking to inform them of something you want them to know, to explain something that they want to understand, to persuade them to think differently, or to challenge them to act in a certain way.

PUBLIC SPEECH PRESENTATION A *public speech presentation* is an oral message given in a formal setting in which anyone is free to attend. Because the speech is open to the public, a variety of listeners may be present. Purposes may be the same as for an informal speech, but adding the word "presentation" gives a more formal connotation. Preparation for a public speech may require a good bit of research for information and the creation of supporting visual materials.

ORAL BUSINESS PRESENTATION An *oral business presentation* may be given internally to others within the same company or externally to clients, customers, agencies, or government representatives. These often involve *proposals* directed to a decision-making body. Business presentations are very formal and usually rely on visual materials, such as graphs, flowcharts, and storyboards, to present data and ideas in a meaningful way. Supporting visuals may be presented with Power-Point® slides, electronic white boards, or other special electronic equipment.

"To succeed in business, it is necessary to make others see things as you see them."

—John H. Patterson

Whether an informal speech, a public speech presentation, or an oral business presentation, the speaker is charged with

- Preparing for oral speaking before a group.
- Analyzing the audience and the occasion.
- Having a clear purpose.
- Researching and organizing the material to be presented.
- Adding visual support whenever possible and appropriate.
- Delivering in an informative or persuasive manner.

First Steps in Speech Preparation

Before you decide on a subject or plan a speech purpose, you have some preliminary thinking to do. Remember that the communication model includes a speaker, a receiver, and a variety of ideas in each person's brain to be communicated, one to the other. In an audience situation, one person talks and interaction may be minimal. Subtle *nonverbal feedback* may be given in the form of facial expressions, sitting positions, and eye contact. These clues may be your only indication of whether your receivers are processing your message or dreaming in another world. To ensure that your receivers are upright, focused, and showing facial expressions that indicate pleasure, curiosity, or deep interest, you must have a plan.

CONSIDER THE SETTING, OCCASION, AND AUDIENCE If you have accepted an invitation to speak to a group, write down the time, place, and date—you don't want to forget to show up! Then, take time to size up the actual situation in which you will be giving your presentation.

Language trap

Don't say, "Let's divide the tasks between the group."
Say, "Let's divide the tasks among the group."

1. **Check the setting.** Be sure to know the address, building, floor, and room number where you will be speaking. Plan how will you get there and where you will park. Check out the room ahead of time if at all possible. Note its size, the seating arrangement, the podium placement, and the presence of any large plants or other objects that might block the view. Is the room equipped with the technology needed for your supporting visuals? If not, make arrangements to have it equipped for your presentation.

2. **Pay attention to the occasion.** Will you be speaking to your group during one of its regular meetings, or is this a special occasion? Will a meal be served while you are speaking, will there be a short break for refreshments, or will there be a reception afterward? Know how your speech will fit into the event. Will you have a time limit? Ask what will precede your speech—will it be a long business meeting, a lunch, or other speakers? The answer will provide an indication of how ready your audience will be to hear you. Also, consider what will follow your presentation.

3. **Size up your potential audience.** *How many* people are expected to be there? Realistically figure out the number of people you'll be facing. This may save you disappointment when fewer show up or panic when twice as many appear. *Why* are people coming—is this a regular civic club meeting, a community organization, a fundraiser, or a volunteer group, or are they coming just to hear you? *What* are the group's expectations? You have been chosen as speaker probably because the group knows you have knowledge of a topic in which it has interest. *What* does the group want—is it information, a challenge, or a different point of view? Any audience wants to be stimulated by ideas expressed in a unique way and with information from credible sources. Perhaps audience members crave suggestions for action that will support a certain cause in which they have concern.

"*Once you set people laughing, they're listening and you can tell them almost anything.*"

—Herbert Gardner

CONSIDER YOUR TOPIC You may be invited to speak on a specific topic, such as "your travels to Bhutan," "how you got your book published," "ways to get into the college of your choice," or "how to sell houses overnight." If you are known for your expertise or experience, then the topic is ready-made for you. You will feel comfortable because you will be talking about something you know well. Audience members will have asked for the topic and recommended that their friends come to hear you.

However, suppose the person who invited you to speak said, "Speak on anything you want to talk about. We just want you to talk to us." Now you must make a topic decision, and this may be challenging. You are asked to speak because you are you.

Ask yourself how you have made topic decisions thus far in this course. If the topic was not provided for you, you probably chose topics regarding subjects of *interest* to you, causes you *felt strongly* about, or knowledge you *wanted to share* because your research had unearthed helpful information. Inventory your own personal interests, attitudes, and experiences. Find a topic that you enjoy discussing.

EXTEND YOUR SELECTED IDEA Once you have a general idea, extend your topic by making a clustering list. A **clustering list** is a tool that helps you organize your speech by grouping together related key words and phrases. It works like this.

1. In the center of a clean page, write your general topic. (See Figure 10-1.)

2. Brainstorm key words and phrases related to the topic. Jot them down around the center topic as you think of them. Do this without stopping. Don't take time to evaluate these words now—continue jotting ideas until you have exhausted your space or your time. Ideally, you should have about 25–30 items. These items may turn out to be main headings in your speech or key words for later research. Some may not be used at all.

FIGURE 10-1   Brainstorming and clustering key words

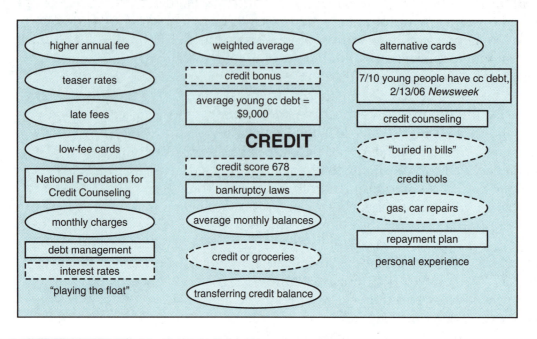

3. Using colored pencils, circle with one color those terms that are closely related. Use a different color for each additional set of related terms (as illustrated by the use of different shapes in Figure 10-1). Each of your groupings represents a subtopic around which you may organize your ideas. The key words within each grouping are ideas to be researched and developed. You are well on your way to preparing your speech.

Find the Link Between Your Audience and Your Topic

Whether you are speaking to a general audience or a specific group of company employees or customers, keep two questions in mind.

- What do I want to achieve with this speech?
- What does the audience want?

Figuring out the wants, needs, attitudes, and beliefs of your audience is like scouting an opposing football team. It pays to know what you are up against.

Your audience will be sitting together as a group, but they will listen to your speech as individuals. Nonetheless, they are people with universal human needs, and they relate to each other through common bonds. To help you understand your audience members, prepare an **audience analysis** by asking yourself questions about their backgrounds, characteristics, and traits.

- Which racial or ethnic group(s) are represented?
- Which age group(s) and gender(s) are represented?
- What educational background(s) do audience members have?

"There are three things to aim at in public speaking. First to get into your subject, then to get your subject into yourself, and lastly, to get your subject into your hearers."

—John Robert Gregg

- From what economic level(s) do they come?
- What is the general family status?
- To what social, political, or institutional groups do they belong?
- What general beliefs or attitudes do they hold about money, education, saving, economic opportunity, patriotism, and the future?
- What common bonds does the group share?

For a specific business audience, answer these additional questions.

- What are their individual occupations?
- What status do they hold in their companies?
- What are their professional concerns?

Not all of these questions are relevant to your particular speaking situation. Select the ones that will help you know your audience better. Then, ask yourself several specific, important questions.

- What does this audience know about my topic?
- How do they feel about it?
- What do they need to know?
- Why?

Shape Your Topic to Fit Your Audience

Once you have brainstormed ideas, you will need to choose those aspects of your topic that meet the needs of your audience. Consider fundamental human needs of which your audience may be concerned and the type of appeal that will most likely capture the attention of this audience.

© 2002 Ted Goff

"Did you skip over the interesting parts of your talk on purpose?"

Audience Analysis

Listening to a presentation should not be like trying to negotiate an obstacle course. When preparing a presentation, learn about your specific audience and design your presentation just for that group. You should appeal to an audience's specific needs, be aware of their concerns, and be interested in them as people. Find out what the audience expects to gain by listening to your presentation. The better you prepare for a certain audience, the more the audience will be interested in and accept what you have to say.

Andrew Hallson is a financial planner for a large investment firm. Andrew has many clients whom he advises about saving money, investing money, and planning for retirement. Andrew must keep on top of a great deal of financial information. Then, he must draw from that knowledge and tailor his advice to the specific, individual needs of each client. He analyzes assets and financial goals of each of his clients and frequently informs them of the status of their investments. He relates dollar figures and rates of return slowly and clearly, since he knows that his clients are probably taking notes. When talking to a client, Andrew answers questions and reassures them about their investments. Although Andrew handles a great number of clients, he treats each of them as if they were the single, most important account with whom he deals.

©Digital Vision

UNIVERSAL HUMAN NEEDS Psychologist Abraham Maslow categorized universal human needs into a pyramid. At the base, Maslow listed **physiological needs** for food and shelter. When these basic needs are met, people focus attention on matters of safety and security. Feeling secure, humans reach to satisfy **social needs** in which they are able to form relationships and to find a sense of belonging. Next are **personal esteem** needs in which one feels a sense of self-worth and finds recognition among peers. At the top of the hierarchy are the needs for **self-actualization**, or the drive for exploring "who I am and what makes me happy and fulfilled." Consider how your speech topic helps your audience satisfy any of these universal desires.

BASIC SPEAKER APPEALS Recall that people are moved or affected by well-reasoned argument (logos), by an appeal to their emotions (pathos), and by the credibility of the speaker (ethos). Regarding ethos, audiences tend to judge the message by the speaker's competence, trustworthiness, poise, and enthusiasm. Will your speech be a logical and well-documented proposal requesting support? Will it be a speech that catches the emotions of the audience and moves them into a new attitude? Or, do you feel so strongly about your topic that you will move the audience with the passion you feel?

Audience research is never wasted. Knowing as much as possible about your audience turns unknown faces into friendly receivers, eases stage fright, and facilitates the decision of choosing the right appeals to accomplish your speech purpose.

Personal CHECK-UP

Draw a triangle and label it with Maslow's pyramid of needs. In what order would the needs appear, from bottom to top?

Take Time to Research

There you sit with a topic, a purpose sentence, and perhaps a thesis statement. You have prepared your clustering list. Now it's time to fill in the details. You will already be knowledgeable about your chosen topic, but you need to conduct research for information to make your speech credible. Where should you look?

People

If you can, interview an expert on your subject. Even a carefully planned phone call to a government officer, businessperson, professor, or author could provide real-world explanations that you won't find elsewhere. Ask for permission to quote your interviewee.

If you conduct an in-person interview, plan carefully. Call to make an appointment, show up on time, and bring a notebook. In advance, write down questions you want to ask, and leave space to jot down answers. Ask specific, probing questions that will get you the information you want.

- "What are your thoughts about . . . ?"
- "Please tell me more concerning . . ."
- "I'd like to know where you stand on . . ."

If appropriate, ask to record the interview; but, always listen carefully. Remember to paraphrase important points for clarification and ask follow-up questions based on answers you receive. Catch key words on paper. Write a summary of the interview immediately afterward, while everything is still fresh in your mind.

Libraries

Libraries are the major source of information when doing research. A library is staffed with reference librarians to assist you with finding special collections, databases, web sites, and collections of books, government documents, and microforms. You could find yourself drifting helplessly unless you have a plan for using the library.

First, consider a library as a group of print collections, including

- Books.
- Magazines (called **periodicals** because they are published periodically—weekly, monthly, and so forth).
- Newspapers (usually on microfilm if more than a month old).
- Government documents.
- Pamphlets.

For each of these categories, tools for locating material—called indexes—are available. An **index** is a reference book with an alphabetical list of topics or names that gives the source, or original place, where each item can be found. Some useful indexes include

- *Business Periodicals Index.*
- *The Wall Street Journal Index.*
- *Public Affairs Information Service.*
- *Reader's Guide to Periodical Literature.*
- *Education Index*

These reference guides point you to specific publications containing articles on your subject.

"Knowledge is essential, but it's the ability to communicate this knowledge that separates the winners from the losers."

—Virgil Scudder

Internet Sources

The Internet is an amazing collection of information, giving you instant access to millions of computer files. But, because anyone may post materials on the Internet, it is important to plan what you are looking for and use only materials that will make you a credible speaker. You will need to filter out personal opinion pieces, commercial sites that disguise their sales pitches, and pages with predetermined, unsubstantiated biases that pop up in your search lists. Do not spend time randomly searching in the hope of finding reliable material that you can fit into your speech. Ask your reference librarian to point you in the right direction.

ELECTRONIC DATABASES An **electronic database**, such as InfoTrac, is a computerized version of an index. It stores thousands of files in such a way that you can locate information quickly. Libraries often offer a variety of electronic databases. To sort through the records and pull up titles of articles on your topic, you must use key words. A *key word* is an important term having to do with your subject. It may be a person's name, a historical event, or simply a subject, such as *agriculture*. Choose key words wisely when looking up information.

SEARCH ENGINES Another way to search the Internet is to use a **search engine** that compiles information and then indexes web sites where it can be found. Some popular search engines are Google, AltaVista, and Hotbot. You might also select a subject index like Yahoo! or Excite that compiles catalogs by reviewing information and deciding which sites to include. You may wish to use more than one search engine to find a variety of resources. Once you locate web sites on your specific research topic, you may find they contain links to other related sites that provide additional data that you may not have considered.

The amount of information available on the Internet is tremendous. Choose educational search engines to pull up articles that have a scholarly basis rather than those of a commercial interest that may have distracting advertising banners flying all over the screen. When you find an article you want to access later, create an electronic bookmark so you can revisit it with the click of the mouse.

©Digital Vision

The Internet offers instant access to many reliable—and unreliable—sources. Learn to recognize the difference.

EVALUATING INTERNET SOURCES As a credible speaker who is competent and trustworthy, you will want to be sure that the web sites you use are reputable. Remember, the Internet is not regulated—anyone can place information on the Web. Look for the following characteristics when evaluating an online source for use.

- **Authority**—Who is the author? What are the author's qualifications? With what organization is the author affiliated?

- **Accuracy**—Where did the author obtain information? Did the author list sources? Is the information free of errors?

- **Objectivity**—Does the information have a minimum of bias? Does it cite fact or opinion? Who sponsors the site? What is the sponsor's motive—is it to sell something?

- **Purpose**—Is the site meant to be educational, to provide entertainment, or to sell a product?

- **Coverage**—What topics are included? Is the topic explored in depth? Are links to other sources provided?

- **Currency**—When was the site last updated? Are article publication dates clearly stated? Is more current and relevant information available elsewhere?

Choosing and Referencing Sources

As you choose material on your topic, confirm that the sources are

- Relevant and related to the topic.

- Reliable and provided by a reputable source.

- Timely and current.

- Fair and unbiased.

Keeping track of the sources you use is important in the event that you need to revisit the material. Cite a full reference, including author, title, publication, publisher, date, and page number(s). Track your Internet information by noting the author, title, web site, date of publication, web address, and date of access. You will want to credit your sources as you give your presentation. You must beware of quoting the exact words of an author without crediting the source of information. In some instances, you will need the author's consent. Using another person's words or ideas and passing them off as your own is called **plagiarism**, and it is highly unethical behavior.

What will you do with all of this information you have so carefully accumulated? It's decision time. As you consider the information from several angles, you will begin to see an organizational pattern appear. This will form the skeleton outline of your speech. You will learn more about organizing your speech in the next chapter.

"It is terrible to speak well and be wrong."

—Sophocles

CHAPTER SUMMARY

Speaking situations abound—in community life, public life, school settings, business settings, and professional organizations. Speeches may range from informal talks to formal public speech presentations and business proposals presented before a decision-making body. To help focus your speech topic, answer questions about the setting, the occasion, and the audience. Once you have a general topic idea, expand your thinking by making a clustering list. Consider how the topic may appeal to listeners by addressing one of their needs. Maslow created a pyramid of universal human needs—physiological, security, social, personal esteem, and self-actualization. Careful research adds credibility to a speech. Research may be conducted through interviews, libraries, and electronic searches. Carefully evaluate the reliability of sources before using information. Be sure to credit your sources to avoid plagiarism.

CHAPTER REVIEW

1. Why is it important to analyze a presentation's setting and occasion?
2. Of what value is a clustering list?
3. What basic questions are important to answer about an audience?
4. Identify three major sources of research information.
5. Explain three criteria for evaluating Internet sources.

CAN YOU DEFINE THESE TERMS?

Match each description with the appropriate term. Write the correct letter in the blank preceding the sentence. Some terms will not be used.

1. ___ Food and shelter

2. ___ Publications issued on a regular schedule, such as weekly or monthly

3. ___ A tool that helps you organize your speech by grouping together related key words and phrases

4. ___ Using another person's words or ideas and passing them off as your own

5. ___ Feeling happy and fulfilled

6. ___ Compiles information and then indexes web sites where it can be found

7. ___ Asking yourself questions about potential listeners' backgrounds, characteristics, and traits

8. ___ A sense of self-worth and recognition among peers

9. ___ A computerized version of an index

10. ___ Relationships and a sense of belonging

Terms:

a. audience analysis

b. clustering list

c. electronic database

d. index

e. periodicals

f. personal esteem

g. physiological needs

h. plagiarism

i. search engine

j. self-actualization

k. social needs

APPLICATIONS

Class Analysis

When preparing a speech presentation, your first steps are to consider the setting, occasion, and audience so that you may plan your speech message to fit the situation. Analyze your classroom setting, the occasion, and your classmates as audience members for an informative or persuasive presentation by answering the following questions. Be sure to include your instructor as a member of your audience.

Setting Analysis

1. How will the physical arrangement of the room affect your presentation?

2. How can you ensure that all students will be able to see and hear from where they usually sit? Can the speaker's stand or table be moved as needed to make you and the audience more comfortable?

3. Will your visual aids be visible from the back of the room? Are sufficient materials, such as markers, thumbtacks, a flipchart, tape, and so forth, available? Can you confirm that all electrical outlets are working if needed?

Occasion Analysis

4. Are you presenting during a regular class period or for a special event?

5. What will precede your speech?

6. What will follow your speech?

7. Do you have a specified time limit? Will there be a timekeeper? How will you know how much time you have left to speak?

Audience Analysis

8. How many people are in the class?

9. What is the average age level of class members? Are there exceptions?

10. What is the general educational background of class members?

11. To what social groups or other affiliations do class members belong outside the classroom?

12. What general beliefs does the audience hold about business? About money? About speaking? About working? About school?

13. What additional characteristics do your classmates have in common?

14. How well do your classmates know each other?

15. What does the class know or think about you?

16. What topics would be of interest to your classmates?

Universal Human Needs

Your company manufactures a beverage product sold through local grocery stores. You have been asked to come up with a different campaign slogan for people at each level of the universal human needs pyramid. With a partner, write a slogan you might use for each target market.

1. Those struggling to meet basic physiological needs.

2. Those focused on safety and security.

3. Those focused on social needs.

4. Those focused on personal esteem.

5. Those focused on self-actualization.

Shaping Your Topic to Fit Your Audience

Think of four different audiences to whom you might speak. On separate paper, write a brief analysis of each of them using the list of questions on pages 174–175. Report what assumptions you had to make and how your speech would shape up differently for each audience.

MAKING CONNECTIONS

Marketing

Advertising is designed to target a specific group of people. Choose a television, newspaper, or magazine advertisement. Write an audience analysis of the specific group of people for whom the ad was designed.

_____

_____

_____

_____

_____

_____

Public Relations

You have been asked to serve on a fundraising committee for a special project for your school. You will be presenting your project to both a parent group and a local business association and appealing for their assistance. The local business association has many members who are former alumni. Describe ways in which your fundraising appeal may differ for each group.

_____

_____

_____

_____

_____

_____

_____

Psychology

Conduct research to find more information on Maslow and his theory regarding human needs. Use at least two different methods of research. Remember to properly cite your sources.

_____

_____

_____

_____

_____

_____

_____

_____

PROJECT

Search and Find

A presentational speaker works comfortably in a library to verify sources, look up new information, and find interesting supporting material for a speech. Working with a partner, use the resources in your library or media center to look up the answers to the following questions. Write the answers in the space below each question. For each answer, you must cite a source. Include author, title, publication, publisher, date, and page numbers for print sources and author, web site, web address, and date of access for Internet sources.

1. In what year of last century did the United States switch from a military draft system to an all-volunteer force?

2. For which race did Apolo Anton Ohno of the United States win the gold medal in the 2006 Olympics in Turin, Italy?

3. What is a "dashiki"?

4. Who is the author of *The House on Mango Street*?

5. For whom was Harvard University named, and when did he live?

6. For more than 100 years, Hawaii had a policy of involuntarily exiling anyone who had a particular disease. What was the disease, and where were people permanently sent?

7. Who was Cicero, and when did he live?

8. What does "eructate" mean?

9. Which four states in the United States join at one border?

10. What is the story of *Paradise Lost*?

11. What was the Harlem Renaissance? Name two individuals who contributed to it.

12. What is "insider trading"?

13. In the Foja Mountains on New Guinea island, scientists discovered a biological treasure trove. What did they find?

14. Who said, "All modern American literature comes from one book by Mark Twain called *Huckleberry Finn*"?

15. The present capital of China, Beijing, was formerly known by what name?

16. How is hantavirus carried, and how do humans get it?

17. Who is Dr. Michael Oppenheimer, and what concerns him about the environment?

18. Who is the discoverer of the proteins angiostatin and endostatin, and how are these being used?

19. What is the LSAT, and who must take it?

20. What was Sputnik, and how did it affect the United States?

DECA Travel and Tourism Marketing Management Team Decision-Making Event

Assume that an active hurricane season has devastated Florida's state tourism industry. You and your partner have been hired by the Florida Department of Travel and Tourism to develop a promotional strategy to revive the flailing tourism industry. Your presentation should

- Explain the economic impact of travel and tourism for the state of Florida.
- Describe the top target markets of Florida tourism.
- Describe the fears of travelers and strategies to overcome those fears.
- Identify top tourist attractions in the state of Florida.
- Describe a promotional strategy for Florida travel and tourism.
- Explain incentives to be offered to encourage individuals to choose Florida as their vacation destination.
- Explain how the plan will be carried out.

You will have 30 minutes to study the situation and organize your analysis. You may use a laptop computer and handheld digital organizer. However, no additional time will be allowed for computer setup. Both members of your team must actively participate in the oral presentation. You will have 10 minutes to present your strategy to the tourism board (judges).

The board will have 5 additional minutes to ask questions.

Performance Indicators Evaluated

- Identify clearly the top target markets.
- Provide solid arguments to counteract objections to vacationing in Florida.
- Demonstrate realistic knowledge of advertising principles.
- Give examples of promotions to bring more tourism back to Florida.
- Explain the financing of special promotional activities and the financial return.
- Demonstrate effective communication and organizational skills.
- Demonstrate critical-thinking and problem-solving skills.

For more detailed information, go to the DECA web site.

Think Critically

1. Who is your audience for this presentation?
2. List the key characteristics of your audience.
3. Which universal human needs should your presentation address? Why?
4. What sources of information will you consult to prepare your presentation?

http://www.deca.org/

Organizing and Supporting Ideas

CHAPTER OBJECTIVES

After completing this chapter, you should be able to

- List and describe patterns by which speeches can be organized.
- Develop an outline using standard format.
- Explain the various types of supporting materials and the appropriate uses for each.
- Discuss types of visual aids, appropriate uses for each, and problems to avoid.
- Prepare a proper speech closing.
- List the steps of a speech introduction that stimulates interest.

KEY TERMS AND CONCEPTS

parallel structure	cause–effect organization	visual aids
topical organization	transitions	model
spatial organization	quote	mock-up
chronological organization	testimony	cut-away
problem–solution organization		

IDEA BOX

To begin preparations for a persuasive speech, list three issues you feel strongly about—for or against. Then, choose one that you can develop into an effective presentation. Remember, persuasive speeches use selected information to cause an audience to change its thinking or take some form of action. Consider the types of supporting materials that you will need to convince your audience.

Stories	Facts and statistics
Examples	Explanations and descriptions
Comparisons	Quotes and testimonies

Preparation Review

If you are required to choose a topic for a speech or presentation, the first hurdle is to decide what to talk about. This calls for creative thinking. If it is to be an informative speech, you will need to think about topics you know well, such as a hobby, a sport you play, an item you collect, or a place you have visited often. If it is to be a persuasive speech, not only must you choose a topic, but you must also relate that topic to the audience's needs and interests. What, exactly, do you want to convince your audience to think? What do you want to stimulate them to do?

Choosing a Topic

Once you have brainstormed ideas, you must narrow down your list to just one topic. Ask yourself the following questions.

1. *Can I cover the whole subject in one speech?* If not, think smaller and more specifically. It is more interesting to present a fully developed subtopic than to try to broadly cover the entire scope of a general topic. Keep in mind that you will have a time limit.

2. *What aspects of this subject will best fit this particular audience, and what do I really want to say?* Remember to think about your audience as you determine the purpose of your speech. Be sure that your intended purpose matches audience members' interests and concerns. Make certain that you know what your purpose is.

Remember to think about your audience as you determine your purpose. Does your intended purpose match the audience's interests and concerns?

Stating a Purpose

To clarify your purpose, state your topic and your goal in one sentence. For example, "I want to explain the procedure for obtaining a passport." This is a purpose sentence for an informative speech. A purpose sentence for a persuasive speech might be, "I want my student audience to be prepared for travel outside of the United States."

Creating a Thesis Statement

Turn your purpose sentence into a thesis statement, or key idea. This involves simply restating your "I want" sentence into a specifically worded form to be developed or explained. For example, the informative purpose sentence could become, "Applying for a passport consists of three major steps." The persuasive purpose sentence might become, "When you cross the border, it's important to have a passport." When you word your purpose sentence in this way, the pattern for developing your idea becomes clear.

Pausing for Research

You have established a topic, a purpose sentence, and a thesis statement. Now it's time to fill in the blanks of your presentation. You may already be knowledgeable about your topic, but you will still need to research supporting material that will make your speech memorable. Then, you will organize your information into a logical pattern to make it understandable.

FINDING INFORMATION Successful presentations sparkle with definitions, examples, stories, comparisons, facts, statistics, descriptions, and quotations. Where do such treasures come from? Some come right out of your head, of course, but you don't have to depend solely on yourself. You can collect a mass of material out of which you can select those snippets that clarify, explain, and illustrate your points. Although all of the material may not be your own, the way you organize it together with your own thoughts and deliver it will put your unique stamp on the subject.

COLLECTING INFORMATION Keeping track of your sources during the research process is very important. When you discover something that you want to review more closely, be sure to note the full reference—the author and title of the book or article, the publisher or the periodical, the date of publication, and the page numbers. You will need this information to revisit your source and to give credit if you use it in your presentation.

As you collect sources for your presentation, skim the articles or book sections to make sure they have what you need. Later, when you actually sit down to read the most useful sources, record facts, data, and statistics on index cards to keep track of them. If you use anything word-for-word, be sure to enclose it in quotation marks and accurately cite the source. When you use an online source, list the author's name, the title of the article, the publication's name, the date of publication, and the date of access. Also, specify the path to the information, as follows.

> Hu, Jim. "AOL's Pop-Up Sacrifice." *CNET News.com,* October 17, 2002. http://news.com.com/2100-1023_3-962345.html (May 3, 2006).

USING COLLECTED INFORMATION Keep several things in mind regarding the research materials you collect.

- **A speech is not a research paper**—A speech is an oral message that will be heard by a group of people. Your audience has little time to critically analyze the material of your speech, nor to be impressed with the quantity of factual information you present. Auditory signals fly past. Be selective in what you present, but make sure the points you do make are memorable.

Language trap

Don't say, "This t-shirt smells badly."
Say, "This t-shirt smells bad."

- **Beware of limiting your research to one article**—When you find material that says exactly what you think, the temptation is to use only that material in building your speech. What if individuals in your audience have already read the article? You will not have anything new or interesting for them to hear.

- **A speech is not a copy of already printed material**—It is a unique arrangement of your ideas, supported by bits and pieces from others. You read widely to enlarge your topic. You select wisely to support your ideas.

What in the world will you do with all of this information you have so carefully accumulated? Now it's decision time. You must consider the information from several angles and decide what to use in your speech. You will not use all of it, but that's okay. It is better to have more than enough information than to fall short and end up with an incomplete or inaccurate presentation.

Organizing Your Presentation

When you are satisfied with the information you have on hand, the process of organization begins. Now you want major points that will develop your thesis statement. In other words, you must find the best way to achieve your purpose. It is time to pull out your research information and decide what to use and what to toss out. At the same time, you must decide on a framework that will make sense to your audience and upon which you can hang all the ideas and supporting material to make your speech memorable.

You can choose from several organizational patterns. It is helpful to be aware of them as you plan your speech.

Organizational Patterns

A speaker often has three to five major points in a speech. Why? Because no more than five points will be remembered, and it often takes only three points to effectively persuade an audience.

You will identify your main points with Roman numerals in your outline. Your main points should be created with **parallel structure**, or worded in the same statement format, to help the audience remember them. It also helps if the main points form a logical pattern. Suppose you want to talk about environmental issues. Here are several useful examples of basic organizational patterns from which you might choose.

- **Topical organization**—Simply list each main point as I., II., and III., often with the most dramatic or climactic point coming last. Example:

  THESIS: Take care of Planet Earth.

  I. Conserve water and gasoline.

"If you have an important point to make, don't try to be subtle or clever. Use the pile driver. Hit the point once. Then come back and hit it again. Then hit it a third time; a tremendous whack."

—Winston Churchill

II. Protect natural resources.

III. Recycle everything.

- **Spatial organization**—Arrange the subject matter in terms of space relationships. This pattern is useful when giving directions beginning at a point the audience knows. Example:

    THESIS: From coast to coast to coast, our country is shrinking.

    I. On the east coast, a rising ocean nibbles away our land.

    II. In the south, hurricanes and floods strip away acres.

    III. On the west coast, earthquakes and mudslides wash soil away.

- **Chronological organization**—Organize material by date, from past to present to future, or reverse. Example:

    THESIS: Nations develop in a pattern.

    I. Early years are an agricultural economy.

    II. The second period is industrial production.

    III. Technological development follows.

    IV. Outsourcing is a new development.

- **Problem–solution organization**—Explain a problem, describe its effects, and offer a solution. Example:

    THESIS: Consider a hybrid car.

    I. Our nations' dependence on oil is a major problem.

    II. This dependence jeopardizes our future.

    III. Hybrid cars consume less fuel.

- **Cause–effect organization**—Show the causes and discuss the effects of a problem. Example:

    THESIS: Our nation is a giant dump.

    I. Industry pollutes our lakes and rivers.

    II. Human agriculture spoils the soil.

    III. Buried nuclear waste is still a threat.

Personal CHECK-UP

Why is it important to organize the main points of a speech in a logical pattern?

Preparing an Outline

Once you choose the organizational pattern that works best for your topic, prepare an outline. Use your three to five major points as the main headings in your outline, as shown above. You should then flesh out the outline. To get started, add one or two details, or subheadings, under each of your major points. These details might include important quotations, anecdotes, or statistics that you will use to make your point. Keep in mind that what you want your audience to remember are the three to five major points in your outline, so make sure they are really the most important pieces of information.

Label your major points with Roman numerals. Use capital letters for subheadings, and label details beyond that with Arabic numerals. This is a standard outline format. A speech outline frequently contains complete sentences for the thesis and main points, but subpoints and supporting details are usually filled in with abbreviated notes using key words. Look at the outline form of the speech on pages 206–207. Note that the speaker has included important transition words in parentheses in her outline. She has also categorized her supporting details to remind herself when to use visual aids, when to launch into an anecdote, and so forth. This helps to ensure that she has a variety of support for her presentation.

Transitions

Now talk through the main points of your speech, using the outline as a road map. As you move from one major point to the next, help your audience understand where you are going by using transitional words and phrases. **Transitions** indicate relationships between thoughts or ideas. Following are some words and phrases you might find useful for your transitions.

- "First," "Second," "Third," and so forth
- "In the first place," "In the second place," and so forth
- "For instance," "For example," "To illustrate"
- "In addition to," "Next," "Likewise"
- "In the same way," "Just like this"
- "In other words," "To restate"
- "To summarize," "In conclusion," "Finally"

Supporting Materials

To be interesting and fully understood, each subpoint must be made clear by definition, specific instances, or examples, or it may be expanded by explanations, facts, testimony, or quotations. The more varied the kinds of support, the more ear-catching your words will be. Many types of supporting materials can be used to bring clarity and interest to your speech.

DEFINITIONS A word can be defined in several ways.

- Use word history (etymology).
  "'Vertigo' comes from a Latin word meaning 'to whirl around'."

- Make an analogy comparing two things that are alike in several ways.
  "Gossip is a deadly microbe. It has neither legs nor wings. It is composed entirely of tales, and most of them have stings." (FCC Newsletter)

Language trap

Don't say, "I will get the report to you by Friday, like I promised."
Say, "I will get the report to you by Friday, as I promised."

■ Tell what the object is not.

"A man is not a machine nor a puppet. A woman is not a slave nor a pincushion. A child is not a possession. A person is a person." (R. W. Sims)

NARRATION Narration is storytelling. Few people can resist a brief, well-told story with a point. If a story drags out, listeners may lose interest.

EXAMPLES Examples are short stories or personal experiences designed to shed light on an abstract idea in listeners' minds.

"Dr. Albert Einstein explained how time is not absolute under his relativity theory. 'When you sit with a nice girl for two hours, it seems like only a moment. When you sit on a hot stove for a moment, it seems like two hours. That's relativity.'"

ILLUSTRATIONS An illustration is usually a longer example or story. Guide your audience with clues such as "To illustrate," "For example," or "Let me give you a specific instance." Remember to use transitional words and phrases as you weave in and out of examples and stories so your audience can follow along.

COMPARISON/CONTRAST Comparison makes an idea clear by showing similarities between it and something the audience knows. Contrast clarifies an idea by presenting differences between it and something the audience understands. Speakers sometimes use quotations to make comparison and contrast points.

"It is better to be painfully alive than comfortably dead." (Leland Sonnischsen)

FACTUAL DATA Facts must be presented in a credible manner to win belief. Statistical information is often presented visually and interpreted precisely. Giving the source of the data is essential. People are usually curious about where information came from. Citing sources also reassures the audience that you have done your research and that you are not just estimating or guessing. It is important to build your credibility in this way.

"Southern Louisiana is losing land at the rate of a football field every thirty-eight minutes. The area is shrinking by a large desktop's worth of ground every second, or a tennis court's worth every thirteen seconds." (Kolbert, 2006, 755)

EXPLANATION In an explanation, the speaker restates an idea for clarification and/or for emphasis.

"He wanted to get out of jail. In fact, he was so eager to be free that he was willing to lie, testify, or turn state's evidence."

Personal
CHECK-UP

Why should a speaker include different types of supporting materials in a presentation?

DESCRIPTION A speaker who uses description includes words that create sensory experiences. Rather than "the car," say, "the sleek, red Porsche." It's not just "a smell," it's "the mouth-watering odor from the barbecue grill."

QUOTATIONS When you use a quote—someone else's exact words, spoken or written—you must credit the original speaker or writer. The best quotations to use are brief, pithy statements—often humorous—that support your idea. Transitional phrases such as "Ben Franklin once wrote" or "As Bill Gates says" can lead both you and your audience into a quotation.

TESTIMONY Testimony is information that comes directly from someone who has firsthand experience with the subject. For example, a consumer complaint letter could be used as testimony to the fact that a product is faulty or unsafe. Testimony can also come in the form of a formal, sworn statement made by someone in the presence of a lawyer or an authorized public official. The credibility or status of the individual giving the testimony also supports your point.

"Congressman George Mahon gave this advice to new Congress members: 'Don't talk too often, do your homework, don't ever lose your credibility by using statements that are tricky or deceitful.'"

Adding Visual Impact

In this visual age of plasma TVs, picture cell phones, and video iPods, we expect to see as well as hear. In fact, most presentation points will be more interesting if visually illustrated. Don't just tell them, show them. If more than one sense is involved, the audience will be more

© 2002 Ted Goff

"Snowballs? I thought we were discussing coconuts."

Visual Aids

One picture is indeed worth a thousand words—but only if it is a good one. What is a good picture? It is large enough to be clearly viewed by everyone in the audience, it accurately illustrates the point being made by the speaker, and it adds impact to the message. Every presentation should have visual aids (besides the speaker), but the aids must add information, understanding, sensory awareness, or drama to the point being made.

stimulated and likely to retain what they hear. A car salesperson, for example, doesn't sit in the showroom and talk about a car. He invites the customer to sit in the vehicle, feel the upholstery, smell the new-car odor, peer into the engine, slam the hood, and take the car for a drive. It is more difficult to provide hands-on experience when speaking in a conference room. Nevertheless, a speaker should plan audience participation by using **visual aids**, or support for a message that engages listeners' eyes in addition to their ears. Visuals should highlight most speeches, but the aids must add information, understanding, sensory awareness, or drama to the speaker's point.

The type of visual aid a speaker uses depends upon the speech topic, the size of the audience, the setting, and the equipment available. The secrets for the success of any visual aid are that it is easily viewed by the entire audience and it supports the point of the message. Keep these secrets in mind as you read about the different types of visual aids.

Realistic Representations

If you can't use the real thing as a visual, sometimes a three-dimensional copy or image will help make the point. Of course, the item must be big enough to be easily visible, yet small enough to be portable.

MODELS An architect might display a reduced-size model of a shopping mall. A salesperson should display and possibly demonstrate the use of an actual product. Any three-dimensional representation, whether actual size, reduced, or enlarged, qualifies as a **model**.

MOCK-UPS A **mock-up** is a simulated or nonfunctional device. A pilot trainee might get an introduction to flying by means of a mock instrument panel. The buttons and dials may turn, but the panel isn't hooked up to any other device.

CUT-AWAYS A **cut-away** is a figure with removable parts, such as an engine or an anatomical model, that allows a speaker to remove sections to reveal other portions of the device or model as he or she speaks.

Graphic Images

Whether your visual aid is a simple word chart, a photograph, or a computer-generated animated model, it can add impact to your presentation. Even sophisticated charts and graphs have become relatively easy to produce on a computer. Desktop publishing, drawing, photo-enhancing, and multimedia software programs provide various means of creating graphic images for display during a presentation.

©Getty Images/PhotoDisc

Visual aids must be large enough to be seen by all members of the audience.

©Digital Vision

A favorite of business presenters, charts, graphs, and tables show relationships among the parts of a whole, represent and compare numerical data, and show trends over time.

PHOTOGRAPHS, DRAWINGS, AND CARTOONS These kinds of visual aids can enhance the spoken message and generate audience interest. Remember that they must be large enough to be easily seen. You can design large poster boards that can be displayed prominently or project electronic versions of your visuals from your laptop computer.

CHARTS, GRAPHS, AND TABLES Planned visuals of statistical information can show relationships among the parts of a whole; represent and compare numerical data; show trends over time; demonstrate growth, decline, or change; and so forth. These types of visuals are easily produced using software and can be professionally displayed during a speech. Tools such as Microsoft® Excel and PowerPoint® software make it possible to produce charts, graphs, and other visuals that can be displayed on a laptop computer and projected on a large screen. New tools can convert information from any slide into a graphic that can be refined with an easy-to-use menu of ready-made options. You might use a digital remote with a built-in laser pointer to click through and highlight your slides as you speak and move about, allowing you to maintain close eye contact with your audience.

Displaying Your Visuals

Supporting information and graphics may be shared in a variety of ways. Choices will depend on the audience size and the type of visual.

WORD CHARTS, POSTERS, AND FLIPCHARTS These visuals can be prepared carefully in advance, and you can add to them as you speak. These inexpensive aids are most effective when shown to small groups in which listeners can position themselves to see well. Slip a covering sheet of poster board in front of a visual until you are ready to show the information. Prepare a flipchart in advance, and then flip the pages to expose the supporting material at the appropriate time. You can also use blank pages to record ideas offered by listeners during the session. A new type of related visual aid is an electronic, erasable whiteboard that requires special markers and allows the user to print out a hard copy of what is written on the board.

COMPUTER-GENERATED SLIDES Computer-generated slides, such as those produced by PowerPoint software, have replaced traditional slides and the carousel used for displaying them. A laptop with a projector attachment does the job. Business speakers often plan, create, and organize their presentations using PowerPoint slides. The speaker frequently puts the title, introduction, body of the speech (complete with complex graphs and tables), and conclusion on separate slides and clicks through them during the presentation. The audience can see the whole speech just like it might be outlined on a sheet of paper—numbers, letters, and all. The computer has become a tremendous tool for presenters, but a few considerations must be made to use a slide show effectively.

With slide show presentations, speakers may easily click through supporting visuals as they talk.

©Digital Vision

- Too much information on slides confuses the audience. Keep slides simple. Limit each bullet point to six words. Limit your bullets to five per slide.

- You may embed streaming video, pictures, and even music into your slides, but try to avoid clip art and posed photos.

- Text and pictures must match the speaker's words.

- Time and effort are required for preparation.

HANDOUTS Distribute handouts that outline your speech at the beginning of your presentation if you want the audience to follow along and take notes. Pictures, brochures, samples, or advertising pamphlets also provide a good follow-up to your presentation. However, these types of handouts should never compete with the oral presentation. Do not pass them out as you speak. Your audience will stop listening. Show the handouts during the speech, discuss the information provided, and tell the audience that the materials will be available at the end of your presentation.

VIDEO Playing a video requires special equipment. Timing is critical. The video must be carefully cued so that the speaker doesn't waste time and lose the audience while searching for the right segment. Viewing time should be short. Video should be used as an aid, not as the entire presentation.

Problems with Visuals

1. Without proper preparation, selection, and timing, visuals can distract from, rather than add to, the message.

2. Too many visuals overload sensory impressions.

3. If the room is darkened for videos or slides, the audience may slip off for a brief nap.

4. The room may not be properly set up for a technology-driven presentation.

5. The speaker may become overly focused on the visuals, fail to make eye contact, and lose connection with the audience. The speaker may face the visual, read aloud what is already displayed, fiddle with electronic gadgets, or leave an expired visual displayed after moving on to another main point.

6. Handouts distributed during the presentation may steal the focus from the speaker.

It is important to remember that *you are your most important visual aid*. Your appearance, poise, gestures, and friendly eye contact with your listeners all provide visual impact. Be sure your visuals enhance and support rather than distract from you and your message.

A Dynamic Ending

You've said your say and time has run out. This is the climax. Your next job is to tie your ideas together and focus on your purpose. The conclusion should meet two major goals.

1. It should summarize your thesis and main points.
   "I've told you ..."

2. It should focus on your purpose.
   "I hope you now know more about ..."

   "Remember, the next time you say, 'I don't have time,' you are in charge of the time you have."

Work hard to create a strong finish. Write the conclusion out completely beforehand. Don't assume you will come up with something appropriate and clever on the spur of the moment. Use a well-prepared closing to cement your message in the listeners' minds.

COMMUNICATION AT WORK

To secure work contracts, Joan Lopez, a public relations consultant, plans five or six interviews each month with local business owners. In well-planned presentations, she presents her qualifications, shows a plan for advertising the business, and demonstrates how she has aided other companies. Joan knows that potential clients want to see what she has done for other customers. She has two types of visual aids she uses to make her point. First, she shows examples of previous advertising campaigns, whether in print or video format. Second, she shows graphs to indicate the sales growth that her other clients have experienced. Her visual aids are always directly related to her presentation, never just decorative. In the sight-driven world of advertising, Joan's visual aids are the most powerful tools she has when it comes to approaching new clients.

An Irresistible Opening

Now that your speech is otherwise fully prepared, you know where you are going and can invite the audience to come along with you. The opening should be designed to introduce your thesis to the audience, but it must be cleverly executed. You must "bait the hook" to grab the listeners' attention and set them up to hear what you have to say. Choose an unexpected remark, a brief story, or an unusual statement to do this. Avoid "telling a few stories" as an audience warm-up. These stories often have little to do with the main message and purpose. Don't say, "Before I start...," because the minute you open your mouth, you have started.

Involve the audience right away by relating to their needs, attitudes, or beliefs. Try to think in their terms. Say "you," and speak specifically to them. Establish your credibility by sharing a bit about yourself. Tell why the subject is important to you, how you got interested in it, and/or why you think the topic relates to your listeners. This step should answer the question, "Why should we listen to *you*?" Then, state your thesis and move into the body of your speech.

The opening is often outlined and labeled, as shown here, to remind the speaker of the steps needed.

INTRODUCTION

Get Attention:

(Visual—show pink paper)
Have any of you ever been awarded a "pink slip"?

(Visual—rattle keys)
What about the keys to the "executive washroom"?

Involve Audience:

In between these two extremes, most of us just get up and go to work day after day.

Establish Credibility:

I worked in the steel industry, and my job was to plan and execute the massive layoffs that were in the offing. What I didn't know was that I was among those to be laid off. Based on this painful experience, I want to share a bit of advice.

Thesis Statement:

Take charge of your own career!

This speaker chose to show an actual pink slip and shake keys to get the audience's attention. For most introductions, sounds, visuals, or cleverly focused words will pique the audience's curiosity and involve them in your subject. Can you see why you should plan the introduction to your thesis after you have worked out the body of the speech? Now, you can get a flying start!

CHAPTER SUMMARY

When preparing a speech, first choose a topic, state a purpose, create a thesis statement, and research/collect information. Next, outline your speech in a logical manner. Organizational patterns of arranging main points include topical, spatial, chronological, problem–solution, and cause–effect. Main points are identified with Roman numerals, subpoints with capital letters, and supporting detail with Arabic numbers. Transitions indicate relationships and lead the audience from one point to another. Types of supporting materials include definitions, narration, examples, illustrations, comparisons/contrasts, factual data, explanations, descriptions, quotations, and testimony. Visual aids must add information, understanding, sensory awareness, or drama to the point being made. Visuals may include representational images (models, mock-ups, and cut-aways) and graphic images (photographs, drawings, cartoons, charts, graphs, and tables). Supporting visuals may be shared through posters, flipcharts, computer-generated slides, handouts, and video. The closing should summarize your thesis and main points and focus on your purpose. The introduction should be prepared last and should catch attention, get the audience involved, and identify your relationship to the topic.

CHAPTER REVIEW

1. List and describe three types of organizational patterns for main points.
2. Name five types of supporting materials and appropriate uses of each.
3. Why should a speaker use visual aids?
4. What are some of the possible hazards of using visuals?
5. What should the speech closing accomplish? The introduction?

CAN YOU DEFINE THESE TERMS?

Match each description with the appropriate term. Write the correct letter in the blank preceding the sentence. Some terms will not be used.

Terms:

1. ___ Worded in the same statement format
2. ___ Organizational style that arranges material by date, from past to present to future, or reverse
3. ___ Organizational style that explains a problem, describes effects, and offers a solution
4. ___ Indicate relationships between thoughts or ideas and lead audience to the next point
5. ___ Someone else's exact words
6. ___ Information that comes directly from someone who has firsthand experience with the subject
7. ___ Any three-dimensional representation
8. ___ A simulated or nonfunctional device

a. cause–effect organization
b. chronological organization
c. cut-away
d. mock-up
e. model
f. parallel structure
g. problem–solution organization
h. quote
i. spatial organization
j. testimony
k. topical organization
l. transitions
m. visual aids

APPLICATIONS

Organizational Patterns

Practice dividing a key idea into main points arranged in a recognizable pattern. Work with a partner to create an example of each type of organizational pattern identified below and on the next page.

TOPICAL ORGANIZATION Some ideas divide easily into topical categories. You may decide to organize a topical arrangement according to aspects, qualities, reasons, steps, branches, or departments. Write a key idea and main points in full sentences using topical organization. Consider the following suggestions for key ideas, or choose any topic that interests you.

- The qualities of a good manager
- The duties of a child care professional
- The branches of government
- The aspects of marketing

Key Idea:

Main Points:

   I.

   II.

   III.

SPATIAL ORGANIZATION Sometimes it is convenient to explain a subject through geographic relationships (space order). Write a key idea and main points in full sentences using spatial organization. Consider the following suggestions for key ideas, or choose any other subject that lends itself to spatial organization.

- An orientation to the various departments on different floors of a hospital or medical center
- The sales areas around the country for a particular company
- The state of the economy in different regions of the country

Key Idea:

Main Points:

   I.

   II.

   III.

CHRONOLOGICAL ORGANIZATION Some subjects are explained most effectively in a time sequence (chronological order). Write a key idea and main points in full sentences using chronological organization. Consider the following suggestions for key ideas, or choose any other subject that lends itself to chronological organization.

- The history of instant printing
- The development of the shoe industry
- The growth of the popular music recording industry
- The development of the Internet

Key Idea:

Main Points:

   I.

   II.

   III.

PROBLEM–SOLUTION ORGANIZATION When addressing a problem for which you have a recommended solution, problem–solution organization is a recommended approach. In this speech framework, state the solution as your key idea. Main points will cover the problem, its effects, and the solution. In this case, the key idea is provided for you. Develop the key idea with main points in full sentences using problem–solution organization.

Key Idea: *Floss teeth and gums regularly.*

Main Points:

   I.

   II.

   III.

Supporting Materials

Use interesting supporting materials in your presentations. People listen to details that make ideas clear, sparkling, and vivid. Below are eight types of supporting materials on the topic "Trachea." Choose a topic of your own, and create a piece of supporting material for each of the following categories. Record your notes on the next page.

1. **Definition**—Use words to tell what something is.

   "*The trachea (tray-key-a) is the principal passage for conveying air to and from the lungs in humans and air-breathing animals with backbones.*"

2. **Visual Aid**—Present a realistic representation or graphic that shows where the subject is, what it looks like, and so forth.

   "*This is a cut-away illustration of a smoker's lungs and trachea.*"

3. **Example**—Give a general or specific example.

   "*Feel the top of the trachea by putting your fingers gently on your Adam's apple, located just below the chin, and swallow.*"

4. **Comparison**—Relate something unknown to something the audience already knows.

   "*The trachea is a muscular tube similar to the esophagus, which is the tube that connects the mouth to the stomach.*"

5. **Contrast**—Show how two things are different.

   "*Although both tubes start in the mouth, the esophagus takes food to the stomach while the trachea carries air to the lungs.*"

6. **Explanation**—Provide pertinent facts about the subject's purpose or relevance.

   "*This air passage is essential for life, and the larynx (lar-in-gks) or voice box, which makes speech possible, is located in the trachea.*"

7. **Quotation or Testimony**—Use the words of someone else to strengthen your point.

   "*'A tracheotomy is an emergency surgery that frees the passageway in order to help someone breathe,' said Lucy Kavanagh, a registered nurse.*"

8. **Factual Data**—Give numbers to clarify the point you are making. Cite the source of the figures.

   "*In the month of October, our paramedics were called nine times because of someone choking.*" (Southwestern Emergency Ambulance Service)

My Topic:

1. Definition:

2. Visual Aid:

3. Example:

4. Comparison:

5. Contrast:

6. Explanation:

7. Quotation or Testimony:

8. Factual Data:

Speech Introduction

The introduction of a presentation should prepare an audience to hear the key idea and a discussion of it. An effective introduction should

- Capture attention and interest.
- Involve the audience.
- Establish credibility.
- Create a strong statement of the key idea.

Work with a partner to select an idea for a presentation. The purpose may be either to inform or to persuade. Carefully word the key idea (thesis statement). Write it in the space below. Now, plan and write the way you would introduce this statement in a speech to your class. Fill in the three steps below. One of you will deliver this introduction, which may be as short as 30 seconds, to the class.

Get Attention:

Involve Audience:

Establish Credibility:

Thesis Statement:

MAKING CONNECTIONS

Journalism

Select an article from the editorial page of your local newspaper. Find the thesis statement and main points. Arrange them in outline form. Make a list of the types of supporting materials that appear in the article.

_____

_____

_____

_____

_____

_____

_____

English—Bibliography

Choose three magazines. Select one article from each, and write a bibliographic note for each article that includes author, title, magazine, date, and page number.

_____

_____

_____

_____

_____

_____

_____

_____

_____

PROJECT

Model Audience Analysis with Outline

The analysis and outline on the following pages are from a presentation that was delivered by Shari J. Dorris, a loan officer of Southwest Mortgage Company. Review the audience analysis and the outline on the following pages. What elements of the outline show that the speaker has tailored the presentation to her audience? Write your answers in the space below.

Title of Presentation: Your Credit Rating and You

1. Who is my audience? Where is the speech setting?

   The audience is 20–30 male and female college students from mixed economic backgrounds. All will graduate from college within two to three years and plan to enter the workforce immediately. We are meeting in a classroom.

2. What does my audience know about my topic?

   These students have some general knowledge of the topic. They have probably acquired credit cards, and possibly have school loans, car loans, mortgages, and rent payments.

3. Why do I think my audience is interested in my subject?

   This is a seminar that the students have chosen to attend during the school's Financial Awareness Week. Their choice indicates their interest.

4. Why do I think my audience needs to know about my subject?

   Credit is a means of developing purchasing power and establishing oneself as a responsible citizen. These young people are ready to think of themselves as independent individuals. They need to be prepared for the future.

5. What does my audience know or think about me?

   Because the speakers for Financial Awareness Week are invited from the business community to speak to various groups, they will recognize my credibility as a female loan officer in a local business organization. I assume they will be very open to the ideas I will present.

6. What specific strategies do I need to use so that my audience will react as I want them to?

   I will use logical reasoning and a variety of supporting materials. My purpose is to convince these students of the importance of credit.

OUTLINE

Introduction

(Get attention)	A. *How many of you live in a house?* (Ask for a show of hands.)
(Involve audience)	B. *How is the house being paid for?* (Get answers.)
(Establish credibility)	C. *I have worked as a loan officer at a mortgage company for five years, and I want to tell you about credit.*

Thesis Statement

I want to tell you three things about credit. It is essential to understand, establish, and maintain a good credit rating.

Development of Key Idea (Body of Speech)

Transition: (First, . . .)

Main point	I. *It is important to understand the basics of credit.*
Definition	A. *Credit rating is the evaluation of how you handle financial obligations.*
Explanation	B. Explain why a business wants to know your credit rating.
Subpoint	C. *Credit rating is needed to finance wants and needs.*
Specific instances	1. Buy car, furniture, place to live
Example	2. Invest in business opportunities—ski shop
Explanation	3. Bail out of tight situation—accident, hospital costs

Transition: (Understanding credit is important. Now, my second point . . .)

Main point	II. *Establishing a good credit rating depends on two major factors.*
Subpoint	A. Permanency
Example, definition	1. Employed, salary, collateral
Example	2. Time in residence, moving about, "skip town"
Subpoint	B. Reputation
Contrast	1. Solid citizen versus less than reliable
Contrast	2. Coworkers speak highly versus unflattering character assessment
Contrast	3. Involved in community work versus lawsuit

Transition: (In review, I've been talking about . . . Now I would like to make a final point.)

Main Point	III. *Maintaining a good credit rating requires effort, caution, and common sense.*
Subpoint	A. *Making payments on time requires effort.*
Explanation	1. Do not use the "grace period"
Illustration	2. Can develop bad habits
Subpoint	B. *Do not co-sign on a loan—use caution.*
Definition	1. Define co-sign
Illustration	2. Story of Rashad and his brother
Subpoint	C. *Use credit cards with common sense.*
Visual aid	1. Show cards
Illustration	2. Story of my roommate
Explanation	3. "Playing the float"

Conclusion

Transition: (Let me summarize for you.)

(Summary)	A. Review three main points: Understand credit, establish good credit, and maintain a good credit rating.
(Focus)	B. *Start out right in handling money as you begin your careers, and your credit rating will work to your advantage in the future.*

FBLA Public Speaking I

Leadership is marked by effective speaking skills. You are challenged to prepare a four-minute business speech developed from one of the following topics.

- Business Ethics in the Corporate Setting
- Outsourcing U.S. Jobs
- Employee/Employer Loyalty in a Dynamic Business World
- Interdependency in a Global Economy

You must work individually rather than with a group for this activity. Facts and working data may be secured from any source. The speech must be well organized, contain substantiated statements and supporting materials, and be written in proper business style.

Notes and note cards may be used during the delivery of the speech. No microphones may be used, and no visual aids are allowed. The order of speakers will be drawn at random. The length of the speech should be four minutes. Five points will be deducted for any speech under 3:31 minutes or over 4:29 minutes.

Performance Indicators Evaluated

- Demonstrate research skills by citing credible sources of information.
- State the purpose of the speech clearly.
- Demonstrate knowledge of and inform the audience about the topic.
- Communicate clearly a viewpoint about the topic.
- Demonstrate critical thinking and organized analytical skills.
- Persuade the audience to a desired conclusion/response from the information presented.
- Adhere to speech time constraints.

For more detailed information, go to the FBLA web site.

Think Critically

1. How will you organize your presentation? Why did you choose that pattern?
2. What types of supporting materials would be most effective for your presentation? Why?
3. If you could use visual aids for this speech, what types would you use? Explain how you would use them.

http://www.fbla-pbl.org/

CHAPTER OBJECTIVES

After completing this chapter, you should be able to

- Identify different styles of speech delivery and know when each is appropriate to use.
- Prepare effective note cards.
- Describe principles for effective PowerPoint® presentations.
- Explain rehearsal and performance guidelines for a successful speech presentation.
- Describe how to prepare for and handle a question-and-answer session.
- Discuss how to provide constructive verbal and written critiques.

KEY TERMS AND CONCEPTS

impromptu	extemporaneous	neutralizing restatement
manuscript style	imaging	positive restatement
memorized style	negative question	

IDEA BOX

We have all listened to speakers who moved us emotionally, challenged us intellectually, or affected our lives in some way. Jot down names of a few people whose speaking style you remember. List the qualities that made them memorable. What is it that makes certain speakers stand out?

Genuine concern for people?

Delivery style?

Passion for the subject?

Other?

Prespeech Advice

It's almost time to present your persuasive message! "But wait," you may protest, "I'm not ready! There are important things we've only touched on. We need to discuss what I may take up front with me and how I should stand when speaking. Is it alright to move about?..."

You're right. We still need to talk about styles of delivery, choices of outline notes, rehearsals, delivery guidelines, and question-and-answer sessions.

Styles of Delivery

How does an oral message get from the speaker to the listeners? How does an audience receive the audio message? What is the visual impact? Because audiences and speaking occasions differ, styles in delivery can range from casual, spontaneous chats delivered with no notes to lengthy, formal lectures read from manuscripts. The style of delivery must suit the speaker and the message, but also the live audience. Televised speeches with a teleprompter at camera level make it possible for anchors and reporters to appear as if they are just talking, not reading printed text. Looking right at the camera and talking directly to it, the delivery style of these "talking heads" comes across as personal and conversational.

A live audience tends to expect much the same from a speaker. Delivery that appears natural and unconstrained depends upon thorough preparation of subject content and careful rehearsal. When you are the speaker, and your audience is seated before you awaiting your message, your delivery style becomes your lifeline.

IMPROMPTU STYLE Experts on a topic are frequently interviewed on television. We watch them speak in an **impromptu** manner—no notes and with little or no advance speech planning—because they know very well what they are talking about. They field questions in

---

© 1996 Ted Goff

"All those who understood the topic I just elucidated, please vertically extend your upper limbs."

Delivery

Some audience members may understand what this speaker said, but not many would want to hear such language. It is unnecessarily complicated. One of the responsibilities of a speaker is to express ideas and provide information at a language level that the audience understands. Talking down to listeners is poor judgment. Talking over their heads is unforgivable. Audience members want the speaker to talk *with them.*

their area of expertise, provide facts and data in support of their point of view, and are able to talk in an engaging manner when invited to do so, even unexpectedly. They make it look easy. This is not a style recommended to novice speakers for their first presentations. Impromptu speeches rarely provide audiences with well-formed ideas or carefully worded arguments. Vocalized pauses, such as "uh" and "ah," fill up the dead spots while you frantically fumble for something to say and ways to say it clearly. Later, the words will come as you review your misery. Now you think, "I should have said ..." It takes time and preparation to express ideas well. However, impromptu speaking is frequently used as a challenging classroom exercise to promote ease in "thinking on one's feet."

MANUSCRIPT STYLE With manuscript style, a speech is completely written out to be read to an audience. The double-spaced pages should have pauses marked for phrasing and words underlined for emphasis. Whether a manuscript speech is delivered from printed sheets or a teleprompter, it is practiced aloud to make the delivery sound less like reading and more like speaking. How does an audience see it? If the ideas are not supported visually, audiences find manuscript speeches difficult to pay attention to for long. If the speaker gallops along with little concern for the audience's ability to consider the message, the listeners are soon lost.

Speaking from a manuscript has several advantages if the speaker is highly placed in government or business. The manuscript limits the message to explicit content. Language can be carefully chosen, ideas skillfully structured, offensive references avoided, and an advance copy released to the media. There are also disadvantages. Often such speeches sound as if someone else wrote them. The speaker's eye contact will be limited, and the stack of paper appears as a communication barrier between speaker and audience. However, a manuscript may be necessary to deliver a lengthy, technical paper or an official statement, such as a speech made during a press conference.

MEMORIZED STYLE Relatively few speakers deliver a prepared speech from memory. Using memorized style requires writing, studying, committing to memory, and delivering the speech with no notes. This style is used infrequently for major speeches because memorizing takes amazing effort and creates great preparation pressure. It is, nonetheless, desirable for short goodwill or courtesy speeches. Talks such as introductions, welcomes, farewells, award presentations, and acceptance speeches are most memorable when planned in advance and delivered without notes. Although the delivery seems impromptu or "off the cuff," these brief speeches are carefully planned and practiced.

EXTEMPORANEOUS STYLE The words *impromptu* and *extemporaneous* are often used as synonyms. However, an impromptu speech usually means delivery without planned preparation. A carefully researched and

"The speech needs to have clarity, power, and purpose. It needs the ring of personality. It needs to be delivered well."

—Elinor Donahue

Personal
CHECK-UP

Which delivery style do you most enjoy as a listener? Explain.

prepared speech, delivered in an informal communicative style with minimal notes, is considered **extemporaneous**. The goal is to communicate naturally and conversationally while referring infrequently to an outline. Although the opening and closing may be memorized for added security, extemporaneous speakers take only a few note cards to the speaker's stand. Resembling the impromptu speech in its appearance of spontaneity, extemporaneous delivery allows eye contact and permits an opportunity for clarification if the speaker sees puzzled expressions in the audience. This style also promotes friendly, interactive contact with audience members.

Supporting Notes

Because no one expects a well-prepared speaker to deliver a speech without any notes, this is the time to decide how much information you will need with you. Will you put notes on cards to take with you to the podium? Will you take your outline sheets up front? Will you write out your whole speech? Take too much, and you'll be tempted to read. Don't take enough, and you won't feel as confident as you should. This decision will be yours to make.

If your goal is to speak to your listeners in a warm, relaxed manner, yet provide well-reasoned, persuasive strategies to achieve your speech purpose, you will probably choose the extemporaneous method. Research and outline your speech carefully to give credibility to your ideas. Rehearse orally to make your words flow easily.

NOTE CARDS Since you've gone to all the trouble of carefully outlining your presentation, you don't want to misspeak any of your precisely worded points. Yet, you don't want to have a 52-card deck to worry about dropping. How will you reduce your outline so that you have a minimal number of note cards?

Start with six 3-by-5-inch cards, written on one side only. Number them. Make color-coded notes indicating where to show your visuals.

1. **First card**—Write out the opening sentences in outline form. Protect yourself against memory lapse by including the first few words of each sentence on the card.
   a. *Get attention:* Write the first words of your opening statement or question; refer to a visual if you have one.
   b. *Involve audience:* Use the word "you."
   c. *Establish credibility:* Use "I."
   d. *Thesis statement:* Write it out.

2. **Second card**—Write the first main point out as a complete sentence. Add subpoints in key word format.
   a. Note your supporting material with key words.
   b. If you want to use a direct quote, refer to it on a supporting card. (See "Sixth card.")

3. **Third and fourth cards**—Prepare cards for your second and third main points in the same format as the second note card.

Language trap

Don't say, "We have in stock all the items which you ordered." Say, "We have in stock all the items that you ordered."

4. **Fifth card**—The fifth card should contain your closing.
   a. *Summary:* Review your thesis and main points. Write out only the first words.
   b. *Focus:* Restate the purpose of your message (what you want the audience to do or believe).
5. **Sixth card**—Write out quotations fully on the sixth card, and include sources of information.

Some speakers find that a different size of card works better for them—4-by-6-inch, for example. Much depends on whether you hold the cards or rest them on a speaker's stand. Don't worry about a mixed outline style. Just write down the few words you need to trigger your memory as you speak. You will probably use your cards only for brief reference. When quoting directly or citing specific statistics, look at your card. Listeners expect accuracy and will not mind your referring to the information. Use your note cards openly, but beware of twisting, shuffling, or mangling them while talking. Your audience will watch this activity instead of listening to you. Figure 12-1 is a sample note card for the first main point of a presentation.

POWERPOINT® SLIDES Across the United States, from business headquarters to the White House, conference rooms are set up for PowerPoint presentations. Speakers turn down the lights and click through slide after slide of carefully prepared information, graphs, and charts. Be cautioned that a darkened room, the rhythmic click of the digital remote, and too much information can lull an audience to sleep. For vitally important decision-making information, the audio is the message and the visual is the supporting material.

FIGURE 12-1   Sample note card

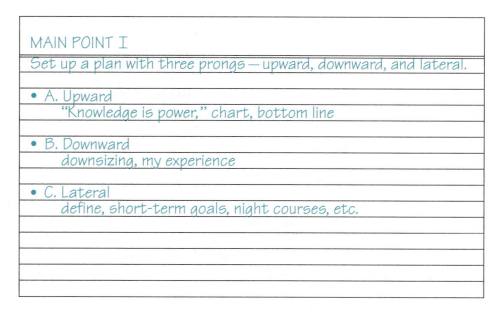

If you speak as you stroll about the platform and occasionally glance at the PowerPoint slides, your style will appear extemporaneous and well prepared. You've likely seen business presentations where a speaker uses a wireless clicker to advance the slides even when the speaker is standing across the room. If that's what you'd like to do, follow some important guidelines.

Use the same outline for your PowerPoint slides as used for your note cards, but avoid putting your introduction on the first slide. Instead, deliver the first steps of the introduction orally to establish your connection with the audience. Once you have set up your key idea, let the thesis statement be your first slide.

The slides that follow will be your main points and your visual support. You will click to display each slide as you are ready to talk about its contents. Create several slides supporting each main point. Your visuals—pictures, graphs, and even video clips—can be embedded in the slides for display at the appropriate times. Be careful to keep the type large, the word count low, and the charts and graphs simple.

You will need very few notes. Each slide will prompt you of what to say as you expound on its contents. You can make an oral transition, click the next slide, and look at the next point as the audience does. Finalize your presentation orally. Deliver the closing with passion.

Delivery Rehearsal

You probably have read through your speech a number of times by now. You are thoroughly familiar with your subject and what you want to say about it. Just looking through the outline is not enough! You must actually practice speaking your message out loud in the privacy of an empty room. Use the outline form you've worked on so diligently.

Have you decided to use PowerPoint slides? The secret to success with PowerPoint slides is practice, practice, practice. Practice clicking through your slides as you speak. Don't leave a slide in view while you talk about something else.

Audio or video record yourself. Are you talking too fast, making frequent filler sounds, or looking down at your notes too often? Time your practice presentation. Are you within your specified time constraints? Stop and adjust the rough spots. Go through it, out loud, again. Try practicing in front of a mirror.

Prior to your speech, mentally rehearse it using a process called **imaging** in which you imagine just how you want your presentation to go. Visualize yourself walking confidently to the speaker's stand. Check out the view of the room. Then, imagine it from the other point of view. Picture your audience looking at you and waiting for your words. What will they see as they look at you? View yourself nodding with assurance, making eye contact, speaking, and gesturing appropriately. The point of imaging is to help you feel more comfortable with the actual presentation. When you stand up to speak, you may feel that you've done it all before.

Performance Guidelines

For your performance, you will want to pay careful attention to your appearance, movement, gestures, eye contact, and voice.

Clothes

Your audience will appreciate your efforts to look nice for them, so be clean, neat, and well groomed. However, don't choose anything new to wear. An unfamiliar outfit may make you self-conscious, and it may not be as flattering as you hope. Pick a familiar outfit that you know is comfortable and attractive on you. For a speech to your class, choose something slightly dressier than normal, everyday wear. Avoid clothes that are particularly short, flashy, low cut, or tight—they will detract from your speech. Remember, you are your own best visual aid.

Movement

Your body posture and walk convey how you feel about delivering your speech. Remember, from the time you stand up, you are communicating. You want to try to be as natural as possible. Watch out for common mistakes such as nervous pacing, wandering about, or shifting from side to side. These actions reveal uncontrolled anxiety. Plan some small, specific movements to relax tense muscles, such as tightening and releasing your shoulders as you walk to the speaker's stand.

When you first face your audience, take a few seconds to "center" yourself. Square your shoulders, take a deep breath, and smile (if your topic is one for which a smile is appropriate). Don't be afraid of the few moments of silence that occur before you speak. Taking an extra pause is better than rushing the start of your speech.

Rehearse some kind of movement between major sections of your speech. You might shift your weight, take a few steps toward the audience, or step to the side of the speaker's stand. Of course, showing a visual aid—be it an object, chart, or projected slide—gives you a reason to move. Work with your visual aid in advance, and remember to look at your listeners as you present it. Do *not* talk to the visual aid.

Gestures

Hands, arms, and shoulders—as well as face and body—express ideas or emotions. Meaningful movements, called *gestures*, are both planned and unplanned. For example, holding note cards gives you something to do with your hands. Concentrating on getting the audience to understand your ideas allows your facial expressions to support your message. Move as you talk only if the gestures feel natural and comfortable. Remember that eyes follow movement. If you tug at your clothing, push up your glasses, twist your rings, run your fingers through your hair, or play with your note cards, the audience will watch that movement and may tune out what you are saying.

©Getty Images/PhotoDisc

Pointing to a visual aid as this woman is doing is helpful, but speakers must be sure to speak to their listeners, not to their visual aids.

Eye Contact

Probably the most essential communication strategy you can learn is to look at those to whom you are speaking. Deliberately focus on one side of the audience and slowly sweep across the room with your eyes. Hold eye contact while you finish a sentence. Don't watch the back wall or look out the window—nobody is listening there. If you are speaking from a stage or podium under a spotlight and the audience area is darkened, try not to squint or hold your hand up to shade your eyes. If you have difficulty seeing your audience, just remember they are there. Visualize them and speak out to them.

Voice

If people can't hear, they rarely make the effort to try. To be sure your voice reaches everyone, send your message out to the listener seated at the greatest distance from you. Speak out (project) to that person, and everyone else will hear you.

Postspeech Guidance

Your carefully delivered speech is finished. Some polite applause—or maybe even enthusiastic applause—may follow. You acknowledge the applause briefly and walk back to your seat. Right? Maybe not. If you've just given a business presentation for coworkers or customers, a question-and-answer session will likely follow.

Question-and-Answer Sessions

In a question-and-answer session, the speaker converses with the audience in impromptu style. It's impossible to know what audience members might ask. You can think about a few things beforehand to prepare yourself for those questions. First, it is helpful to recognize the different kinds of questions that might arise. Types of questions to anticipate include the following.

- **Hypothetical**—Worded in the form "What if...?" or "What happens if...?"

Personal CHECK-UP

What can a speaker do to feel comfortable and to look confident and poised while speaking?

- **Nonquestion**—The listener does not seek information, but wants to send a message of his or her own.

- **Attack**—Designed to challenge the speaker, force the speaker to take a stand, or put the speaker in an awkward position.

- **Either/or**—May try to force the speaker to make a commitment.
  "Which do you support—a conventional work week or four 10-hour days?"

- **Information-seeking**—The listener really wants to know something.

It is a good idea to control a question-and-answer session yourself rather than let someone else select questioners. Point to the questioner and listen carefully with your eyes fixed on the person speaking. If the audience can't hear the question, repeat it. Restating the question lets you make sure you have understood it correctly, gives you time to sort out the content, and helps you mentally prepare an answer.

If the question is stated negatively, rephrase it in a neutral or positive form.

- **Negative question**—Implies that there is something undesirable about the subject of the question. Example:
  "Why are your hiring practices so bad?"

- **Neutralizing restatement**—Rephrases the question in a way that diffuses the negative implication. Example:
  "The questioner would like me to explain our hiring practices."

- **Positive restatement**—Rephrases the question in a way that not only removes the negative implication, but also puts emphasis on a positive aspect of the subject. In this example, the emphasis is on making improvements.
  "What can be done to improve our hiring practices?"

Throughout the question-and-answer period, it is important to be as polite as possible. Maintain a positive attitude. Never argue. If a question designed to put you on the spot causes an uncomfortable situation, turn the moment around by asking that person a question yourself—respectfully, of course. Build credibility by earning respect as a speaker. Here are some additional tips for responding to questions appropriately.

- Try to agree with questioners who seek approval.

- Rephrase questions to fit your speech purpose.

- Rephrase a challenging question in your own words.

- Handle attack questions with good humor.

- If you don't know the answer, admit it, and if appropriate, advise the questioner of where the information might be found.

> **"The very best financial presentation is one that's well thought out and anticipates any questions . . . answering them in advance."**
>
> **—Nathan Collins**

COMMUNICATION AT WORK

Ted Martin works two shifts a week as a police officer. The rest of the week he works as the community liaison for the Police Department. Ted gives frequent public speeches to community organizations and clubs. In addition, he talks to school children, speaks to news reporters, and, in general, represents the Police Department in the community. Depending on his audience, Ted's focus varies. For school children, he emphasizes drug abuse prevention and child safety. When he's in front of news cameras, he listens carefully to the reporters and provides the basic information that makes up most news reports. In many cases, Ted must respond to questions, whether from children, news reporters, or city government officials. He answers questions confidently and completely. If he doesn't know the answer to a question, he says so, and if appropriate, he indicates that the matter is under investigation.

Listening and Critiquing

Your friends will say your speech was good. Your best friends will say, "Great job!" What you really want to know is, what part was effective? What do they remember? What you want is a *critique*—a review with comments about good points and areas to be improved.

Consider the following critique questions as you listen to the presentations of others. Be specific when you make comments. Ask others to use these questions as a guide as they critique you.

Language trap

Don't say, "Your presentation was real good."
Say, "Your presentation was very good." or "Your presentation was excellent."

1. Was the introduction carefully planned to get attention? To involve the audience? To establish the speaker's credibility?
2. Was the thesis stated clearly?
3. Did the purpose of the speech become obvious?
4. Were the main points easily understood?
5. Did the speaker use helpful transitions?
6. Were the visual aids well prepared and easily seen? Did they add to the presentation and support key ideas?
7. Was the speaker's voice loud enough to be heard easily?
8. Did the speaker pronounce words correctly and articulate clearly?
9. Did the speaker control nervous mannerisms?
10. Did the speaker maintain eye contact with all sections of the audience?
11. Did the speaker stand and move confidently?
12. Did the presentation meet the time requirement?
13. Did the closing summarize the thesis and main points?
14. Did the final sentence focus on the desired audience response?

In offering a verbal critique to speakers in learning situations, it is always helpful to give a positive account of high points in organization, research, or delivery. Some parts of a presentation will almost always meet or exceed your expectations. Point these out specifically. Limit your suggestions for improvement to a few, well-chosen remarks. The speaker won't remember much more than that. For example, make one suggestion for polishing delivery and one for improving content.

"Speak to students seated in the back so everyone will hear you."

"I didn't quite catch your third point. You might add a clearer transition next time."

If the critique is written, follow the same advice. State two or three things you liked, then state specific suggestions for techniques that could be improved.

Checklists for Speech Preparation, Practice, and Delivery

For your next speech presentation, use the checklists in Figure 12-2 to remind yourself how to prepare thoroughly.

Proper preparation, practice, and delivery will make your next speech a success!

FIGURE 12-2 Speech checklists

Steps for Preparing a Speech

1. Analyze the audience and occasion.
2. Decide on a topic.
3. Narrow the topic to fit audience and group interests.
4. Clarify your speech purpose.
5. Turn your purpose sentence into a thesis statement, or key idea, to be developed.
6. Research the topic. Find articles, references, and experts.
7. Collect a variety of supporting materials.
8. Identify three to five main points.
9. Choose an organizational pattern and outline the body of the speech, listing the main points.
10. Divide main points into several subpoints.
11. Select the best supporting material for each subpoint from your collected resources.
12. Include transitional phrases in the outline.
13. Write a closing that summarizes the thesis and main points.
14. Complete the closing with a statement that focuses on your desired audience response or action.
15. Develop an attention-getting introductory statement or story.
16. Plan a step to involve the audience.
17. Decide how to establish your credibility.

Steps for Practicing

1. Plan several visual aids for the speech.
2. Prepare note cards or PowerPoint® slides to guide you.
3. Practice the speech out loud using the cards or slides.
4. Practice the speech with visuals.
5. Record your practice, if possible.
6. Time the speech.
7. Smooth out the rough spots.
8. Practice again.
9. Use the imaging technique to visualize the setting and yourself as the speaker.

Steps for Delivery

1. Plan to wear something flattering, familiar, and comfortable.
2. Plan specific actions and gestures to relax tense muscles and to avoid unconscious, nervous movements.
3. Arrive in plenty of time to set up the presentation.
4. Make eye contact with the audience.
5. Project your voice to the farthest listener.
6. Be prepared for a question-and-answer session if giving a business presentation.

CHAPTER SUMMARY

After completing your outline, you will need to practice the delivery of your speech. Prespeech preparation should include a decision about the style of delivery. Delivery styles include impromptu or unprepared delivery, reading from a manuscript, memorizing the presentation, or extemporaneous. Extemporaneous speeches are carefully researched and prepared, but are given in an informal, "audience-connected" manner with minimal notes. Note cards should be carefully prepared to remind you of your points and supporting materials. PowerPoint slides may be used to structure the speech framework and provide support for both you and your audience. Rehearsal is critical and involves practicing out loud with supporting visuals, timing yourself, and imaging. Performance guidelines include paying careful attention to appearance, movement, gestures, eye contact, and voice. Be prepared for question-and-answer sessions by anticipating likely questions. Know how to recognize question types and how to best handle each one. When critiquing a speech, provide positive comments, mentioning effective speaking points. Limit your suggestions for improvement to a few, well-chosen remarks.

CHAPTER REVIEW

1. What are the four styles of speech delivery? Briefly describe each.
2. List guidelines for an effective PowerPoint presentation.
3. How can imaging help a speaker give a more relaxed delivery?
4. In general, how should a speaker respond to audience questions?
5. What is the most helpful way to structure comments when critiquing a speech?

CAN YOU DEFINE THESE TERMS?

Match each description with the appropriate term. Write the correct letter in the blank preceding the sentence.

Terms:

1. ____ Speaking with no notes and little planning
2. ____ A mental rehearsal in which you imagine just how you want your presentation to go
3. ____ Rephrases a negative question in a way that diffuses the negative implication
4. ____ Giving a speech that is completely written out
5. ____ Style in which a carefully prepared speech is delivered informally with a minimum of notes
6. ____ Implies something undesirable about the subject
7. ____ Requires writing, studying, committing to memory, and delivering the speech with no notes
8. ____ Rephrases a negative question in a way that removes the negative implication and emphasizes a positive aspect of the subject

a. extemporaneous
b. gestures
c. imaging
d. impromptu
e. manuscript style
f. memorized style
g. negative question
h. neutralizing restatement
i. positive restatement

APPLICATIONS

Manuscript Style of Speech Delivery

Abraham Lincoln delivered the famous Gettysburg Address in November 1863 at Gettysburg, Pennsylvania, the site of one of the Civil War's bloodiest battles. Read the speech until you feel that you can *talk* it through as President Lincoln must have spoken it from the back of the envelope on which he had scribbled the words. Make the delivery sound as though you were thinking up the ideas as you talk. Be prepared to deliver the speech to your class if your teacher asks for volunteers.

The Gettysburg Address

Fourscore and seven years ago our fathers brought forth on this continent a new nation, conceived in liberty, and dedicated to the proposition that all men are created equal.

Now we are engaged in a great civil war, testing whether that nation, or any nation so conceived and so dedicated, can long endure. We are met on a great battle-field of that war. We have come to dedicate a portion of that field as a final resting-place for those who here gave their lives that this nation might live. It is altogether fitting and proper that we should do this.

But, in a larger sense, we cannot dedicate . . . we cannot consecrate . . . we cannot hallow . . . this ground. The brave men, living and dead, who struggled here, have consecrated it far above our poor power to add or detract. The world will little note nor long remember what we say here, but it can never forget what they did here. It is for us, the living, rather, to be dedicated here to the unfinished work which they who fought here have thus far so nobly advanced. It is rather for us to be here dedicated to the great task remaining before us . . . that from these honored dead we take increased devotion to that cause for which they gave the last full measure of devotion; that we here highly resolve that these dead shall not have died in vain; that this nation, under God, shall have a new birth of freedom; and that government of the people, by the people, for the people, shall not perish from the earth.

—Abraham Lincoln

Acceptance Speech

President Lincoln's Gettysburg Address is an example of oratorical excellence using repetition and two less-familiar patterns—antithesis and tricolon.

- **Antithesis**—Opposition and contrast. Example: "The world will little note nor long remember what we say here, but it can never forget what they did here."

- **Tricolon**—Division of an idea into three harmonious parts, usually of increasing power. Example: " . . . of the people, by the people, for the people, . . ."

What do these two techniques add to the Gettysburg Address? Do you think Lincoln used these techniques deliberately? Why or why not?

Write a brief acceptance speech in which either the antithesis or tricolon technique is used. Polish the words until they shine. Share your speech with a group of classmates.

MAKING CONNECTIONS

Speech Contests

Judges are always needed for academic speech or debate contests. Find out if your school or community holds such competitions, and offer to serve as a judge. Write about your experience in a one-page essay. Jot notes here.

_____

_____

_____

_____

_____

_____

_____

_____

History

Early famous speeches sound very different than present-day speeches. Compare an early speech presentation with a current-day speech. What differences do you note in organization, composition, and delivery? Explain your findings.

_____

_____

_____

_____

_____

_____

_____

_____

_____

PROJECTS

Acceptance Speeches

Read the following excerpts from two Nobel Peace Prize acceptance speeches, or look up ones given more recently. Choose one. Practice and deliver at least a part of the speech to your class. Put yourself in the shoes of the original speaker. Remember, you are receiving an immense honor.

"Peace is not a matter of prizes or trophies. It is not the product of a victory or command. It has no finishing line, no final deadline, no fixed definition of achievement.

Peace is a never-ending process, the work of many decisions by many people in many countries. It is an attitude, a way of life, a way of solving problems and resolving conflicts. It cannot be forced on the smallest nation or enforced by the largest. It cannot ignore our differences or overlook our common interests. It requires us to work and live together."

—Oscar Arias Sánchez
Accepting the 1987 Nobel Peace Prize

"I feel honored, humbled and deeply moved that you should give this important prize to a simple monk from Tibet. I am no one special. But, I believe the prize is a recognition of the true values of altruism, love, compassion and nonviolence which I try to practice, in accordance with the teachings of the Buddha and the great sages of India and Tibet."

—The 14th Dalai Lama
Accepting the 1989 Nobel Peace Prize

Questions

1. Critique your own delivery. Include suggestions for improvement where appropriate.
   a. Did you establish your position at the speaker's stand before you began speaking?

   b. Did you prepare thoroughly enough that you didn't have to read the message word-for-word?

   c. Did you make eye contact with the entire audience?

d. Did you speak slowly and clearly?

e. Did you stand up straight?

f. Did you briefly acknowledge the applause and return gracefully to your seat?

2. These excerpts are very brief. How did that affect the way in which you delivered the speech?

3. Most of us have seen awards ceremonies in person or on television. What common errors do you think people make when they give acceptance speeches? What general suggestions for improvement would you give?

Persuasive Speech

You have been preparing a persuasive speech to present to your class. Complete the planning for your speech using the outline form provided on the next page. Adjust it as needed. Your speech must be five to six minutes in length. Remember, you want to persuade your classmates to think or do as you suggest. Use your audience analysis to help you select the appropriate appeals. Use at least one visual aid. Practice your speech orally a number of times. Stay within the time limit.

Your evaluator may use the critique sheet provided on page 227.

OUTLINE FORM FOR PERSUASIVE SPEECH

Introduction

(Get attention)   A. _____

(Involve audience)   B. _____

(Establish credibility) C. _____

Thesis Statement

_____

_____

Development of Key Idea (Body of Speech)

Transition _____

Main point   I. _____

Subpoint   A. _____

                     1. _____

                     2. _____

Subpoint   B. _____

                     1. _____

                     2. _____

Transition _____

Main point   II._____

Subpoint   A. _____

                     1. _____

                     2. _____

Subpoint   B. _____

                     1. _____

                     2. _____

Transition _____

Main Point   III._____

Subpoint   A. _____

                     1. _____

                     2. _____

Subpoint   B. _____

                     1. _____

                     2. _____

Conclusion

Transition _____

(Summary)   A. _____

(Focus)   B. _____

CRITIQUE SHEET FOR PERSUASIVE SPEECH

Speaker: Give this page to your instructor or student evaluator before you speak.

Evaluator: On a scale from 1–10 (with 1 being "poor" and 10 being "excellent"), rate the speaker on each of the following elements by circling the number of points awarded.

Total Possible Points: 105 (The first ten questions are worth a maximum of 10 points. The last question is worth an extra 5 points.)

Speaker's Name: _____

Subject of Speech: _____

Speaking Time: _____

The Verbal Message:
1. Did the speaker catch your attention and involve you in the subject?   1   2   3   4   5   6   7   8   9   10
2. Did the speaker establish his/her own credibility and concern about the subject?   1   2   3   4   5   6   7   8   9   10
3. Was the thesis effectively stated and the purpose of the presentation clear?   1   2   3   4   5   6   7   8   9   10
4. Did the pattern of the main points clearly develop the thesis?   1   2   3   4   5   6   7   8   9   10
5. Was a variety of supporting materials used?   1   2   3   4   5   6   7   8   9   10
6. Were visuals handled well?   1   2   3   4   5   6   7   8   9   10
7. Were you satisfied with the closing?   1   2   3   4   5   6   7   8   9   10

The Nonverbal Message:
8. Was the speaker enthusiastic, poised, and communicative?   1   2   3   4   5   6   7   8   9   10
9. Did the speaker maintain eye contact? Was the speaker's voice loud enough to be heard easily, and were language and pronunciation correct?   1   2   3   4   5   6   7   8   9   10

Effectiveness of Communication:
10. Did the speech persuade you?   1   2   3   4   5   6   7   8   9   10

Bonus:
11. Did the speaker relate the material to the needs and interests of the audience?   1   2   3   4   5

Total Points: _____

Comments:

_____

_____

_____

Communication Skills Inventory

This is a self-test. Read the following statements, and score yourself honestly. Place in the blank an "A" for always, an "S" for sometimes, or an "N" for never, depending on how the statement applies to you.

_____ 1. I tend to qualify my statements by adding such phrases as "It seems to me...," "In my opinion...," "To the best of my knowledge ...," or "I think..."

_____ 2. I feel comfortable speaking to any audience.

_____ 3. I am usually careful to check the accuracy of my perception before I make comments about a topic.

_____ 4. I generally verify my perception by making comparisons to previous experiences, repeating the experience to be sure, using several of my senses, or checking with other people.

_____ 5. I listen to other people express opposing viewpoints without getting angry, insisting that I am right, or tuning them out.

_____ 6. I try to view people as individuals who are unique and therefore different from myself, rather than stereotyping them into rigid categories based on their behavior or appearance.

_____ 7. I feel comfortable working with a group to meet a common goal.

_____ 8. I listen to the opinions of others but withhold my personal judgment until I check other sources.

_____ 9. I ask questions to check my interpretation of what was said before I comment on the statements of other people.

_____ 10. I try to express myself in specific, descriptive terms that other people can check through observation, rather than making broad, general statements.

_____ 11. I am willing to change my behavior when I perceive that my attitude or actions prevent me from getting along with others.

_____ 12. Before coming to a conclusion, I wait until I have enough information to justify my decision.

_____ 13. I try to use empathy before I discount another person's opinions.

_____ 14. I am well prepared to speak before an audience.

_____ 15. I listen to myself as I talk to see if my attitude is appropriate for the particular situation.

Questions

1. Based on your evaluation, in what areas do you think you need to improve?

2. What do you think this evaluation says about your communication skills?

BPA Presentation Management—Individual

Major universities are offering an increasing number of courses and degrees online for the convenience of students. While many individuals are interested in earning college credit at home, they have major concerns about online courses and degrees. Since online courses allow students to create their own schedules, some students worry about their ability to be self-disciplined and motivated to complete the coursework. They also have concerns about a lack of face-to-face communication with the instructor when they have questions or difficulties. Some students worry about how future employers view degrees earned online. Finally, students are concerned about getting feedback from instructors in a timely manner.

You are challenged to create a presentation using desktop technology that promotes e-learning and effectively addresses all of the concerns. The presentation should show how the benefits outweigh the detriments of online college courses and degrees. Your speech will be evaluated for oral presentation as well as effective use of current multimedia technology. Charts and other visual aids should be incorporated into the speech.

You will have ten minutes to set up your multimedia presentation. Your speech must be seven to ten minutes in length. Judges will have an additional five minutes to ask questions.

Performance Indicators Evaluated

- Explain the delivery of online courses.
- Describe the benefits of online courses and degrees.
- Define the interaction that online students will have with their teachers.
- Give examples of successful online degree recipients and their employment.
- Provide convincing arguments for students to sign up for online courses and degrees.
- Demonstrate effective oral communication skills.
- Use current multimedia technology to effectively enhance the oral presentation.

For more detailed information, go to the BPA web site.

Think Critically

1. Describe how you will get the audience's attention and involve them in your presentation.
2. Why is it important to give examples of successful online college graduates in this presentation?
3. How will you effectively diminish students' fears of online courses?
4. How will you prepare for the judges' questions at the end of your presentation? List three questions that the judges might ask you and provide answers.

http://www.bpa.org

adrenal system releases chemicals to stimulate the body's nervous and muscular systems to prepare for fight or flight

agenda a planned list of items to be covered in a meeting

aggressive response a reaction that is unnecessarily harsh and forceful

articulation errors occur when you do not make sounds clearly and accurately

assertion a claim that something is true

assertive firm and confident without being harsh or disagreeable

assertive response a reaction that communicates your preferences and feelings in a firm but positive way

assumptions conclusions reached when we take for granted that others perceive things as we do

attitudes the way you think or feel about an object, person, event, and so forth

audience analysis asking yourself questions about audience members' backgrounds, characteristics, and traits

autocratic style style in which the leader exerts high control, makes decisions, and tells others what to do and how to do it

beliefs firm convictions about something

briefing a short meeting in which precise instructions, a summary of goals, or essential information is given, often in preparation for an upcoming event

cause–effect organization organizational style that shows the causes and discusses the effects of a problem

channel a means of sending and receiving messages

chronological organization organizational style that organizes material by date, from past to present to future, or reverse

clichés overused expressions

climate the tone of the meeting affected by the physical setting

clustering list a tool that helps you organize your speech by grouping together related key words and phrases

codes symbolic ways of representing ideas or feelings

communication apprehension the larger and more general anxiety covering many fears relating to communication

conflict a clash of differing attitudes, behaviors, ideas, goals, or needs

connotations the feelings that people attach to words because of personal experiences

consensus a harmonious agreement of all group members

constructive argument a logically planned presentation in support of an affirmative or negative view

counseling interview a one-to-one business meeting with the purpose of giving/seeking guidance and advice

covert body movements slight or hidden expressions of the face and eyes

cross-examination an opportunity to ask questions of the opposing side in a debate

cut-away a figure with removable parts that allows a speaker to remove sections to reveal other portions of the device or model as he or she speaks

debate the discussion of an issue through the consideration of opposing arguments

decoding the mental process of converting sound into meaning

democratic style style in which the leader starts the meeting, but group members are expected to initiate discussion, suggest procedures, and make decisions

denotations specific definitions generally agreed upon by educated speakers of a language

diction the care and precision with which you use your tongue and jaw to create clear speech sounds

directive questions questions that can be answered "yes" or "no"

dyad the smallest communication unit, made up of a group of two

dynamics the way people function together and interact with each other to make decisions or reach goals

ego conflicts arise from the perception of an attack on our abilities or on who we are

electronic database a computerized version of an index

emotional appeal (pathos) a persuasive speaking strategy in which the speaker plays on audience members' personal needs for survival, good health, safety, appreciation, and recognition

empathetic listening listening that is concerned with the person speaking rather than the message being spoken

empathy the ability to perceive another's point of view and to sense what others are feeling

employment interview a one-to-one business conversation with the goal of securing an entrance into the job market

encoding the process by which an idea or message is transformed into oral language

energy potential develops as a result of the body changes from the fight-or-flight response

etiquette accepted social behavior

evaluation interview regularly scheduled "check-ups" on employees

exit interview an informational interview that takes place when an employee leaves a position in a company

extemporaneous delivery style in which a carefully researched and prepared speech is delivered in an informal communicative style with minimal notes

feedback the verbal or nonverbal response the receiver gives back to the sender

fight-or-flight response in response to a threatening situation, the inborn instinct in which our bodies gear up to either fight or run

gesture an expressive movement of any part of the body

give-and-take meeting a meeting in which group members are expected to speak up, listen, disagree, express their views, compromise, and reach consensus

hearing when the ear responds to vibrations caused by sound waves and transmits nerve impulses to the brain

hidden agenda an individual's set of needs that are different from those of the group and its goal

hygiene cleanliness and care of self and personal belongings

imaging a mental rehearsal in which you imagine just how you want your presentation to go

impromptu delivery style that involves no notes and little or no advance speech planning

index a reference book with an alphabetical list of topics or names that gives the source, or original place, where each item can be found

inferential language statements that draw conclusions by a reasoning process that may or may not be faulty

informational interview a one-to-one business meeting to gather specific information

informative speaking a form of speech presentation in which the speaker knows more about a topic than the audience and endeavors to share information in which the audience has interest

interpersonal skills those behaviors you need in order to develop relationships with other people

interview a conversation—formal or informal—with one of a number of business purposes

interviewee the person who answers questions, provides information, and helps achieve the goals of the meeting

interviewer the person who plans the meeting, sets the goals, asks the questions, and generally controls the direction of the conversation

involuntary movements movements that you make without realizing it

judgmental language statements that evaluate good/bad, right/wrong, ugly/pretty, and so forth

listening when the brain focuses on the meaning of the sounds being heard

listening for intent zeroing in on the unspoken "why" in the spoken message

logical appeal (logos) a persuasive speaking strategy in which the speaker appeals to listeners with critical thinking and sound reasoning

main motion an issue or question that is under discussion in a meeting

manuscript style delivery style in which a speech is completely written out to be read to an audience

memorized style delivery style that requires writing, studying, committing to memory, and delivering a speech with no notes

mentor an experienced, knowledgeable person who offers guidance and advice to help you reach your goals

message made up of words carried by sound waves and gestures or movement carried by light waves

mixed message when the words say one thing and the voice indicates another

model any three-dimensional representation, whether actual size, reduced, or enlarged

negative question question that implies there is something undesirable about the subject

neutralizing restatement rephrases a negative question in a way that diffuses the negative implication

nondirective questions open-ended questions that allow you to probe gently to get the information you need

one-way meeting a meeting called by a leader to provide information to others about business issues, benefits, or procedures

overt body movements easily noticed actions

paralanguage clues to meaning revealed by the tone of voice, volume, rate of speaking, pauses, and so forth

parallel structure worded in the same statement format

paraphrase to repeat in your own words the message you heard

parliamentary procedure a set of rules and practices used by large groups to maintain order during meetings

passive response a reaction that is weak and lacks energy

perception the process of making sense of the world through the use of your senses to observe and be aware of your surroundings

performance appraisal a meeting between an employee and direct supervisor to discuss how well the employee performed job duties over a specific time period

periodicals magazines published on a regular basis (weekly, monthly, and so forth)

permissive style style in which the leader offers little guidance to the group

personal esteem a sense of self-worth and recognition among peers

personal space an area with invisible boundaries within 1½ to 3 feet of you in which others are generally not welcome

persuasive speaking a form of speech presentation in which the speaker tries to change listeners' thinking or urge them to take some kind of action

persuasive style style in which the leader makes a decision and then works to move the group to accept the decision

physiological needs food and shelter

pitch the variation in relative vibration frequency—high to low—of the human voice that contributes to the total meaning of speech

plagiarism using another person's words or ideas and passing them off as your own

positive restatement rephrases a negative question in a way that not only removes the negative implication, but also puts emphasis on a positive aspect of the subject

problem–solution organization organization style that explains a problem, describes its effects, and offers a solution

problem-solving interview a one-to-one meeting that is often the basis for airing concerns

process-oriented roles roles assumed by group members that serve to smooth interactions and maintain relationships

pronunciation errors occur when you do not make the correct sounds or you place the accent on the wrong syllable

proposition a statement to be argued in a debate

protocols norms of behavior that you are expected to learn and follow in the workplace

public distance a range of 12 feet or more between the speaker and listeners, such as for presentational speaking

quote someone else's exact words, spoken or written

rate the speed with which words are spoken

rebuttal a speech that serves to refute and disprove the other side's argument

receiver the person who hears or sees the message sent

referents the items to which words refer

reporting language statements based on observation

reports organized presentations of factual information

reprimand interview a one-to-one meeting in which some undesirable behavior or problem with your work is brought to your attention

search engine a tool that compiles information and then indexes web sites where it can be found

self-actualization being happy and fulfilled

self-esteem the way you value yourself

self-image how you see and think about yourself

sender the source of a verbal message (words) or nonverbal message (actions, gestures, tone)

small talk light or casual conversation about such topics as the weather, sports, or current events

social distance a distance from 3 to 12 feet within which we feel comfortable standing when conversing with colleagues or new acquaintances

social needs relationships and a sense of belonging

socializing process a time for group members to get acquainted and learn about each other

spatial organization organizational style that arranges the subject matter in terms of space relationships

speaker appeal (ethos) a persuasive speaking strategy in which the audience may accept a message simply because of the speaker's personal qualities and attractiveness

speech putting words into sound waves

stage fright the nervousness felt at appearing before an audience

task-oriented roles roles assumed by group members to serve to move the task along and get the assignment done

territory an employee's invisibly identified workspace

testimony information that comes directly from someone who has firsthand experience with the subject

thesis statement a purpose sentence for a speech restated into a specifically worded key idea that needs to be developed or explained

timbre the distinctive qualities and tone that make your voice uniquely yours

topical organization organizational style that lists each main point as I., II., III., often with the most dramatic or climactic point coming last

training the delivery of "how to" information in the form of instructions, explanations, or demonstrations

training session a one-to-one business meeting to go over procedures or to orient an employee to new surroundings

transitions words and phrases that indicate relationships between thoughts or ideas

values ideals or views held dear

visual aids support for a message that engages listeners' eyes in addition to their ears

volume/intensity the degree of loudness with which a message is spoken

voluntary movements movements that are under your control in that you consciously make them

word whiskers frequent "uh," "ah," or "um" sounds that punctuate conversation

Feedback (*Continued*)
   in conversation, 91
   in empathetic listening, 37
   on interviewee critique sheet, 125
   in listening, 20
   from receiver, 9
   in speech, 8
Feelings, effect of, 5
Fight-or-flight response, 70, 71
Flipcharts, as visual aid, 196
Flowcharts, for oral presentations, 171
Follow-up, for interviews, 118
Ford, Henry, 95, 112
Formal debate, 156–158
Formal situations, communication type appropriate for, 40
Friendships, close, conversations in, 39

G

Gardner, Herbert, 173
Gatekeeper, as group-member role, 137
George, Elizabeth, 15
Gestures and hands, as nonverbal communication, 54–55, 198, 215
Gettysburg Address (Lincoln), 222
Give-and-take meetings, 132
Goals
   of informative presentations, 152
   of interviews, 108
Goodwill talks, 154
Google, 178
Government documents, use of, for research, 177
Graphic images, for presentations, 171, 195–196
Gregg, John Robert, 174
Grooming. *See* Personal grooming, as nonverbal communication
Group decision making, 134
Group dynamics, factors affecting, 132–134
   team players and, 138
Group identification and status, as nonverbal communication, 52
Groups
   action, 129
   leadership roles in, 137
   leadership styles in, 137–138
   member roles, 136–138
   negative behaviors in, 135
   problem-solving in, 158–159
   size of, and group dynamics, 133
   social, 129
   See also Meetings

H

Handouts, as visual aid, 197
Hands and gestures, as nonverbal communication, 54–55

Handshaking, 60
Haney, William V., 23
Harmonizer, as group-member role, 137
Hearing
   definition of, 18
   difficulty of, due to speaker's volume/intensity, 34–35
   listening vs., 18
   process of, 18
Help, seeking, at work. *See* Counseling interview; Informational interview; Problem-solving interview
Hidden agendas, in groups, 135
Hotbot, 178
How? questions, 90
Human needs, satisfying, in presentations, 176
Hygiene, as nonverbal communication, 52
Hypothetical questions, 216

I

Idea Box features, 2, 14, 31, 49, 68, 86, 107, 128, 150, 170, 187, 209
Ideal solutions to problems, 159
Illustrations, as supporting material, 193
Image
   personal, effect of, 5
   voice as element of, 32
Images, mental, in communication, 8
Imaging, 214
Impromptu speaking, 66, 210–211
Incidental motions, in meetings, 131
Inconsiderate behavior, 92–93
Index (reference book), 177
Inferential language, 17
Influencing others, speech used for, 7
Informal situations, communication type appropriate for, 40
Informal speeches, 171
Information
   appropriate and accurate, 152
   finding, collecting, and using, 189–190
   See also Research, for speeches
Informational interview, 111–112
Information exchange, speech used for, 7
Information giver, as group-member role, 136
Information seeker, as group-member role, 136
Information-seeking questions, 217
Informative presentations, 154
   accuracy and appropriateness in, 152
   briefings as, 153
   definition of, 151
   evaluating effectiveness of, 153
   goal of, 152
   purpose sentence for, 151
   reports as, 152–153

Testimony
    definition of, 152
    as supporting material, 194
Thank you, importance of, 89
Theroux, Phyllis, 40
Thesis statement
    creating, from purpose sentence, 151, 188
    examples of, 190–191
    writing out, on note card, 212
Thinking
    effect of experience on, 5
    as key to effective communication, 5
Thoreau, Henry David, 9
Timbre, of voice, 35
Time
    of meeting, and group dynamics, 133
    use of, as communication, 58
Titles, correct, importance of learning, 88
Topical organization, for presentations, 190–191, 201
Topics
    appropriate, for conversation, 90
    link with audience, 174–175
    narrowing of, 188
    organization patterns for, 190–191
    selection of, for speeches, 173, 188
    shaping to fit audience, 175–176
    statement of, 188
Tracy, Brian, 4
Training, group dynamics and, 134
Training presentations, 153
Training sessions, 110
Transition words, for presentations, 192
Tricolon, 222
Trustworthiness, as speaker characteristic, 155
Two-person decisions, in groups, 134

U

Unacceptable behavior at work, 92–93
Uncommon abbreviations, avoiding, 91
Unwritten rules of behavior, at work, 92–93

V

Value conflict, 95
Values, definition of, 4
Verbal codes, 3, 15
Verbal messages, from sender, 7
Videos, as visual aid, 197
Visual aids
    displaying, 196–197
    effective, 194
    examples of, 171
    graphic images, 195–196

importance of, 195
problems with, 197–198
realistic representations, 195
speaker as, 198
Visualizing. *See* Imaging
Vocal messages, elements of, 33–36
Voice
    as communication tool, 32–36
    diction and, 35
    dysfunctional clues and, 36
    level (sound of), 18
    as part of image, 32
    pitch of, 33–34
    projection of, during presentation, 216
    rate of speaking, 34
    timbre, 35
    tips for improving, 33–36
    volume/intensity, 34–35
    See also Paralanguage
Volume, of voice, in speaking, 34–35
Voluntary movements, as nonverbal communication, 53–54

W

Wall Street Journal Index, 177
Welcome speeches, 83
What, when, where, who, why? questions, 90
White boards, for oral presentations, 171
Whiting, Percy H., 154
Winans, James, 155
"Win-lose" approach, to settling conflict, 96
"Win/lose-refuse" approach, to settling conflict, 96
"Win-win" approach, to settling conflict, 95–96
"Win-yield" approach, to settling conflict, 96
Withdrawer, as group-member type, 135
Withdrawing, from conflict, 96
Word charts, as visual aid, 196
Words
    changing meanings of, 15–16
    as connotations, 16–17
    as denotations, 16
    journalistic, 90
    power of, 15–17
    as symbols, 15
    types to avoid, 91
    See also Language
Word whiskers, 73
Work
    conversation skills for, 87–91
    listening skills for, 19–20, 36
    as team-oriented activity, 112
    unwritten rules of behavior for, 92–93
Worry, stage fright and, 70, 71